THE
CENTURION
PRINCIPLES

To
Rob
May the Lord
guide you with His
wisdom + protect you
with His strong arm

Jeff O'Leary

PSALMS 27:1-5

THE
CENTURION PRINCIPLES

Battlefield Lessons for Frontline Leaders

COLONEL
JEFF O'LEARY
(RET.)

NELSON BUSINESS
A Division of Thomas Nelson Publishers
Since 1798

www.thomasnelson.com

Published in Nashville, Tennessee, by Thomas Nelson, Inc.

Author is represented by the literary agency of Alive Communications, Inc., 7680 Goddard Street, Suite 200, Colorado Springs, CO 80920.

Unless otherwise indicated, Scripture is taken from the New King James Version. Copyright © 1982 by Thomas Nelson, Inc. Used by permission. All rights reserved.

Other Scripture references are from the following sources:

New American Standard Bible (NASB), © 1960, 1977 by the Lockman Foundation.

The New Revised Standard Version Bible (NRSV), © 1989 by the Division of Christian Education of the National Council of the Churches of Christ in the USA.

The *Holy Bible*, New Living Translation (NLT), copyright © 1996. Used by permission of Tyndale House Publishers, Inc., Wheaton, Illinois 60189. All rights reserved.

The World English Bible (WEB).

Library of Congress Cataloging-in-Publication Data
O'Leary, Jeffrey.
The centurion principles : battle lessons for frontline leaders / Jeffrey O'Leary.
p. cm.
Includes bibliographical references.
ISBN 0-7852-6196-6 (hardcover)
1. Leadership. I. Title.
HD57.7.O42 2004
658.4'092—dc22

2004010966

Printed in the United States of America
04 05 06 07 08 QW 9 8 7 6 5 4 3 2 1

To you—the brave ones:
Cast your dreams like jewels
Across the ocean of your
Heart's desire;
Seek your destiny in waters
Deeper than yourself,
And you will find your Destiny Maker there.

CONTENTS

—·—

THE OATH OF A CENTURION

A BATTLE-HARDENED LEGIONNAIRE WAS PROMOTED TO THE rank of Centurion based on at least sixteen years of combat service and valor at the point of the spear. He was able to carry ninety pounds of equipment at least twenty miles per day and train under the harshest of conditions. The Centurion was required to equip himself at his own expense and pay for his own food, clothing, bedding, boots, arms, armor, and pay dues to the burial club. He was a skilled engineer and builder in addition to being the finest combat soldier. He held ultimate sway over the welfare of every man who served in his hundred-man century. The enlistment period was for twenty-five years, after which a cash payment and small plot of land were provided (unless the treasury was short of cash, in which case, commitment to service was involuntarily extended).

Punishment in the legions was swift and severe and within the discretion of the Commander of the Legion. Death was the penalty for fleeing during battle or feigning illness to avoid battle. Minor offenses were often punished by the loss of a body part.

To rise to Centurion was considered the highest honor a legionnaire could attain. The Centurion always led his troops from the front.

THE OATH OF A CENTURION:
"STRENGTH AND HONOR"

This country thirsts for a new kind of leader. A yearning for integrity has become a groundswell of desire to find strength and honor again among those who rise to the pinnacle of government, clergy, business, and the military. As a nation, we have lost our way and we know it. Following the last presidential election, 57 percent of voters described the "moral climate of the country" as "seriously off on the wrong track."[1]

Now more than ever, America is in need of leadership that guides by what is right rather than what is popular; what is honorable rather than what is legal; what is self-sacrificial rather than what is merely self-serving. More than ever, we are looking for strong, virtuous leaders whom we will not be ashamed to call our own.

We live in an age where "image is everything." In leadership, this model has produced empty shells, from presidents to parents, senators to schoolteachers, and politicians to pastors. A particularly pertinent example of this moral callousness was recalled by a former crewmember of *Marine One*, the presidential helicopter:

> I vividly remember my flight over the tornado-devastated region in the Midwest during my tour of duty. The terrible tornado that had taken the city by surprise had left a path of destruction nearly two miles long. Everything within its path had been destroyed. Our mission was to fly the president over the destruction in order for him to see the damage first hand. This was my first flight as his personal crew chief and I was overwhelmed with pride and honor as he appeared out of Air Force One and headed my way. I was so nervous; I knew millions were watching, as this was a nationally televised event.
>
> After we had boarded the helicopter and took off, the president began to move the furniture. He turned his back to

the window and began to deal cards out to the other passengers. During the entire flight I watched with amazement as the president played hearts. Only once did he ever look out his window. He made a quick glance over his shoulder and immediately turned back with a shrug.

After twenty minutes, we prepared to land at a school near the worst of the damage. I looked out the window and saw a massive crowd of mourners. They had gathered in order to walk with their president through their destroyed neighborhoods. Some had lost their loved ones but all had lost their homes. My attention was pulled back into the helicopter suddenly as an aide asked for a glass of water. I quickly produced one and handed it to the aide. The water was then handed to the president who did not drink it. Instead, I watched in amazement as he dipped his fingers in the water and dabbed a bit under each eye. Smiling at his fellow card players, he then changed his expression to that of sorrow and turned his chair toward the window.

As I opened the doors, the president stepped out and approached the crowd looking very distraught, tears apparently rolling down his face. To the crowd, the president appeared to be crying and struck with grief. How would they have known differently?[2]

Gratefully, those traumatized families were not aware the tears came from the bottom of a glass. Yet this kind of hollow leadership cannot long be hidden. We have learned this all too well as the corporate dominoes continue to fall.

People are beginning to realize that the easy way will no longer suffice, and that the merely "legal" way will no longer satisfy. They have learned leadership by deceptive and sordid means brings only sorrowful and shameful ends. People are ready for great new leaders who rise above their peers—like those in history who went beyond the call of duty and still inspire us today.

The Centurion was a leader who earned his promotion by proving himself in battle for nearly two decades. He rose from the ranks of one hundred men through mental and physical toughness and self-sacrifice. There were no "positional" Centurions, men appointed for political reasons or cash contribution. Centurions led their troops from the front—from the pointed end of the spear in position, character, and valor.

The Centurion is a metaphor for those who have led others with strength and honor across the centuries. "Strength" incorporates the best qualities of decision making, technical competence, business and spiritual wisdom, vision, and an unrelenting commitment to excellence, as though they were a painter ready to sign a canvas. "Honor" encompasses the virtues of integrity and honesty, self-denial, loyalty, and a servant's humility to those in authority above as well as a just and merciful heart to those below.

Timeless leadership principles carried these brave warriors through the most desperate circumstances. These principles have proven true under fire, where life and death were but a breath apart. If they were useful then, they will surely serve those in ministry, military, or corporate leadership today. They will also be beneficial for every mom and dad struggling with growing teens testing the limits of their endurance. Leaders come in all shapes and sizes—men and women—and the world is critically short of Centurion leaders.

Military leaders are forced to make life-and-death decisions affecting those serving below them. Yet other leaders also make decisions that may mean the life or death of a nation, a church, or the continued existence of jobs in a company. You may already be a busy executive. You may already be "in charge." What you must decide is whether you will lead like a Centurion.

This book presents models as a means to teaching leadership principles. Principles are often forgotten in the heat of the battle while models are not. We emulate that which we admire—even in dire circumstances. I have chosen eleven portraits and the principles that helped define their leadership greatness. For many, examining leaders through a "one-principle looking glass" cannot possibly do them justice. Yet, this should spur you to study these and other models that intrigue or inspire you. None of these men and women was perfect, but they possessed qualities of greatness while they led their armies like Centurions. The models and principles in these portraits have withstood the test of time, beginning just before the emergence of the Roman Empire.

This is not a book for those seeking ten quick ways to succeed in leadership without really trying. Instead, it is a collection of narratives of Centurions in crisis, Centurions holding fast to strength, honor, and virtue while at the point of the spear. Life-changing lessons are best absorbed through observation rather than instruction. Standing in their shoes will allow you to discover leadership as a dynamic living concept. Whether your world is clashing among corporations, fighting for freedom, or ministering to the misguided, principles remain constant while circumstances change with every tick of the clock.

This book is written in memory of those who have led like Centurions and for you who soon will. Centurions are not easily forgotten. They leave a legacy without trying to do so and leave footprints for the generations to follow. Their voices and actions will live here once again.

Though technology has made obsolete what once was commonplace, it has yet to replace the intangible value of an inspirational leader. The world is desperately seeking great leaders again. The world needs Centurions who are strong in both their competence and their character.

I invite you to lead with the strength of a Centurion and the honor and integrity of one as well. I invite you to lead like a Centurion.

"Strength and Honor."

CHAPTER I

HANNIBAL
CHAMPION OF CARTHAGE

*Great leaders don't think outside the box—they bury
it. And then they make darn sure none of their
followers are tempted to dig it up again.*

MOST BOOKS IN THIS GENRE START OUT WITH THE PREMISE
that everyone can be a leader. I don't think that is true, and I believe
the plethora of sorry leadership examples in corporate America bear
this out. Of those leaders who are fitted to their calling, very few
are willing or able to become Centurions. The weight of the leader's
mantle weighs too heavily on most shoulders to be borne ably or
for long. So it is not uncommon then for many to settle for "managing" situations rather than rising to leadership.

Too many leaders focus upon the trappings rather than the sub-
stance of their office. Headlines continue to reveal a corporate
parade of CEOs living dissipated lifestyles, consumed by greed,
lacking a moral compass, and willing to sink to any level to reach
their ends. They leave no positive memory of their tenure, much
less a legacy to follow.

Centurions have no illusions of such "trappings," but gather the courage and will to set out through dark forests and dangerous waters while inspiring others to follow them. If you've picked up this book to learn their secrets, then you possess a willingness to test your mettle, your limitations, and your heart.

If we believed as the ancient mariners once did, that there was an edge to the ocean beyond which "great sea monsters live," few would be stout enough to venture beyond the water's edge. It takes a courageous heart, an adventurous spirit, a quick mind, and a visionary soul to become a Centurion.

I encourage you to begin by deciding whether you *want* to be such a leader—whether you will risk traveling into the waters where those sea monsters live. With a stout enough heart you will find your dark fears vanish in the light of dawn's greater reality. You will discover that your toughest foe to overcome is not the enemy before you but rather the enemy of great achievement that is *within* you. That is where your journey begins and is the focus of this book. It is what people know about themselves that ultimately defeats them. It is also what makes them afraid. That is why we begin with the box. Defined. Confined. Safe. Comfortable. Approved.

> *M. A. Rosanoff:* Mr. Edison, please tell me what laboratory rules you want me to observe.
>
> *Edison:* What? There ain't no rules around here! We're trying to accomplish somep'n!
>
> Thomas Alva Edison, 1847–1931[1]

Go outside the box? You're on your own. Unlimited risk. Job security—zero. A place littered with failure. On your own and unapproved. No known road maps. Potential? Achieve what all before you thought was impossible.

When you look at the risk and potential, is it any wonder so few are willing to go outside the box? Most large organizations, wittingly or not, force their employees to fit into predefined boxes or suffer the consequences. It begins with the simple and obvious, such as dress, and escalates to unwritten rules that the brightest figure out in a battle for survival. The results produce a cookie-cutter workforce that seeks to replicate those at the top—if they want to get to the top. Creativity is limited to the wall posters of corporate culture—mantras to repeat during evaluations, but never apply.

When I was a fellow at Harvard University, I loved listening to the undergraduates telling each other, "The first rule of Harvard is: break all the rules." It was simplistic, leaning toward anarchy, but had the effect of inspiring each other to be creative. In corporate, military, or civilian cultures, it takes leaders, not the "undergraduates," to instill that kind of culture.

The barriers you face today may appear to be insurmountable. But it may just be that you've been searching within a small, safe "box" for solutions when they don't exist there. Until you are willing to cross the line to "where sea monsters live," you will just "manage" the situation, rather than conquer a nearly impassable mountain.

In Hannibal's day, there were barriers and hurdles that no one could surmount. Hannibal's challenge was to find solutions to those barriers—the same as any leader today. The soon-to-be great Carthaginian general had to find a way to bring the war home to the empire of Rome. To this point, the war was a distant news event for the Romans as Hannibal rampaged far away in Spain. Rome felt safe behind the Alps to the north and with a strong navy protecting the eastern and western shores. But Hannibal wasn't a bureaucrat just managing the situation while carrying the title of "General." He was devising a plan to penetrate formidable Rome by doing something no army had ever done since Hercules (the Greek). He was going to take an army across the Alps.

ROME AND CARTHAGE—CLASH OF EMPIRES

Rome and Carthage grew side by side, clashed steel against steel, and acquired allies from Spain to North Africa before facing each other in three major wars. The decisive one, the Second Punic War, lasted from 219 to 202 BC. Against the growing military might of Rome stood the great commercial empire of Carthage, which was located in what is now Tunisia. Its commercial wealth came from Spain, its largest possession.

In 219 BC, Rome began to hear of a fearsome general whose very name provoked fear in the streets wherever he approached.

"*Hannibal ad portas!* Hannibal is at the gates!" was the ancient equivalent of the Cold War cry, "The Russians are coming!" No general or nation had ever shaken Rome as much, or would again until Alaric the Visigoth in AD 408.

In the First Punic War, Rome defeated Carthage, whose allies were led by Hannibal's father, Hamilcar. Carthage spent the next twenty years preparing to wrest itself from the heavy burden of Roman tribute and rule. Hamilcar built Carthaginian commerce and power in Spain: New Carthage in the east, and Lisbon in the west. From these two great cities, the Carthaginians were able to amass great wealth, power, and the potential to confront Rome again.

At the age of nine, Hannibal went to Spain with his father. Before departing, his father took him to an altar and, placing his hand on the sacrifice, made him swear that he would never be a friend to the Romans. At an early age, Hannibal was devoted to his father's successor, Hasdrubal, who led the Carthaginian army in Spain. On the death of Hasdrubal, Hannibal was appointed to command the Carthaginian army in Spain and quickly conquered the remaining Spanish tribes in that region.

"When I compose I sit down to the piano, shut my eyes and play what I hear."

ERNST THEODOR "AMADEUS" HOFFMANN, COMPOSER, 1776–1822[2]

Alarmed at his success, the inhabitants of Saguntum, a small city in Spain, sent a cry of help to their long-standing ally, Rome. Accordingly, a Roman ambassador was sent to Hannibal, who was passing the winter at Carthage Nova.

He reminded Hannibal that a treaty between the Carthaginians and Romans guaranteed the independence of Saguntum. He emphasized that any attack upon Saguntum would be viewed as a declaration of war upon Rome. Hannibal's response was to lay siege to Saguntum in 219 BC and conquer it eight months later.

Instead of declaring war, the Romans sent another envoy to Carthage itself, demanding that Hannibal be removed from command and punished. If this was not done, Rome would declare war on Carthage. Fabius, the Roman envoy, "laid his hand on the fold of his toga . . . and said, 'Here, we bring you peace and war. Take which you will.' Scarcely had he spoken when the answer no less proudly rang out: 'Whichever you please, we do not care.' Fabius let the gathered folds fall, and cried: 'We give you war.'"[3] Hannibal was appointed commander in chief at that moment—he had not reached twenty-five years of age."[4]

The easiest way for Hannibal to get his considerable forces to Italy would have been by sea. He had enough transports, and Carthage could have provided more. Even animals as large as Hannibal's war elephants that he used to terrify the enemy's infantry could have been transported. Further, landings upon hostile coasts had rarely been opposed, but then few had even tried against Rome.

Hannibal's major impediment to successful invasion by sea was Rome's superior navy. Hannibal could have risked slipping by the Roman fleet, but he needed something more than a safe landing zone. Hannibal needed allies. He needed the help of Rome's enemies, the Gauls, to resupply his army and provide him fresh troops.

CROSSING THE ALPS

At fifteen thousand feet at the highest point, the Alps presented a formidable challenge. Above ten thousand feet, oxygen is insufficient to sustain human life. Finding a path well below that would be difficult, yet that was where Hannibal pointed his armies.

Rome quickly sent the consul Publius Scipio to intercept Hannibal before he could reach the critical mountain pass. Because of the speed of Hannibal's army, Publius was unable to reach them in time and returned to Italy to await Hannibal, should he make it through the mountains—an occurrence Rome considered highly unlikely.

Along the way, Hannibal decimated tribes that opposed him, gathered allies that assisted him, and built roads where none existed. He widened many narrow roads so that fully equipped elephants could now pass. He left Spain in June of 218 BC with ninety thousand infantry, twelve thousand cavalry, and thirty-seven elephants.[5] By the time Hannibal crossed the Pyrenees and Alps, he was reduced to half his infantry, two-thirds of his cavalry, and only a few of his elephants.[6] It was a costly journey compared to what would have been a comparatively easy journey by sea. Yet, in addition to crossing the Alps, Hannibal accomplished the one goal he desperately sought—an alliance of Gauls to fight Rome.

Hannibal spent the winter resting his men and successfully recruiting thirty thousand Gauls (French) to meet the forces Rome was rushing into northern Italy. His moment of testing had arrived. Would he be known as "the son" of the great Hamilcar or a great leader in his own right? A modern-day comparison might be two presidents whose sons were also elected U.S. presidents—John Adams in the nineteenth century and George Bush in the twentieth. While an incumbent father would be a useful counselor, the weight of office can be placed upon only one pair of shoulders, which must be strong enough to bear the crushing weight of circumstances that test each leader.

Hannibal's strength rested in his ability to think beyond ordinary conventions and methods. Crossing the Alps was the first example of Hannibal's unique leadership creativity that couldn't be defined by any particular style, method, or "box." Rome faced Carthage in dozens of battles during the Second Punic War and was time and again baffled and beaten by an inscrutable leader who always seemed one step ahead of the Romans—one step out of the box.

First Contact—Rome Rushes to Disaster, 218 BC

When your enemy rushes at you in haste, step aside and his own weight and speed will offer the opportunity to trip him up. (Axiom of martial arts)

Rome faced Hannibal almost immediately upon his arrival in December as the Romans found his army in the hills across the River Trebia (west of modern Piacenza). Against the advice of Scipio "the elder," the Roman Consul Sempronius hastily crossed the river with forty thousand infantry. Hungry to be the commander who defeated Hannibal, he hurriedly prepared his army for battle. The historian Alexander recorded the short battle from the hills above the two armies.

> Now with the River at their back and unable to retreat in case of defeat, the Romans faced an attack by Hannibal, his infantry in the center advancing directly and his main cavalry force, elephants, and missile-throwing light troops on each wing driving away the weaker Roman horses and falling on the Roman flanks. While the Roman army was completely occupied with these assaults, a hand-picked Carthaginian cavalry and infantry force of two thousand . . . descended on the rear of the Roman Army. The converging assaults to the front, sides, and rear shattered the Romans. Only ten thousand (out of forty thousand) were able to escape, most cutting their way through the Carthaginian center. The remainder died. Hannibal probably lost only about five thousand men.[7]

Surprise at Lake Trasimeno, 217 BC

Battle in war is inevitable. When outnumbered—outthink. When outthought—outfight. When outfought—disengage and vanish to fight another day. Always leave one ace in your pocket to be used when all else is lost. Once you've used it, you've used it. You'll need a different ace for another day.

Licking its wounds that winter, Rome prepared two armies to block Hannibal's army from threatening Rome itself. The Roman leaders expected Hannibal to soon march on Rome, and the road through the Po Valley was the easiest and most direct route. With two armies consisting of forty thousand under Nepos and twenty thousand under Geminus, they blocked his path with a formidable force.

Like Robert E. Lee of the Confederate Army, Hannibal knew he had limited resources in men and equipment. He elected to confuse rather than confront. "He turned away from the waiting Roman armies, climbed over the Apennines north of Genoa, reached the coast and marched south along it. The Romans were surprised but not worried, because Hannibal would have to turn towards them to go south or cross the marshes of the Arno River, which were nearly impassable in the spring floods. So the Romans took no precautions to block that route."[8]

> "The freedom to make mistakes provides the best environment for creativity."
>
> ANONYMOUS

Hannibal then did what no one believed could be done. Hannibal sent his army and elephants into the flooded swamps. As they tried to tread through the soft mud, many died of exhaustion. Hannibal himself, riding upon an elephant, caught an infection and permanently lost the sight of one eye. Four days later, however, his army emerged south of Rome's legions under Nepos. Hannibal's losses were heavy, but he had done what the Romans thought impossible. Nothing stood between Hannibal and Rome.

Terrified by the news, Nepos ordered his army to pursue Hannibal. Though counseled to wait for the arrival of reinforcements under Geminus, Nepos's pride and fear of Hannibal drove him as mercilessly as he drove his army. Yet Hannibal had no intention of marching on Rome. Instead, like Sherman in the U.S. Civil War, he instituted a scorched-earth policy devastating the countryside while gathering supplies to sustain his army. This infuriated Nepos, who whipped his army with greater fury, following Hannibal's path from one burnt village to another.

With Nepos hot on his heels, Hannibal finally turned to face the forty thousand Romans as he marched past Lake Trasimeno. On the hills in the west were enough vegetation and trees to conceal a part of his army. He placed his Gauls, cavalry, and lead-throwing slingers in the hills, while displaying his African and Spanish infantry in sight of the Romans just beyond where his hidden army waited. Alexander described the outcome of this battle in 217 BC (see map):

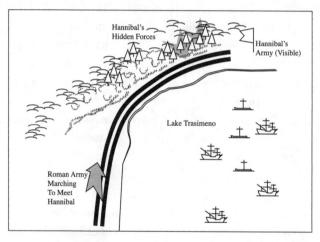

In the early morning the Romans, in column formations, pressed over a pass just west of the lake and marched along the lakeshore road. They had made no reconnaissance, and heavy mists from the water made visibility poor. When the front of the column reached the massed Carthaginian heavy infantry, it halted and the rest of the column closed up behind. Hannibal ordered his cavalry to prevent a Roman retreat by blocking the pass on the west (behind Nepos), then directed his light infantry to strike from mountainside. The Romans were utterly surprised and panicked. With nowhere to go and in march, not battle, order, they were slaughtered like cattle, thirty thousand of them, including Nepos. About ten thousand fled in scattered groups through the mountains to notify Rome of the disaster. Hannibal lost twenty-five hundred men.[9]

In this battle, Hannibal demonstrated a skilled use of geography and tactics. However, he employed another element of battle that the Romans would long remember. It was enough that an army should face men of valor, equally trained and armed. But that day, the Romans saw what dozens of rampaging, armored elephants could do on the field of battle. As these enormous beasts rampaged toward the Roman lines, the effect must have been truly terrifying. The thundering herd shook the ground under the enemy well before the dust kicked up by their feet rose a hundred feet into the air. Once they fell upon the precise Roman formations, they stomped to death many in their ranks, oblivious to the spears and arrows shot into them. Only one in four Romans survived the battle, and Hannibal's name and army were no longer being joked about. And the worst was yet to come.

THE BATTLE OF CANNAE, 217 BC

Strength against strength weakens both—leaving the outcome gravely in doubt. Use your strength against weakness to produce confusion and panic. Never be afraid to allow your enemy to underestimate you, but prepare to respond when he acts upon his miscalculation.

During the summer of 217 BC, Hannibal rested his army along the Adriatic coast and continued to ravage cities and towns in the heel of Italy. Rome was in no position to confront him after the devastating losses of the year before. However, Rome appointed a new leader as "dictator" for six months—Quintus Fabius Maximus. His name became synonymous with a strategy of early guerilla warfare known as "the Fabian strategy." Rome, like the supposedly "great and powerful Oz," was reduced to projecting the illusion of power. Harass, attack, and withdraw while waiting for a better day. As a guerilla fighter, Fabius performed well, but Rome found it a bitter pill to swallow.

Since Hannibal was stronger in cavalry, Fabius kept his forces in the hills as a way of nullifying this advantage—choosing to strike and retreat, strike and retreat. This was both wise and effective considering the shifting balance of power following the disasters at Trebia and Trasimeno. "The Romans hovered in the vicinity of the Carthaginians, cut off stragglers and foragers, and prevented them from founding a permanent base. The strategy avoided Roman defeat and dimmed Hannibal's glory. It successfully kept Rome's allies from declaring for Carthage, but it aroused great opposition among Romans themselves, for their state had thrived on a tradition of offensive warfare."[10]

At one point, Fabius made a bold attempt to corner the Carthaginians in the area of Falernia. Fabius did what no commander had done before him; he surprised Hannibal. That night, recognizing his situation as desperate, Hannibal ordered all of the cattle in his camp gathered together. He tied torches to each of their horns and sent them stampeding into the Roman camp. Panic and confusion ensued. Under the cover of darkness, with fear rampant in the camp of the Romans, Hannibal extricated his entire army without the loss of a single man. How many leaders, in the few hours available, could have envisioned and executed such an escape of seventy thousand soldiers?

DISASTER AT CANNAE

From every disaster comes the power to reshape a stagnant bureaucracy—from corporations to armies. Remake them while the bitter taste of defeat still lingers on the lips.

For six months, Fabius kept Hannibal at bay, but the Senate refused to extend his tenure as commander and instead appointed two consuls "who would make Rome proud by taking the fight to Hannibal." One cautious leader, Paulus, was teamed with a more impetuous consul, Varro. They had learned that to face Hannibal without overwhelming superiority would be courting disaster. So they brought massive forces with them. "Rome assembled the largest army they had ever placed in the field, eighty thousand infantry, and seven thousand cavalry. They marched towards Hannibal, Varro and Paulus alternating command each day."[11]

> "When Alexander the Great visited Diogenes and asked whether he could do anything for the famed teacher, Diogenes replied: 'Only stand out of my light.'"
>
> JOHN GARDNER, 1912–2002[12]

The two commanders argued along the way about how to confront Hannibal; Paulus arguing for favorable positioning, while Varro took advantage of his day of command and launched his attack on what he believed would be his "day of glory."

Hannibal crossed over the Aufidus (modern Ofanto) River to the western side, this time leaving his back to the river. Though it was summer, and at low tide, it did form a barrier in the event of defeat. Actually, Hannibal hoped to use this positioning to entice the Romans into attacking him. A further enticement, though unplanned, was that by this point in the war, all of Hannibal's elephants had died. It would be a battle upon the open plain between two superbly trained armies, Rome having the numerical advantage.

> Both armies were arrayed in customary order, the infantry in the center and cavalry on both wings. But Hannibal pushed forward his less dependable Gauls and Spanish foot soldiers in the exact center, while holding back his strong African infantry on either side. This provided a natural magnet for the advancing Romans, who struck at the Gauls and Spaniards, forcing them back, just as Hannibal had intended.

The convex Carthaginian line, therefore, became concave, sagging ominously inward. The Roman legionnaires, flushed with apparent success, crowded into this opening believing they were breaking the enemy front.

At this moment Hannibal gave the signal and the African foot soldiers suddenly wheeled inward from sides, striking the Roman flank and enveloping them into a tightly packed mass. Meanwhile Hannibal's heavy cavalry on the left wing had broken through the weaker Roman cavalry on that side and had swept around the Roman rear to drive away the cavalry on the Roman left flank. Leaving the lighter Numidian (Algerian) cavalry on the right wing to pursue the Roman horsemen, Hannibal's heavy cavalry delivered the final stroke by bursting onto the rear of the Roman legions, already enveloped on three sides and so compressed they were unable to offer effective resistance.[13]

Cannae was a greater massacre than any of the combined losses up to this point. Of the eighty-seven thousand Romans that gave battle that day, only six thousand escaped to survive to tell the story, including Scipio (one day Scipio "Africanus"). Hannibal lost about six thousand men.

From this point on, the war in Italy settled into a stalemate. Hannibal did not have the siege trains and engines required to breach Rome's walls while Rome lacked the stomach to confront Hannibal again after so many disasters. Consequently, Rome returned to the Fabian strategy, and for the next eight years, Hannibal ravaged the country. In Spain the situation was nearly as bad. Most of the Spanish tribes formerly allied to Rome had abandoned them, and Rome lacked the leadership there to reverse their fortunes.

Far from home, Hannibal used strategies and tactics never before faced by the Romans. His ability to outthink his enemy, while outnumbered by a well-trained, superior force, made him one of the first, and best, outside-of-the-box thinkers. It was also what caused the Romans to reshape and reorganize their military leadership.

THOUGHTS FOR TODAY'S CENTURIONS

IF SCIENCE IS RIGHT, HUMAN BEINGS ONLY USE 10 PERCENT of the mind's capacity. That those who suffer from stroke and permanent brain impairment can relearn tasks associated with the specific area of brain atrophy confirms this belief. The mind is capable of much more than we've discovered. There is creative energy there, but how do we begin to uncover it and bring it to life within ourselves and those around us? Hannibal lost an eye crossing what was once thought to be an impassable swamp. Even that didn't dim his ability to outthink and outvision Rome.

There are a number of ways to increase personal and organizational creativity. It takes effort, but the benefits are well beyond bottom-line considerations, because creativity influences every aspect of life—even its quality and length.

Increasing creativity requires challenging the mind to stretch itself beyond what it believes it is capable of achieving. It was Pablo Picasso who noted, "I am always doing that which I cannot do, in order that I may learn how to do it." Even simple exercises can increase creativity and brain activity.

In 1991, *Life* magazine ran an article on nuns who were in their eighties and nineties. None of them showed any signs of what is common in the very aged—Alzheimer's disease. The one common thread between all of these women was that they worked on jigsaw puzzles each day. In doing so, they apparently held off the ravaging effects of brain deterioration. Science concludes that unless humans create new neural connections as they age, brain atrophy is inevitable. For those in leadership, the use it or lose it principle is just as applicable.

Most of us have formed definite neural pathways of thought. Habits and ways of approaching situations in life create impressions and deep ruts in the brain. "We have truly hard-wired our mechanism for thought . . .We can see that we need to create flexibility in the brain to have flexibility of mind."[14]

If you want your organization to develop creative solutions to previously unsolvable problems, you are going to have to change old ways of thinking by leading the way. That means some rigid structures need to become more fluid. To achieve employee buy-in, they need to know they are going to be rewarded for creative solutions, even if they ultimately fail.

Why not introduce games, puzzles, questions, or trivia competitions—not necessarily related to the present working environment? Such activity will begin to stretch the minds of those who work with and for you. This isn't as random as it sounds because some puzzles stimulate right-brain activity (creativity and intuitive thinking), while others stimulate the left (analytic and logical thinking).

A second means to encourage and develop creativity is through humor. Yes, funny, silly, seemingly irrelevant, and absurd humor. Ever flown on Southwest Airlines? Instead of worrying about taxi times and delays, you feel that you've booked a seat in the audience of Comedy Central. The punch lines from the microphone seem to lighten the atmosphere without undermining the serious nature of the business of flying. Do they script their lines like a Disney ride? Hardly.

Herb Kelleher, twice named CEO of the year by *Financial World* magazine, says creating a culture is their number-one priority. What kind of culture? "We decided we were going to hire good people and let them be themselves, let them be individualistic. We were going to create an environment where we pay a great deal of attention to them, their personal lives, as well as their business lives. We wanted to show them that we don't regard them just as work automatons. We wanted to create an environment where people can really enjoy what they're doing."[15] Southwest has successfully survived and profited while other airlines went into bankruptcy after the economic downturn and stock market decline. Herb Kelleher and those at Southwest Airlines show that creativity doesn't have to be an economic sinkhole.

The AT&T plant in Norcross, Georgia, celebrated achieving a major milestone (a contract changed) by holding a parade throughout the plant. Employees working on their own time made the floats from leftover supplies. Last in the parade were the operations manager and the president of the CWA local not just shaking hands, but hugging in congratulations of their joint accomplishments. Why do these things? To increase morale. To lessen stress. To enrich camaraderie and teamwork. To make work fun and something people look forward to each day.[16]

Improving productivity and creativity through thinking outside the box can involve something as simple as wit. Laughter and humor change the atmosphere, lighten the heart, and increase company morale. Any one of those would make most employees rejoice, but here is something else that CEOs can rejoice over. This kind of environment has been shown to "have a direct effect upon the bottom line. Lower turnover, absenteeism, lateness, error rates, increased production, accuracy (and) finer quality. The overall results . . . higher profits and greater staying power when things get tough."[17]

In addition to exercising your brain, your body also needs exercise to increase creativity. Time out of the work environment, away from the phones and computers, can do a lot to clear the mind and stimulate new ideas. Exercise is known to increase oxygen to the brain, and enough exercise releases endorphins into the body, increasing productive output while creating what is known as a runner's high.[18] Are you, as a leader, willing to encourage, even demand, your organization exercise daily—even if it's just a half-hour walk around the plant, base, or building?

"I am always doing that which I cannot do, in order that I may learn how to do it."

PABLO PICASSO

Be prepared for those moments when your mind is open and new ideas pour in. Carry a notebook and write down your thoughts. Many great inventors have done this and found that most of what they wrote was useless. But on occasion, there was a treasure buried among the pages of worthless thoughts.

Finally, read everything you can get your hands on. Fill your mind with the knowledge of many fields, not just your own. For in some field, far from your own endeavors, you may find a new way of approaching a formerly unsolvable problem. If nothing else, you will have learned a great deal that will be stored as "potential" for your unwritten future.

You might say to all of this, "I'm not the creative type." You do a disservice to yourself in believing that, for each of us has been endowed with creative energy. And even if I were to believe you, I would remind you of something Warren Bennis said: "There are two ways of being creative. One can sing and dance. Or one can create an environment in which singers and dancers flourish." Perhaps your creativity will be evidenced in creating an organization in which future Thomas Edisons create the technologies of tomorrow. Perhaps you will be the general whose captains feel free enough to walk into your office and say, "I've got a lot smarter, cheaper, faster, better way of doing this," without fearing for their position.

Fear has a tendency to paralyze. Creativity and fear seldom co-exist. Fear will sometimes produce short-term results, but rarely long-term solutions. Creative minds believe they can devise the plans and methods needed to overcome anything—anything. How much are those kinds of people worth in your organization?

I remember reading about a math problem that had never been solved. A college professor gave the class a final exam and put two problems on the board. The first one was for their grade. The second one was the unsolved problem they could work on for personal enrichment and extra credit. One of the brighter students in the class (who seemed to lack the skill of punctuality) arrived late and saw the two problems on the board. It was a take-home exam and so he picked up the problems and walked out. The student didn't hear the instructions and assumed both problems were part of the exam. He went home and worked nonstop on both and then turned them in on the day they were due. While grading the papers, the professor was astonished to see that this student had solved not only the first, but the second as well. The student was pleased by the instructor's compliments, but didn't understand the significance because he never realized the problem had been unsolvable. Too often we look at problems that have never been solved and join the rest of the world in agreement. Creative people don't focus on limitations; they focus on possibilities.

As leaders, we must allow our subordinates to develop creativity if our organizations are to break new ground in the face of stiff competition. It takes a creative and fearless leader to cultivate such talent and provide the necessary resources to achieve such breakthroughs.

If you want to be a great leader, you're going to have to destroy the box within which many sit and make their decisions. I provided some examples of what companies have done to increase corporate creativity. But what about your own? Studies show that even during sleep, the brain continues to work on solving problems. So, your own creativity could be increased by taking the time to hike along a mountain ridge, or walk along the beach and feel the wind in your face as the water washes over your feet. Then maybe you will be given a fresh approach to pursue; one that will change your world and the world of those around you. Hannibal changed the face of war during his lifetime. What might you do?

A PAUSE FOR A SPIRITUAL REFLECTION

Most of us never produce a life of creative achievements because we have not connected to the Great Creator Himself—the source of all creative energy. If God endows each of us with that energy, then it is up to us to find it within ourselves and use it. If you leave it lying dormant, you miss those moments we define as extraordinary. If we settle for common wisdom, then we cannot produce uncommon ends. If we listen to what God is saying to us, then we open ourselves to the possibility of living exceptional lives.

Take a breath. Maybe it's been a long time. Reflect back upon the dreams that once lived in your heart. Perhaps it's been decades and you've given up all hope of achieving what you once desired. Those creative dreams are seeds that have been waiting for you to water them. If you would be a creative leader—a Centurion leader—you must begin by being a creative individual. Like anything worthwhile, it takes time. The oak tree takes nearly a century to reach its full height but begins as an acorn. Those who are too fearful, lazy, or busy, end up growing, if at all, to the size of a bush, stunted by a leadership philosophy called "expediency."

Your future can be so much greater than that. God is a destiny shaper and destiny maker, and scatters seeds of creativity freely. The question is whether you believe it and whether you are willing to water the seeds planted inside you. At the end of your life, as you examine the significance of your days, will you see an oak tree or a bush growing there?

PATHWAY TO CREATIVITY

We began with "the box"—a mystical box. But if it exists only in the imagination, why do so few break out of its confines? While we can't hold up this box and see it with our eyes, it is still as real as gravity. It's real because we as leaders translate it into a reality that is defined, confined, safe, comfortable, and approved.

Go outside the box? You'll be on your own facing nearly unlimited risk. Forget about job security because at times you'll be out on the limb all by yourself. There are no known road maps where you're going, but it is the road that all Centurions must take. What awaits you? Potential—potential for an extraordinary life that leaves a memorable legacy. Why? Because it is our nature to admire the oak tree rather than the bush.

CHAPTER 2

SCIPIO AFRICANUS
GENERAL OF ROME,
CONQUEROR OF HANNIBAL

*Victory teaches the simple, failure the wise; success
teaches a few lessons, failure a thousand.
Study the lessons of the defeated.*

WHEN THE FOUNDATIONS OF A NATION ARE TORN, ALL SENSE of future is lost as well. By the year 210 BC, Hannibal had ravaged Rome's countryside and most of Rome's allies in Spain as well. Rome's "Fabian strategy" of hit-and-run left the once proud nation further devoid of any hope to ever achieve a decisive victory. Rome was in danger of descending into an indecisive malaise. The continued losses forced Rome to order the conscription of all its remaining able-bodied males, thereby further depleting an already faltering economy.

In Spain, the situation was even worse. In addition to losing numerous battles to Hannibal's brother, Hasdrubal, the Roman army lacked competent and courageous leadership. The increasing erosion of Roman power demanded a strong proconsul to reverse the decline—which was easier said than done. The qualified were unwilling to present themselves as candidates for such responsibility. The potential to end one's career aspirations abruptly, not to mention the real risk of an early death, weighed heavily on the minds of young officers eligible for the post.

The first reference to the son of General Publicus was under less than auspicious circumstances. Scipio was one of the six thousand Roman survivors who lived to tell of the Carthaginian massacre at Cannae. From that moment forward, Scipio began serious study of the tactics of Hannibal. Time and again, he watched as numerically superior Roman armies were carved up by the Carthaginian magician; for that is how Rome came to view the feared Hannibal—a warrior who against the odds, time and again, snatched victory from defeat.

In spite of his youth, Scipio distinguished himself early at the age of seventeen.

> He was stationed with the Roman army under the command of his father, one of the consuls for the year (218 BC). His father had placed him with a reserve detachment on a hill, away from the presumed center of the battlefield. During the course of the engagement, however, his father became separated from the main unit, was surrounded by the enemy, and sustained serious wounds. Upon seeing his father's plight, the young Scipio immediately galloped to his rescue. His comrades followed his gallant lead and the enemy dispersed upon their advance. The episode gained him considerable popular fame, which led to rapid advancement up the military and civilian ranks.[1]

While Scipio was a serious student of the profession of arms, he certainly wasn't a one-dimensional figure. He had considerable civil leadership skills as well.

> In 212 BC Scipio made his first attempt at public office. His elder brother, Lucius, was a candidate for *curule aedile*, a lower

officer responsible for police and market supervision. There were two open positions and multiple candidates for this office. Sensing that his brother stood little chance of being elected, while fully aware of his own budding popularity, Scipio devised a plan for them to run together for the offices . . . When the appointed time for elections arrived, both he and his brother appeared before the people as candidates. The sight of the popular Publius Cornelius "Scipio," next to his brother Lucius, aroused the crowd's enthusiasm and they were both elected *aedile* for the year."[2]

By 210 BC, Scipio's father, Publius, and uncle, Gnaeus, had made significant gains against the Carthaginian army in Spain.

Most Roman leaders, however, were not greatly impressed by the brothers' victories, [and] considered Spain a sideshow while Hannibal was at the gates in Italy. Consequently, they did not send substantial forces to Spain, and in 211 BC the Carthaginians defeated the Romans and killed Scipio's father and uncle in two separate battles in southern Spain.[3]

The stench of defeat now permeated the halls of the Roman Senate. While the Senate gave short shrift to Spain, the loss of their two top commanders was a tough pill to swallow. Who would fill their place? Precious few stepped forward to seek the title of proconsul in Spain—most weren't interested in taking the helm of a sinking ship. The Senate had already demonstrated their disdain for the army's needs there, so the silence was deafening. At that moment, Scipio stepped forward.

He had several reasons to seek the position. His father had been killed in service to Rome in Spain, and he felt a deep family obligation to right this wrong. Further, he had avidly studied Carthaginian battle strategy and desired to test his mettle against those who had defeated all previous consuls. He felt he possessed the acumen and stamina needed to shore up the Roman army and prepare it to one day face Hannibal himself. The first opening for leadership was in Spain and so he offered himself for service. It was a well-known saying then that "if you want to rise up in the world, do the difficult." So, that day, Scipio rose up and placed his name before the Senate. He was twenty-four years of age.

The fact that he was so young made his subsequent appointment almost unprecedented. However, he had a number of supporters in the Senate and now headed one of the most powerful families in Rome. The Senate thought the son of the fallen Publius might be able to bind up various alliances threatening to unravel in Spain. Scipio was appointed proconsul and Commander of the Legions in Spain and landed there at Emporion with about ten thousand infantry and one thousand cavalry during the summer of 210 BC.[4]

THE BATTLE FOR SPAIN—FIRST BLOOD

Surprise and deception can make a smaller army appear larger, a larger army appear invisible and achieve victory while greatly limiting casualties. Thomas Bacon said, "In the end, no matter the facts, man will believe the truth that most pleases him." Make your enemy believe the truth that pleases him, and then you can do anything.

Upon arriving, Scipio made a survey of Rome's field positions and visited his allies along the Iberian Peninsula rallying support and inspiring confidence. He also *commended* the remaining Roman leadership there rather than berating them—noting that they had prevented a complete annihilation.

At this time, there were three Carthaginian armies dispersed throughout Spain, yet they had not moved to defend their supply depot in the city of New Carthage in southern Spain. Too much victory can lead to complacency, and Scipio took advantage of their oversight, attacking New Carthage in his first major offensive.

Scipio's father had repeatedly been denied adequate resupply by

Rome, and Scipio saw the effects—an inability to take the offensive, leading to ultimate defeat. Now, it was his turn. The Carthaginian armies under Hannibal in Italy were dependent upon Spain and Tunisia for resupply. If he could cut off and isolate the Carthaginian armies in Spain, perhaps he could turn the tide of war in both Spain and Italy.

New Carthage was the only Spanish port fit for the Carthaginian Empire to land its fleet and resupply its armies. Moreover, the Carthaginians kept the bulk of their bullion, Spanish hostages, and war material there. The city had strong walls and natural defenses situated on a peninsula connected to the mainland by a four-hundred-yard strip of land to the east. The most enticing consideration was the Carthaginians had left only one thousand trained soldiers guarding it.[5]

> "It's not work, if you love what you're doing."
>
> STEVE SEARS

Scipio instructed his naval commander to sail to New Carthage and blockade the city's port. At the same time, he force-marched his army of twenty-seven thousand men to arrive there simultaneously with the navy. For some reason, it didn't occur to Carthage that Rome might attack the only viable seaport in Spain. Whether through arrogance, ignorance, or just complacency, the Carthaginians had left their supply lines to Italy and Africa unguarded.

Scipio launched an initial frontal attack against the eastern gate that failed, leaving many Roman casualties. As the city's dwellers rejoiced at their hated enemy's misfortune, Scipio prepared for a second assault against the same gate. At the same time, he took five hundred men and twenty-five ladders to the opposite side, which was protected by a lagoon now at low tide.

Just as the water reached its ebb, the men raced across the shallow lagoon and flung their ladders against the undefended wall; Scipio launched a simultaneous attack against two other positions. This three-pronged attack "fixed" all enemy forces in place and prevented them from moving to support the main attack against the lagoon. The five hundred men quickly ascended the lagoon wall, cleared it for a substantial distance in both directions, then assailed the rear of the Carthaginians defending the eastern wall, taking them by surprise and opening the way for the main body. To break the resistance of the people, Scipio allowed civilians to be massacred while the citadel held out. But once it surrendered, he stopped the killings. In a stroke the Carthaginians had lost their main base, key to their control of Spain, and the strategic initiative.[6]

Since Rome dominated the sea, Scipio could now threaten the three remaining armies of Carthage marching in Spain. If they moved directly against Scipio, he could choose where to fight, since he could now move his main body by sea and threaten the rear of any approaching army. As a result, a number of Iberian tribes who had supported Carthage joined Rome and tipped the balance of power in Rome's favor.

Hasdrubal, brother of Hannibal and Carthaginian general in Spain, could wait no longer as he lost both allies and the initiative. It was at this moment that Scipio's study of Carthaginian battle tactics paid off. Remembering the disaster at Cannae, Scipio broke with Roman battle doctrine in which massed troops marched directly at the enemy in frontal assault—strength against strength.

It was this heavy thrust that Hannibal had exploited at Cannae, enticing the Roman legions to drive into his sagging center and then turning his heavy infantry against the legions' exposed flanks. Scipio, learning from Hannibal, divided his army into three parts: light troops in the center and heavy troops on each wing.[7]

Facing Hasdrubal, who had the advantage of being above him on a two-step plateau, Scipio sent his light troops forward armed with javelins and darts. In spite of the disadvantage, they drove Hasdrubal back and enticed him to order his main body forward to face what he believed was the main attack. Scipio took half of his heavy troops while his lieutenant took the other half and began to flank Hasdrubal. Scipio's light troops allowed the Carthaginians to advance as they fell back in the center while holding strong along the edges of their formation. Hasdrubal was quick enough to realize he was about to be "Cannae'd" and pulled his troops out of the hole before he was decimated. Even so, he lost a third of his army in the process.

Hasdrubal withdrew, licked his wounds, and rebuilt his army using mercenary replacements to a respectable seventy thousand infantry, four thousand horses, and thirty-two elephants. He now outnumbered Scipio two-to-one.

These two armies faced each other again less than a year later while standing on two ridges overlooking a valley between them. Much like the setting in the first battle of the movie *Gladiator*, the numerical advantage went to Carthage. Scipio used elements of both deception and surprise to even the odds.

The Carthaginians moved forward first, and the Roman army responded in kind. Scipio had placed his heavy troops in the center, as was standard practice. However, as they neared each other, Hasdrubal could find no advantage and instead of engaging Scipio, he retreated. Scipio did the same. Much like two chess masters probing and checking for weaknesses, the two commanders initiated a series of feints for several days without committing their complete armies to battle.

Scipio then took the initiative. He fed his troops late one night and ordered them to arise before daylight. By dawn, his cavalry was attacking the outer rim of Hasdrubal's army, creating considerable confusion. Realizing he was in the middle of a surprise attack, Hasdrubal ordered all of his troops to battle, having no time to feed them.

Scipio had reversed his troop arrangement, now placing the Roman legions along the wings and his Spanish mercenaries in the center. He then waited for almost six hours before engaging in battle to allow the effects of hunger to weaken his enemy. When the time came, he ordered his Spanish troops to move forward slowly, while the legions on the wings marched quickly. When the legions were abreast of the enemy, they wheeled inwardly and began to smash the flanks of Carthage. Although the weaker Spanish center had not yet reached the frontlines of Carthage, they were a threat, and so the Carthaginian center could not disengage to help their flanks. As Rome methodically destroyed the wings, the tired and famished Carthaginian center had nowhere to go except to fall back.

Scipio continued to attack Hasdrubal as his men retreated, placing forces all along the escape routes. The Carthaginians were forced to pass through the Roman gauntlet to get to their ships, and very few of them survived to escape. Carthage's mighty presence in Spain was broken.

The Battle in the Senate

To become a Centurion, a leader must possess martial as well as moral courage. Lack the first and you will find death. Lack the second and you will find disgrace. Lack them both and you will find yourself a politician.

Centurions are often remembered for their great deeds of bravery and self-sacrifice against hopeless odds. Yet to be a great leader, a Centurion must possess two kinds of courage. It is not enough to possess only martial courage; a Centurion must also possess moral courage. In time, each type of courage is tested. Scipio had proven his martial courage in battle and was about to have his moral courage tested in the Senate.

Scipio had cut off Hannibal's supply lines from Spain; however, Hannibal still had Carthage itself to supply his ongoing war in Italy. Scipio returned to Rome with a surprising proposal. He wanted to take his legions to Africa to threaten the capital city of Carthage—the center and the strength of the Carthaginian Empire. By doing so, he hoped to force Hannibal to leave Italy to come to the aid of his homeland.

Because of Scipio's success in Spain he was reelected consul in 206–205 BC. While he had both enemies and friends in the Senate, his success was a breath of fresh air compared to the stench of defeat that had permeated Italy for almost a dozen years.

Scipio stood before the Senate and made his case to take the war to Carthage itself. He had seen the effects of an undersupplied army when he severed the Carthaginians from their supply depot at New Carthage. If he could threaten the capital city of Carthage, the rulers of Carthage might be enticed to order Hannibal home to defend their city. He concluded his arguments by asking the Senate to imagine Italy free of Hannibal for the first time in a dozen years.

His primary adversary in the Senate was Fabius, the consul who had developed the hit-and-run strategy against Hannibal. His answer seemed very modern: when you can't defeat the idea, attack the character or competence of the author.

> The Republic cannot support campaigns in both Italy and Africa. Hannibal is still formidable and experience shows that invading Africa is risky. It is still possible that Hannibal's brother, Mago, will come to join his brother. I myself think that . . . Scipio was made consul for the sake of the Republic, not for his own private gain, and that the armies are enrolled to guard the city and Italy, not so consuls, like kings in their arrogance, to transport them anywhere in the world they wish.[8]

Scipio responded:

> No one had talked of his ambition or of the dangers when he was sent to Spain . . . Hannibal's own example had shown the value of taking the offensive, and there was more likelihood of Carthage's allies rebelling against her than there had been of Rome's allies joining Hannibal. Without allies, Carthage

would find herself without troops, since she had no citizen soldiers. The invasion of Carthage would inevitably compel Hannibal to return to Africa and he [Scipio] could fight him in his own country, which could now be made to suffer as Italy had suffered.[9]

His character, his motives, his competence, and his wisdom were all mercilessly attacked in the Senate; however, Scipio continued to hold his ground, arguing the merits of his strategy. In the end, the Senate, seeing no better alternatives, acceded to his plan. Scipio refused to take the bait to engage in a personal battle with Fabius and focused on winning the Senate's support for his plan.

While Rome finally supported Scipio, the Senate prevented him from raising new conscripts in Italy. He was allowed to take only volunteers and whatever support he could gather in Africa. To guard against Hannibal, Rome insisted that four legions remain in Italy, and Scipio was able to raise only two legions of volunteers, some twenty to thirty-five thousand infantry. He had won the battle in the Senate, but his Carthaginian enemies were pleased that he wouldn't be bringing the five to six legions he would need to equal the forces they would field in Africa.

> "Sign your work at the end of each day. If you can't do that, find a new profession."
>
> AUTHOR

SCIPIO LANDS IN AFRICA, 204 BC

Scipio landed in Africa in 204 BC near Utica, just twenty miles north of Carthage with thirty thousand Roman troops. He faced a Carthaginian army of thirty thousand infantry under Hasdrubal as well as fifty thousand infantry and ten thousand cavalry under the Numidian king, Syphax—ally to Carthage. Beyond being outnumbered, Scipio lacked intelligence as to the exact locations, strength, and weaknesses of the two armies facing him. Facing two armies possessing a three-to-one advantage, Scipio sent ambassadors under the guise of diplomacy to gather intelligence.

> To bring it off, he needed to find out what was in the two camps, where the gates were located and when and where the guards . . . were posted. The visits of his emissaries provided this information. Scipio determined that Syphax's camp was the more vulnerable, especially because some of the soldiers' huts were outside the entrenchments encircling the camp and many others inside were strewn about with little space between them and were built of flammable material.[10]

Scipio now had the information he needed; he halted the negotiations and began a series of movements to confuse the enemy—launching ships, moving siege engines, and sending two thousand infantry up the hill overlooking Utica to simulate preparations to attack. That night as the Carthaginians watched the hills, Scipio marched his legions silently toward their camp, arriving at midnight.

He took half his forces and prepared to attack Hasdrubal while assigning his lieutenant to attack the Numidians and burn their camp. As the Romans reached the Numidians' camp, they torched every structure. In the confusion, the Numidians thought a natural disaster had struck and men rushed out unarmed and in disorder. They were cut down in large numbers. From the camp of Hasdrubal, the soldiers saw the flames and came to assist—again not armed. Now Scipio launched his attack against the unguarded gates of Hasdrubal's camp and set torches to everything. The end result was a massacre. "Perhaps forty thousand Carthaginians and Numidians were killed or died in the flames, and five thousand were captured. Hasdrubal got away with about twenty-five hundred men. Syphax got away with more of his men and retired to a fortified position."[11]

The Carthaginians sent to Spain for reinforcements and, when they arrived, marched out to face Scipio again. This time the numbers were more equal. The Numidians and Carthaginians regrouped with about thirty-five thousand troops to face Scipio's thirty thousand, and fought tenaciously and bravely. However, the end result was the same: a decisive *Romo Victor*—a Roman triumph.

"The frightened Carthaginian Senate frantically called Hannibal back from Italy, just as Scipio had predicted would occur when Carthage was threatened."[12]

The final conflict, between mighty Carthage and its legendary General Hannibal, and Rome, led by thirty-one-year-old Scipio, was about to begin.

SCIPIO VS. HANNIBAL AT THE BATTLE OF ZARMA, 202 BC

Study your enemy until you are absolutely certain of his habits. In his habits you will find his weakness.

While Scipio awaited the arrival of Hannibal, he kept his troops busy in the fertile Bagradas Valley, where the vast majority of food supplies were grown. Marching through this valley, Scipio seized all the grain they could find and sold all they captured as slaves. Little by little, Scipio hoped to reduce the will of the Carthaginians to resist and force Hannibal to take the field with minimal preparations. Scipio understood, being far from home, his own position would grow weaker over time, while Hannibal's would grow stronger. Scipio might expect some cavalry support from Masinissa's Numidian horsemen, but Hannibal could raise many times that with the allies of Carthage so near.

When Hannibal's ships touched the shore, he drove his army at Scipio's with the haste of a general who had received his orders from a frightened and angry king of Carthage. Of course, this wasn't all good news for Scipio. He would face Hannibal's fifty thousand men with his own thirty-six thousand, which included the Numidians—if they arrived in time. Even so, Scipio believed his best opportunity for victory was sooner, rather than later.

Hannibal sent three spies ahead to determine the condition and size of Scipio's army. As things turned out, Scipio's army intercepted all the spies and brought them to camp. Standard practice in such cases was immediate execution. However, Scipio took the spies and gave them a tour of the camp. And then, in a show of gallantry, told them to return to their lines. Hannibal was impressed by this and requested a meeting with Scipio before the battle began. Scipio knew that the spies would report his strength but would also report he lacked any cavalry. This was a calculated risk. He was depending upon the Numidian cavalry to arrive in time to support him in battle. As Hannibal and Scipio stood between their great armies,

> Hannibal spoke first saying he wished their two countries had never gone to war. He adjured Scipio not to be too confident, citing his own case as an example of how rapidly fortunes could change, and ended by saying that Rome should retain Sicily, Sardinia, and Spain and have an addition of the islands between Italy and Africa, and that on this basis they should make peace.
>
> Scipio countered by asserting that Carthage was responsible for both wars, and that no one was more aware than he of the fickleness of fortune. He declared that although his terms might have been acceptable if Hannibal had left Italy before the Romans invaded Africa, they were not so now when he controlled the country. He also pointed out that Hannibal had omitted all mention of conditions like the return of prisoners, the surrender of warships and the payment of an indemnity, which the Carthaginians had agreed upon before their treacherous violation of the peace: why, after all that, should he be prepared to accept less generous terms? He ended by demanding that the Carthaginians be prepared to place themselves at Rome's mercy or fight.[13]

Scipio called his commanders and presented his strategy. Hannibal's elephants had broken the backs of many Roman legions, advancing as fearsome, unstoppable forces overrunning all in their path. Defeat after defeat taught Scipio he must deal with this or face the same ruin. Instead of creating a checkerboard pattern of infantry as was common, he placed his lines with breaks of space between them "leaving unobstructed spaces between each set of companies (*maniples*)."[14] He trained his infantry to maneuver to one side or another upon command to avoid the earth-shaking beasts.

Hannibal placed his elephants in front of his lightly armed troops. He put his eleven thousand mercenaries behind them. In the third line, he placed another eleven thousand Carthaginians and in the last line, he placed twenty-four thousand of his finest veterans, which stood in reserve. On each wing he placed his four thousand cavalry. Hannibal was superior to Scipio in every respect, except cavalry—where Scipio had recruited large numbers of Numidians.[15]

The battle began as Hannibal ordered his elephants to charge the Roman legions. Scipio responded by blowing a large number of trumpets and cornets as soon as the elephants charged. The elephants were terrified. Some stopped in place, others turned and began to trample Hannibal's own troops, and others rushed madly forward. Confusion was the commander for some time. As for the elephants that continued forward, Scipio's infantry order allowed lanes through which the elephants could safely pass. As the troops maneuvered to the right or left, Scipio avoided the mass casualties that usually marked the beginning of each battle with Hannibal.

> "One who knows the enemy and knows himself will not be in danger in a hundred battles."
>
> SUN TZU

While the elephants began their stampede, the Roman cavalry launched an attack against the Carthaginian cavalry on the flanks and forced them into flight. Scipio now advanced against the front line of mercenaries. The mercenaries held the advantage because they were highly skilled in these skirmishes; however, they were unable to break the Roman lines. The pressure and drive of the advancing legions just behind the front lines caused Hannibal's front-line mercenaries to turn to flee. Hannibal's second lines, however, were so disciplined they refused to break ranks and continued to march forward, killing their own front lines who were attempting to retreat through them.

The second Carthaginian line now began to push the Romans back and inflict significant damage. "Although the Romans began to waver, their line was longer than the Carthaginian line and over-lapped it. And they gradually cut the Carthaginians to pieces."[16]

Again, as the second line began to falter and fall back, the third line of Carthaginian veterans refused to break ranks, and those in the second line fell and died or fled around the flanks. "Advance and live or retreat and die" was the axiom for the first half of this day's combat.

The battle now fell to the hard-core Roman and Carthaginian troops. As they faced each other to engage, Scipio recognized that his army was now in great danger. His lines were far less dense than the Carthaginians, and so he ordered his lines re-formed such that his lines overlapped the edges of the Carthaginian lines. In this battle order, Scipio knew he could not endure a sustained battle against the larger forces of Carthage. Yet it would provide him time—time enough to play one last ace. Scipio was awaiting the return of Masinissa and his cavalry, who had left earlier to engage Carthage's cavalry. If Masinissa prevailed and returned in time, they would tip the balance in Rome's favor.

After re-forming his lines, Scipio engaged Hannibal, and "the contest was for long doubtful, the men falling where they stood out of [sheer] determination, until Masinissa and Laelius [returned] at the providential moment."[17]

The fresh cavalry attacked the rear of Carthage's infantry and sealed their fate on the plains of Zarma in northern Tunisia. "Hannibal lost twenty thousand men killed and almost as many prisoners. Hannibal himself and some other survivors slipped away. Scipio lost two thousand."[18]

The battle of Zarma broke the back of the Carthaginian Empire, though Scipio was magnanimous in victory and imposed generous terms of peace. Some fifty years later, disputes between Carthage and Rome over tribute payments resulted in the sacking of Carthage, leaving it without a stone standing.

Following his triumphal return to Rome, Scipio presented the Senate with 123,000 pounds of silver. In return, he became the first Roman general to receive the name of the land he had conquered, Scipio "Africanus."

Scipio spent almost fifteen years studying the habits of Hannibal and the requirements of resupplying armies overseas, and devised the means to defeat him. Even at that, the battle hung in the balance for nearly two days of hand-to-hand combat against the legendary Hannibal. In the end, Scipio used the habits of Hannibal to overcome a numerical disadvantage on his enemy's doorstep. In doing so, he achieved a victory that became legendary in the annals of the Roman Empire.

THOUGHTS FOR TODAY'S CENTURIONS

THINK BACK TO THE LAST PROMOTION PARTY YOU ATTENDED— perhaps it was your own. What was the theme of the day, the theme of the toasts and congratulations that were given? If it was like most, the theme was: "Congratulations and keep up the great work"; "She's done a great job at X; we know she will do a great job at Y." "He's done a great job and so it should be no surprise that he is being promoted."

Now, what about the time you weren't promoted or were fired or laid off? What were your thoughts and feelings during those events and the period that followed? Those who have been "downsized," or "rightsized" in today's parlance, go through a period of introspection and reflection—a time of reexamining the old ways of doing business. Lots of questions enter your mind about ways you could or should change and ways you might grow and learn. It's a time that you look hard in the mirror to see what is there and, more important, what isn't there. That's what this principle is all about. It's about beginning with learning, rather than failing without it. It's what made Scipio so different.

There is no doubt that he was courageous, but he was also smart enough to "know that he didn't know" enough to beat Hannibal. Isn't that the lesson of many Clint Eastwood movies—"A man's got to know his limitations"? Too many don't. Scipio studied the battles of those who had been defeated by Hannibal, and then devised means to overcome Hannibal's strengths.

What about Hannibal? Why did he fail then after so many years of victory? Most obviously, he didn't realize that Rome, specifically Scipio, "was going to school on him." His methods and strategies were studied and then countered by a resourceful opponent. Beyond that, like all leaders, he served at the behest of superiors— in this case, the military was subservient to the civil authorities. The conflict of funding "guns or butter" caused the same rifts then as they do today. In its prime, Carthage loved its standard of living and jealously guarded it against the costs of maintaining Hannibal's army. Finally, he dealt with many in the civil government who were jealous of his power and fame—a human condition that transcends all borders, cultures, and times.

In the movie *Patton,* General Patton stands watching his allied tanks for the first time put Rommel's tanks to flight. Patton cries out in triumph, "I read your book! You magnificent S.O.B." Those at the top should expect their methods to be studied, which means a Centurion can never stop studying, learning, and evolving. In the end Alexander, the historian, sadly noted, "It is ironic that the man who had shown the ancient world the combination of mobility and shock force that cavalry could provide would himself be defeated by this weapon."[19]

If you are in leadership today, go to school on your competition because your competition is going to school on you. Put yourself in the shoes of your competitors and ask, What would you do? In the U.S. military, we have a group of pilots whose only job is to fly captured or replicated enemy aircraft using enemy tactics. We call them "The Aggressor Squadron." We then send our best and brightest pilots against this squadron to learn the enemy's tactics and how to defeat them.

Most of the early engagements are won by the aggressor pilots, to the chagrin of the hotshots that arrive full of themselves. In time, however, these young pilots learn lessons from defeat that enable them to graduate from Red Flag (a complete air-war battle) and Top Gun with aerial skills unmatched by those who have never had their steel tested. Failure and defeat can be the most powerful catalysts of change—if arrogance and pride can be put aside. William Smithsburg, chairman of Quaker Oats, notes, "There isn't one senior manager in this company who hasn't been associated with a product that's flopped. That includes me. It's like learning to ski. If you're not falling down, you're not learning."[20] In football, a runner will be tackled twenty to thirty times a game. The trick is to keep falling forward. That isn't failure—that's progress.

Some people have become legendary for facing and overcoming their failures. Tom Watson, founder of IBM, used to say,

> To double your success rate, double your failure rate. Many discoveries and breakthroughs are made by accident. The history of innovation is a long list of failures that eventually led to bigger successes. The list includes products like Post-it-Notes, Pyrex cookware, Jell-O, Popsicles, the Walkman, Life Savers, Coca-Cola, Silly Putty, Kleenex, Levi's jeans, Band-Aids, Kellogg's Corn Flakes, and runs on into the thousands. Accidental innovations and unplanned applications happen every day. Few of them ever amount to anything productive and useful. The inventors and companies that are able to capitalize on their "happy accidents" are those that are the most flexible and responsive to the unexpected opportunities before them.[21]

Babe Ruth struck out more times than he hit home runs and yet is remembered as one of the greatest hitters of all time, "The Sultan of Swat." A newspaper fired Walt Disney because he had "no good ideas." Beethoven's music teacher once said of him that "as a composer, he was hopeless."[22] In *Self Help*, Samuel Smiles writes, "We often discover what will do, by finding out what will not do; and probably he who never made a mistake never made a discovery."[23] It takes a lot of faith to pursue success day after day when all you go home with is another day of failure.

IN THE WORKPLACE

Everyone wants to learn from the successful because they believe it will rub off somehow—either their knowledge or their aura. Models of success are very important, but we gravely underestimate the power of failure in propelling us toward success and achievement. It is critical for individuals and organizations to understand the ingredients of leadership failure. Why? Because it is the single greatest unaccounted-for expense in a company's bottom line. Bad leadership drives away and keeps away great talent.

Failed leaders and bad bosses are a boon to cartoonists and blight on business. Polls reveal that half of U.S. workers are unhappy. Discontent spans all age groups and income levels. Fifty-nine percent of the workforce says that their commute to work is the best part of their job![24] Nearly 50 percent indicate their discontent stems from bad leadership. The same survey indicated much higher levels of satisfaction only one decade ago. As conditions at work deteriorate, employee turnover and numbers of sick days increase proportionately. *CIO* magazine noted recently:

> Think you have a retention problem at your company? (Who doesn't in this industry?) Throw away the HR manuals and take a good hard look at yourself and your management team. You and the managers who work for you—not the hot job

market—might very well be the number-one cause of attrition in your organization. Retention studies show that 70 to 80 percent of the reasons why people leave companies are related to bosses, according to John Sullivan, Professor of Human Resources at San Francisco State University. Sullivan consults high-tech companies on retention and says money is not one of the top reasons people switch jobs in the industry. "People either say my boss was a jerk, or I wasn't challenged."[25]

Corporations are losing their lifeblood and talent as their best employees vote with their feet. Study the reasons for it, because it has become a national trend. Ask any human resources manager who's done the math. It's far cheaper to retain qualified personnel by paying them more and offering generous benefit packages than it is to continually retrain new employees on the hiring-and-firing merry-go-round.

If you and your organization aren't willing to examine failure as a means to improvement, other people will be doing it for you—including potential clients and employees. Web sites are beginning to instruct potential employees to screen *you* as a potential "boss from hell." If a leader isn't interested in learning from failure, or improving through professional development, talented employees are going to go elsewhere. In screening out bad companies and bosses, one site advised:

Look for the personal touch: Genuine respect and concern for the individual, not just as an employee but as a person with a life outside work, mark good workplaces across the board. When that's absent, beware.

Screen your questioners: To the extent you can, silently critique your interviewers. If they all ask the same questions, the culture may be rigid and intolerant, quashing individuality.

Scan some Web sites: A growing number of Web sites air employee angst. Vault.com posts e-mail about more than 1,000 companies. Message boards can provide a taste of company culture.

HANG OUT AND SCHMOOZE: Once you have a job offer in hand, spend as much time as possible in the workplace . . . Ask people how long employees typically stay, what they like most about their jobs, and whether they find time to have a life.

PROBE PAST RESPONSES TO PERSONAL EMERGENCIES: Managers' reactions to human crises expose their true colors. Too many stories of unchecked callous bosses should be a warning.[26]

We all face failure at some point in our lives, but not everyone learns or recovers from it. Seeing how others have faced their failures and found a way to survive and thrive in spite of it is critical to becoming an enduring leader in a sea of change. Today, leaders are falling and failing not because of technical incompetence but due to moral vacancy. Ten years ago, society said live and let live to a president caught in dissipation. Not today—not to corporate leaders. One after another, their misdeeds are being uncovered, and prosecutors are bringing them before the bar.

Arthur Andersen LLP was convicted of obstruction of justice for its role in the Enron Corporation debacle. The felony conviction meant the one-time accounting titan could no longer submit certified financial statements for their clients. It put them out of business. Why? Because they certified Enron's statements as true, which was a lie. (Shareholders lost billions of dollars when the truth of Enron was revealed.) None of the business education and professional acumen can save a company that abdicates its integrity for greed. If you aren't interested in learning from the failures of others and applying corrective actions, you will soon join their ranks.

> Convicted Watergate conspirator, John Ehrlichman, wrote, "When I went to jail, nearly two years after the coverup trial, I had a big self-esteem problem. I was a felon, shorn and scorned,

clumping around in a ragged old army uniform, doing pick and shovel work out on the desert. I wondered if anyone thought I was worth anything . . . For years I had been able to sweep most of my shortcomings and failures under the rug and not face them, but during two long criminal trials, I spent my days listening to prosecutors tell juries what a bad fellow I was . . . I'd go back to a hotel room and sit alone thinking about what was happening to me. During that time I began to take stock . . . I was wiped out. I had nothing left that had been of value to me—honor, credibility, virtue, recognition, profession."

But then he began to see himself and to care deeply about his own integrity, his capacity to love and be loved, and his essential worth. He concluded about the Nixon years, "In a paradoxical way, I'm grateful for them. Somehow I had to see all of that and grow to understand it in order to arrive."[27]

If you would be a great leader, study the lessons of the defeated before you study the lessons of the victorious. In the defeated you will find the conditions of human frailty and weakness by which all leaders are affected. In studying Hannibal, Scipio grew in leadership competence. By studying the best, he rose up to the level of the best. He also discovered that which we all have—weaknesses. In battle, he tried to minimize his weaknesses while countering the strengths of his enemy with unique solutions, created well beyond the box. If you can see in your own character a reflection of those who fell into disgrace or defeat—if you can recognize the shortcomings in your professional competence—then you have begun the journey toward becoming a Centurion.

PATHWAY TO MAKING FAILURE YOUR STEPPING-STONE TO VICTORY

Andrew Harvey gives this advice as you think about failure and learning from it. Begin by learning from your own failures.

- Be a lifelong learner. You must continue to educate yourself.
- Don't quit because you see failure as a possibility; have courage in the face of adversity.
- If you make mistakes, acknowledge your responsibility.
- Learn from your errors, so that in the future you're making new mistakes instead of repetitive ones.
- Be open to feedback and criticism. [28]

Before you engage your enemies, like Scipio, you must understand their habits, their weaknesses, and their reasons for success. Like anyone involved in intelligence gathering, you must find the scraps of information upon which lives may one day hang in the balance. If not lives, the jobs of your employees or health of your organization may depend upon your professional approach to "knowing yourself" and "knowing your enemy." When it comes to your opponents:

- Read their writings—many of the brightest aren't shy about sharing their brilliance.
- Consult those who work with and for them—the disaffected are often willing to share.
- Learn from those who have been defeated by your enemy— they may provide the best insight into how and why they lost.
- Discern their vices, habits, and weaknesses—all can prove invaluable in finding the means of defeating a very resourceful, powerful, and resilient enemy.

Failure is a reality for all who risk. But Centurions learn over time that victory teaches the simple while failure instructs the wise. Success teaches us a few lessons, but failure . . . failure teaches us a thousand.

ALEXANDER THE GREAT

CONQUEROR OF THE WORLD

You must unify your people before you can lead them to great ends.

THERE IS NOTHING MORE EXCITING THAN TO WORK ON A team or within an organization that knows where it's going and what it wants to accomplish. Add to that a leader who knows when to add power and focus and when to back off and let the team run with the ball, and you have a group ready to tackle the toughest problems within your organization.

But how do you become such a leader and inspire such followers? How do you achieve such unity of purpose and heart? Is it even possible in a world of increasingly self-serving interests that hobble organizational potential and distract mission focus?

Unity of purpose is a principle that sounds corny at first, like one of the many motivational signs leaders stick up on the walls. And if you're putting up posters to instill culture, you've already lost the battle.

Unity comes from a deeper well than the surface water of motivational slogans, and it begins with you—the leader. The reasons people are working in your organization may span a range from absolute selfishness to stunning altruism. A great majority may just be concerned about keeping their paycheck, and you are going to have to find the means to unify everyone—from those who are true believers in your vision to those with less lofty motivations.

Unity is not motivating a group to speak the same words, but to speak the same language. It's about instilling a high-value common purpose that most will pursue, even if it sometimes comes at the expense of self.

Few world leaders ever faced that as squarely, competently, and successfully as did a young man called Alexander.

YOUNG ALEXANDER—RISE TO NATIONAL POWER

The world in 500 BC is best understood in light of the power and dominion of the Persian Empire under Darius, "the Great King." The Persian Empire extended from Greece to the eastern boundaries of modern Iran.

By the fourth century BC, Greece was tired of being a humiliated vassal and paying tribute to the Persian Empire. It was into this world that Alexander, son of Philip II, king of Macedonia, was born. The Greek cities along the Mediterranean were known as city-states that fiercely protected their independence from one another. This ensured their independence but also enabled the Persians to isolate and conquer them.

Philip sought to end these divisions and built and financed an army in hopes of unifying Greece and Macedonia.[1] He also created an infantry formation, the *phalanx*, with each soldier wielding an eighteen-foot spear, making the wedge nearly impenetrable. His cavalry, made up of the offspring of noble families, wore helmets and fought with short swords meant to wound and unhorse opposing cavalrymen. Once dismounted, they faced the long spears of the infantry.

In 338 BC Philip confronted a coalition of Greek states at Chaeronea and soundly defeated them. The jealously and fiercely guarded independence of the city-states was beginning to wane. Philip assumed control of a forcibly united Greece and was appointed general in chief to lead their united forces. The time had come to begin to liberate the city-states that were governed by Persian *satraps* (literally "guardians of power").

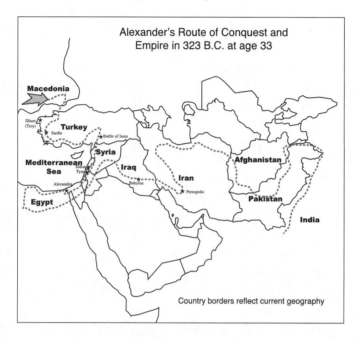

Alexander's Route of Conquest and Empire in 323 B.C. at age 33

Country borders reflect current geography

At a ceremony to commemorate the upcoming expedition, Philip was struck down by an assassin. He died shortly after, leaving his twenty-year-old son, Alexander, in tenuous control.

Alexander was educated in science, literature, and physical training under his early tutor, Leonidas. "Alexander led an austere life under his strict mentor, who allowed him 'for breakfast, a walk before daybreak, and for dinner, a light breakfast.'"[2] He was later tutored by Aristotle in philosophy, political science, poetry, and drama. "By age sixteen, the young prince was considered qualified to act as regent while his father was away on military campaigns."[3] He fought courageously at his father's side during the battle of Chaeronea and earned the respect of the army, before reaching age nineteen.

Upon his father's death, Alexander was named general in chief. His first military action was to march his army north into the Balkans, who rebelled against the new regent. His army successfully crushed the rebels at the city of Thebes. "Terror-stricken, the other Greek cities (including Athens, which voted to congratulate Alexander for his victories) made amends."[4]

Alexander, having solidified the home front, now prepared to liberate the other Greek city-states that were being crushed by Darius and the Persian Empire.

THE POWER OF PERSIA

To call the expedition Alexander was about to lead a "David and Goliath" affair is a vast understatement. "Between 550 and 525 BC, the Persian army had overthrown the kingdom of the Medes, the kingdom of Lydia (in Asia Minor), the Neo-Babylonian kingdom (Mesopotamia and the Levant), and Egypt."[5] The Persian Empire began under the strong hand of King Cyrus the Great, and by the time Darius I ascended the throne, it had expanded substantially in every direction.

The Persian kings built major thoroughfares that connected the major centers of their power. This meant any rebellion in the outer portions of their kingdom could be easily handled within a month of travel. Egypt, one of the farthest countries from Persepolis, the capital of Persia, broke away in 404 BC. Shortly thereafter, it was reconquered by Artaxerxes III, who made a horrific example of the Egyptians to discourage all others.

The Persians installed their own governors, or satraps, in each city to ensure proper "tribute" was paid each year. The wealth of Persia was renowned to be measured in thousands of tons of gold. If Alexander could succeed, he could use some of this money to buy armies and loyalty. But this would not be enough. He needed to build unity.

To bring unity to so many cultures, languages, and religions was an achievement no leader before him had attempted. Even if he succeeded in that endeavor, the odds were against him militarily. He would face a king who could field an army numbering in the hundreds of thousands. As he left Greece, few expected he would ever return.

FIRST BLOOD—TROY, 334 BC

The four-thousand-year-old city of Troy, made famous by Homer's account of the Trojan War, was the landing spot of Alexander's army. They crossed the Bosphorus, the narrow waterway that connects the Aegean and Black Seas along the western edge of Turkey. As they approached the beach, Alexander launched his spear from his boat and stuck it into the sand—symbolically laying claim to the Great King Darius's lands.

Alexander brought forty to fifty thousand infantry and about twenty-five hundred cavalry, mostly Macedonians, supplemented by volunteers from the Greek city-states. Those that were with him were motivated by dreams of wealth rather than by Alexander's desire to free Greece from Persia, thus establishing his name for the ages.

"The Great King Darius III, who gained the throne in 336 BC, had long known of the Macedonian plans . . . At that time, he had entrusted command of his troops to Memnon, who had inflicted several defeats on the Macedonian leaders and forced them to limit their operations to the Trojan plain, where Alexander had now landed."[6] Confident that his armies in Turkey could defeat Alexander, Darius felt little concern.

"Hoping to create a strong defensive position that Alexander might be lured into attacking, the Persians grouped their cavalry on the sloping banks of the Granicus River. In doing so, however, they neutralized their ability to maneuver. When Alexander led a surprise attack at dawn, the collision of the two masses of cavalry was extremely violent. Alexander himself plunged into the fighting at the head of his men. Several thousand Persian cavalry fled from the battlefield."[7]

Upon hearing of Alexander's victory at Troy, the nearby city of Sardis surrendered without a fight. The city was the wealthy center of Persian power in the west, and its inhabitants, "the Mithrines," were the first noblemen to ever surrender to the Greeks. Because of this, Alexander elevated these nobles to serve at his side—the same honor they held under Darius. In Sardis, and the next city he conquered, Dacylium, "the local administrative structures were left in place, although all the major posts (civil, military, and financial) were put exclusively in the hands of Macedonians and Greeks."[8]

> "It is not in numbers but in unity that our great strength lies."
>
> THOMAS PAINE, 1776

His treatment of the conquered began to have its intended effect. Rather than fearing a bloodthirsty army, cities began to send emissaries to arrange agreements of surrender.

Throughout the spring and summer of 334 BC, Alexander moved along the southern coast of Turkey, taking one city after another. Many of these cities chose to ally themselves with Alexander, hoping for the kind of treatment received by those at Sardis. "As a general rule, when Alexander took possession he established democratic government in the cities he had liberated, unlike the Persians, who had installed local tyrants, often loathed by the majority of the population."[9]

Within a year, Alexander had brought the Persian Empire in Turkey to its knees. City after city fell or surrendered to Alexander's army. He used the strategy of liberation from the Persian yoke to weaken the resistance of the inhabitants and the promise of merciful treatment for those who had governed in the name of Persia. Once the city was taken, he replaced the Persian satrap with a Macedonian one, while keeping many of the lower-ranking functionaries to ensure the smooth transition of power. These elements of his leadership proved to be a formidable combination and helped unify his rule once he moved on. However, this could only work in the cities once held by Greece. As he prepared to enter

Syria, a strategy of liberation would be useless. Something else was going to be needed.

ALEXANDER AND DARIUS III IN THE BATTLE OF ISSUS, SYRIA, 333 BC

By now Alexander had the attention of Darius. Having lost the wealth of Sardis and all the Greek city-states along the southern coast of Turkey, he was sufficiently alarmed to order a general mobilization. All *satraps*, save those in Iran and India who were too far removed, were ordered to provide troops to face the Macedonian king.

The army under Darius gathered near the ancient city of Babylon and marched toward the Macedonian position. Alexander was outnumbered two to one in cavalry and three to one in infantry against Darius, who fielded one hundred thousand foot soldiers and eleven thousand horsemen. As Alexander faced the army before him, the news of his impending defeat caused the Greek city-states to assert their independence from his empire.

Alexander had left in Macedonia twelve thousand infantry and fifteen hundred cavalry to maintain order. Nevertheless, the political winds were shifting against him as news spread that the Persian king would personally face Alexander. Preparations were being made for a new order upon his demise.

Alexander's strategy of achieving unity through primarily bloodless conquests was a chapter that had ended. In order to retain the lands he had liberated and regain the unity he built in the Greek city-states, he must win the upcoming battle.

Alexander had been ill following the war in Turkey, but recovered and marched his army to face Darius in Syria. Darius's army had grown to some three hundred thousand soldiers in addition to an equal number of his court—a number exceeding six hundred thousand people.

The armies faced each other across a small river and the battle was joined. Darius stood in his war chariot surrounded by the spearmen of his guard. The armies were flanked by the sea on one side and mountains on the other. This left very little room for the large numbers of Persian cavalry to maneuver.

"Alexander turned his gaze in all directions, seeking Darius. As soon as he saw him, he raced into the field with his horsemen straight for the Great King in person, for more than achieving victory over the Persians; he wished to be the personal instrument of victory."[10]

The cavalry on both sides engaged in close quarter battle, and for several hours the battle hung in the balance. Alexander himself was wounded in the thigh but continued to fight valiantly at the head of his army.

The infantry of Alexander with their eighteen-foot spears and superior maneuverability cut through the Persian infantry and left legions of dead underneath their feet as they pressed forward. The Persian left flank crumbled but bravely fought on, and Alexander redirected his troops toward the Persian mercenaries in the center. The Greek phalanxes pressed in, ripping through the Persian center and causing chaos there as well. At this point, Darius was seized with terror and turned with many of his men to flee.

The Persians suffered more than one hundred thousand infantry and ten thousand cavalry casualties. Alexander escaped with the loss of about five hundred infantry and cavalry. This overwhelming victory sent a thunderbolt of shock upon all the cities of Greece that were preparing to rebel against Alexander's rule. "The Athenians abandoned their intrigues, and with their homelands directly threatened . . . the Persian fleet, broke away and sailed homeward to defend them."[11]

Enormous sums of wealth were strewn upon the ground by the fleeing Persians. "Silver earmarked for enormous payments to the army, vestments of a host of noble men and women, gold place settings, golden horse bits, tents decorated with royal splendor, and chariots were all abandoned by their owners and overflowed with unheard of wealth."[12] But just as important as the loss of wealth was the loss of political esteem Darius suffered that day.

The Great King who had fashioned himself in monuments and temples as the greatest horseman, warrior, archer, and spearman had not merely been defeated in battle. "He had run away leaving behind him the insignias of power, his royal cloak, his bow, and his chariot."[13]

BUILDING UNITY IN A CONQUERED LAND

Imagine such an event occurring in the face of today's media. This story would be spread far and wide within hours of the end of the battle. The shame and the humiliation of an army three times the size of Alexander's going down in defeat would be front-page news. The photos of the gold being picked up by the Macedonians; the royal cloak being held up for display; the family of Darius standing in fear and confusion—all would be grist for the twenty-four-hour news mill. Alexander was wiser than many at that time. He understood he had won more than a battle. He had won a new strategy for undermining the Persian Empire.

Until now he had used the strategy of liberation to unify his growing empire. Each of the Greek city-states had chafed under the tribute and harsh rule of the Persians. While Alexander did not release them from the tribute, at least they would be ruled by Greeks and Macedonians. But what of these new lands that had never known the Greek political system? They certainly wouldn't view Alexander as a liberator, but as a conqueror. How do you unify multiple language groups and cultures in such hostile circumstances?

The first thing Alexander's historians or "publicists" did was to publish stories far and wide of the battle and of the behavior of the Great King, Darius. They tirelessly repeated the epic battle with one aim in mind—to discredit Darius's legitimacy to rule the Persian Empire. They compared the courage of Alexander that day to the fear of Darius, who fled the battlefield and abandoned his army and family.

Alexander rode into Darius's camp to review the booty and the captives. Standing before him was Darius's mother, his wife, two daughters, and his youngest son. "The King spoke and said, 'Fear nothing, Mother . . .' By thus calling the old woman Mother he gave a taste of the kindness with which these women would be treated."[14] His merciful treatment of Darius's family was a story that spread quickly and helped his image immensely as he began his conquest of the cities of Phoenicia (now Lebanon and Israel).

Sidon, Bablos, Aradus, Rhodes, and Cyprus surrendered without a fight while Tyre opposed him, fiercely clinging to its independence. "Phoenician ports supplied the Persian Empire with the bulk of its war fleet and seamen. Tyre was the wealthiest and most powerful of them—hence Alexander's relentless siege of the city, which lasted ten months."[15] Because Tyre was located on an island, Alexander was forced to build a causeway from the mainland to lay siege to it. The Tyreans turned back a series of assaults until finally yielding. Alexander now had supremacy of land and sea in the west.

Nothing stood between Alexander and Egypt, and in the autumn of 332 BC he entered Egypt unopposed, taking possession of the capital, Memphis. This last victory along the Mediterranean meant the Persians had been swept from the sea and land from Syria in the east, Greece in the west, and Egypt in the south. "To mark his possession of the Egyptian shore, Alexander founded a new city in the Nile delta, which he named after himself: Alexandria."[16]

> "We must all hang together, or, most assuredly, we shall all hang separately."
>
> BENJAMIN FRANKLIN, 1776

At this point, Alexander unveiled a new method of creating unity among conquered territory. He decreed that civil government remain in the hands of the Egyptian governor (satrap), while military and economic control was placed under Greek and Macedonian administrators. This was a significant tool that he used repeatedly as he began his march through city after city into the heart of Persia.

Alexander's method served two purposes. It created a smooth transition between the old powers and new, so the average citizen suffered less inconvenience and was less inclined to chafe against Alexander's rule. More important, the message of his treatment of these nations preceded him on his way into the heart of Persia. All in power knew that if they opposed Alexander, he would bring them to their knees and end their days in office. Conversely, those able Persian administrators who capitulated would be kept in their positions. Later, when his trust was proven unfounded in some cases, he did not hesitate to replace the corrupt and disloyal. Again, this method of dealing with the conquered was immensely successful in building loyalty and unity within his growing empire.

BATTLE AT BABYLON, 331 BC

For three years Alexander took city after city, but he had yet to face Darius in his own land, and he longed to defeat him again in battle. In the spring of 331 BC, Darius fielded a new army near Babylon.

Darius called for every available person able to carry arms. His army numbered somewhere between a half million and a million soldiers. Again, Alexander would enter the field of battle at a significant numerical disadvantage. Additionally, Darius fielded a new chariot as a weapon he believed would turn the tide of battle in his favor. "Iron-pointed spears protruded ahead of the horses; three sword-blades were affixed on either side of the yoke; javelin points stuck outward from the spokes of the wheels; scythe blades welded to the wheel rims mowed down everything the horses encountered in their charge."[17]

Remembering the last encounter with Alexander, Darius chose a wide plain to spread out his cavalry and infantry. Moreover, he had the plain leveled and planted iron spikes in the ground to wound the enemy's horses. He felt prepared to repay Alexander finally for his previous defeats. Darius staked everything on his iron-spiked chariots, confidently believing they would tear Alexander's infantry to shreds.

Alexander crossed the Tigris River unopposed and found Darius waiting for him near Babylon. When he saw the chariots, he armed numerous men as archers to rain arrows down upon the chariots before they could reach his own infantry. It was a brilliant move that decimated the new chariots of Darius. Darius was stunned, as were the nearly half a million troops who expected finally to defeat the Greek invader. "Despite a heroic charge by Mazaeus on the Persian right wing, defeat was once more in store for the Persians. Again Darius fled, leaving in Alexander's hands treasure worth roughly four thousand talents (between seventy-five and one hundred tons of silver), his bow, his arrows, and his chariot."[18]

Instead of pursuing Darius, Alexander marched his army into the ancient city of Babylon. Again, his aim wasn't the destruction of the cities he conquered, but their loyalty—their unification with his growing empire. As he entered the city, the opposing commander of Persian cavalry, Mazaeus, came out along with all of his sons to meet him. This was clearly a very courageous act, as many in Alexander's position would have put to death their opposing leaders as well as their entire families. Mazaeus came out bravely to face whatever awaited him.

This act of bravery was reciprocated by Alexander, further endearing himself to the Babylonians. As he met Mazaeus, he declared that his former enemy would be appointed "satrap of the city." Mithrines, the former head of the garrison at Sardis, became satrap of Armenia. These administrative appointments marked a turning point in Alexander's policy, for they were the first time that he elevated Persians to such high posts. Naturally, though, it was to Greeks and Macedonians that Alexander entrusted the military and fiscal control of his growing empire. Nonetheless, his appointment of Mazaeus meant that a certain number of Persians came over to Alexander's side.[19]

Alexander also spent time researching the cultural and religious habits of the people he conquered. As he entered the city, he would pay respect to the icons of their history. He sought to cause no offense to any culture and language group that fell under his growing domain, even in the area of their religion.

Final Battle and Treachery
at Persepolis, 331 BC

While Alexander's conquests continued beyond Persia into India, he made two unusual decisions that cemented his reputation as a master of unifying both his army and his conquests. These occurred before and just after his final confrontation with Darius.

By the summer of 331 BC, Alexander's army had thrust deep into the heart of the Persian Empire. His army had suffered the heat of summer in the Babylonian desert and the cold and snow of the Iranian plateau. Yet his leadership in the face of so many obstacles brought him material support from home. "Macedonian reinforcements and Greek mercenaries had already reached him at Gordium (3,350 men) and Tyre (4,000 mercenaries). [Now] 6,500 Macedonians, 4,100 Thracians, and 4,380 Greek mercenaries [joined his army] . . . The contribution of the western Greek states was particularly noteworthy in view of opposition in Greece to Macedonian rule."[20]

Persepolis, located in the southern portion of modern-day Iran, was the jewel and crown of the Persian Empire. It was well defended by a triple wall that encircled the entire city. "Ten feet in height, the outer wall was set with guard posts in the form of towers; the middle wall was twice as high. The third or inner wall was made of hard stone strong enough to endure forever."[21]

The great highway from Susa to Persepolis was guarded by a series of fortresses and should have provided adequate resistance to any invader. But then again, Alexander wasn't just any invader. Darius had left a blood relative to defend Persepolis while he and a large contingent of his army fled east into the mountains. Alexander split his forces, leaving Paremio to command the assault on the capitol of Persia, while he and his remaining troops took to the hills to engage the Persian army of some twenty- to forty thousand foot soldiers and about seven hundred cavalry. They guarded the pass known as "the Persian Gates," and a bloody battle ensued.

Alexander was unable to pierce these stout defenders, and so he "led his force along a goat trail and came down into the valley behind the Persians. He then crossed the Pulvar River and arrived at Persepolis in January of 330 BC."[22]

But where was Darius? Alexander searched out the city and found the palaces, storehouses, and treasury of the Persian Empire to be beyond their most vivid imaginations. Alexander found some 120,000 talents of silver, 3,000 tons of gold, taking some 10,000 mules and 5,000 camels to transport all the wealth.[23]

Yet the "once" Great King Darius continued to flee to the east, dreaming of revenge. By now, he had only three thousand cavalry and between ten thousand and thirty thousand foot soldiers. More and more, his former satraps refused to assist him. His speedy flight "stirred doubts among his followers. The only way to escape the Macedonian pursuer would be to leave the women and baggage on the spot and press on at top speed for eastern Iran. This time the Great King's prestige was at stake. Entire units lost heart and deserted him, and the Persians from his entourage left to offer their services to Alexander."[24]

Alexander himself had finally had enough and ordered his men on a forced march in pursuit of Darius. Day after day, he drove his men on so relentlessly that many soldiers were left behind and many horses died along the way.

In spite of Alexander's diligent pursuit, it was several of Darius's own men who recognized the warning signs. Hoping to secure their own safety and the goodwill of Alexander, they executed him. For Alexander, Darius's murder was a great political windfall.[25]

Alexander was wise enough to understand that there were many in Persia who reviled him as a usurper of the worst kind. No matter what cowardice their king had shown, Darius was still their king. Consequently, Alexander placated Darius's supporters and solidified his gains in eastern Iran. Alexander assumed the role as the great avenger of King Darius. He ordered Darius's murderers hunted down and killed.

"Alexander handled Darius's body with great respect, bearing it with him to Persepolis to be buried in the traditional Persian style. Meanwhile, the end of Darius had led the Persian nobles of his entourage to go over to Alexander."[26]

Alexander covered more territory and conquered more lands and people than any single ruler in history. Alexander had led his army halfway across the known world to the Indus River of India before he finally headed for home some six years later.

THOUGHTS FOR TODAY'S CENTURIONS

HOW ARE YOU GOING TO CREATE UNITY WITHIN YOUR organization? Alexander faced the most monumental challenge to unity ever encountered by a world leader. He never expected his satraps in Babylon and those in Egypt to align their processes and goals with each other. That was his job! He gave strategic direction, set up the political and military elements, and then expected his guidance to be followed—and enforced his will when necessary. Certainly there were differences between each region, and between every satrap. Some were highly ethical while others were not. Some were efficient while others just muddled through. Yet it was then and is now the Centurion's responsibility to create unity.

Unity is not a body, group, or organization that speaks with one voice. You might be able to get a group of robots to do that, but not human beings. Organizational unity is simply the subordination of personal goals and purposes to those of the organization. It occurs when those who work for the organization are inspired to accomplish something greater than they could alone. It is easier to define than to achieve, and it is almost always fleeting.

Great examples teach important lessons, while bad examples

teach us even more. As we enter an era where terror is on everyone's mind, the U.S. Secret Service couldn't be more important. And yet it appears that the organization is in dire need of finding a Centurion able to instill unity in the ranks. *U.S. News and World Report* broke the following story in June of 2002 and ran a follow-up in the late fall of 2002. As you study the facts, consider what you might do to build unity were you hired to head up the Secret Service. Perhaps the lessons of Alexander still have value today.

A CASE STUDY IN DISUNITY—THE UNITED STATES SECRET SERVICE

You know your organization is in trouble when supporters take out newspaper ads advising people not to work for your company. The nation's largest police union, the Fraternal Order of Police (FOP), published an advertisement advising prospective Secret Service applicants to "Just Say No."

> During recent Secret Service recruiting interviews, informa-tion, believed to be false and misleading, was passed to prospective applicants in order to secure their employment . . . that is why the FOP must strongly discourage anyone from applying for positions in the Secret Service or the Uniformed Division at this time.[27]

Besides the embarrassing ongoing publicity, the problems at the Secret Service are long-standing and deep.

BACKGROUND

The Secret Service is comprised of two separate and very distinct divi-sions: a Uniformed Division and Plainclothes Special Agents. Even though the two divisions work side by side serving the president and leadership of the country, the differences begin immediately.

Although they work intimately together, uniformed officers live in a world very different from that of plainclothes agents. The cultural, social, and financial gulf between the two communities has resulted in distrust, contempt, and hostility, agents and officers say. Disputes between officers and plainclothes agents are legion. They include disparities in pay, promotion, disciplinary structure, and rules regarding carrying of weapons, and the inability to gain collective-bargaining rights.[28]

The agency itself is 137 years old, and not once in its entire history has a senior member of the uniformed division been selected to head the Secret Service.

This caste system can be seen in other ways. Every special agent gets a government car and parking permit; uniformed officers slog to work on public transit or fight for parking around the White House. Each year, at Christmastime, uniformed officers posted to the White House can only stare through the frosted windows of the presidential mansion as special agents attending the annual Christmas party rub elbows with the president and first lady; uniformed officers are not invited to the party.[29]

The major differences between Special Agents and the Uniformed Division begin with education. Entering the Secret Service as a Special Agent requires a BA, three years of work experience in criminal investigations and passing a Treasury or Marshal's Enforcement exam. To enter the Secret Service in the Uniformed Division, whose primary role is protection, requires only a high school diploma, passing a written test and interview, and completion of a polygraph examination. That alone should account for the disparities since it is common knowledge that a college degree results in improved salary and promotion opportunities. But it's not as clear cut as it might seem. There is no degree for understanding the criminal mind. That is why officers across the country on police forces, sheriff's departments, and other police agencies commonly rise up to high levels of authority without a college degree.

In brief, the Secret Service is comprised of two major organizations that are highly segregated, though they still work side by side. While the initial entry requirements for Special Agent are higher and pay more, as would be expected, there is a widespread perception in the Uniformed Division that there is little opportunity to move up into the ranks of Special Agent and receive the commensurate benefits. Further inequities of organizational segregation occur in perks and general treatment, which exacerbate the current tensions.

IMPACT AND CHALLENGES OF CURRENT STRUCTURE

Smart business recognizes that talent votes with its feet—either to follow and lead an organization or to head for the door. In the case of both divisions of the Secret Service, the talent has voted to leave. "The Uniformed Division, consisting of fewer than 1,000 officers . . . have lost nearly 320 uniformed officers and more than one hundred plainclothes agents."[30]

The result is a growing workload for fewer workers. "Secret Service statistics show . . . in 2002 fewer than one thousand officers worked five hundred thousand hours of overtime. That translates, on average, to ninety-hour work weeks per officer."[31] When an organization is unable to retain its employees such that an *average* workweek is seven days long, twelve hours a day—with an extra six-hour shift thrown in somewhere—the results can only be catastrophic.

The current situation in the Secret Service can be summed up as a badly divided organization that is debilitated by a long-standing rift between employees, a lack of equal opportunity to move into the ranks of Special Agent, a lack of vision, and an inability to attract and retain talent. Whether these ever affect the Secret Service's *raison d'être* to protect this nation's leadership remains to be seen. However, the agency's current direction leaves the outcome in doubt.

YOU'RE HIRED—PROVIDE YOUR RECOMMENDATIONS ASAP!

The bitter and sweet of leadership is the reality that you are hired to solve intractable and previously unsolvable problems. Most likely, your boss will ask for solutions in what most would view as an unrealistic timeline. Get used to it because it doesn't get better. This is certainly a particularly difficult case but no more difficult than those many leaders face in their own way.

I would recommend you take some time alone or in groups and provide your recommendations along with barriers, timelines, and consequences for failing to change.

I have some strong sense of the possibilities that exist in this situation if the leadership is willing to approach the problem creatively. There are precedents (not replications) that could be useful to examine in implementing corrections. The medical profession certainly has a two-level system between doctors and nurses while the military has existed with divisions between officer NCOs and enlisted for centuries. What has made them work, caused them problems, and are there take-away solutions for the Secret Service? Your mission, should you choose to accept it, is to build bridges between agents and uniformed officers to restore unity, improve retention, and rebuild morale while continuing to perform the mission of protecting high-ranking members of the government.

> "If a kingdom is divided against itself, that kingdom cannot stand. And if a house is divided against itself, that house cannot stand."
>
> MARK 3:24–25

A PAUSE FOR SPIRITUAL REFLECTION

What is it about unity that is so important? Even Jesus in the last hours of His life prayed, "I do not pray for these alone, but also for those who will believe in Me through their word; that they all may be *one*" (John 17:20–21, emphasis added). What kind of oneness is He talking about? Just looking at creation tells you God isn't interested in creating carbon copies.

"Oneness" is being inextricably linked to a common cause and a common purpose. Paul encourages believers to "fulfill my joy by being like-minded, having the same love, being of one accord, of one mind" (Phil. 2:2). If we are to lead well, we must also be able to follow well. Becoming part of a team and learning how to function and support others is probably one of the first requisites of a future leader. As a leader you will have to find ways to unify elements within your organization that cannot or will not rise above petty differences for the common good.

Begin your evaluation of your own leadership by asking yourself this question, "Have I supported my own supervisor and leaders above him?" Do you give honor to whom honor is due, and are you in the habit of avoiding gossip and slander of peers and leaders?

Another attribute of unity is that members are committed to a common cause and equally committed to resolving conflicts and barriers to reaching that goal. That includes relationship problems. Paul encourages us to make "every effort to maintain the unity of the Spirit in the bond of peace" (Eph. 4:3 NRSV).

Finally, if you believe that you have a Destiny Maker, a greater power who lifts up and humbles, then you won't need to pursue self at the expense of the larger body. The Bible promises, "But God is the Judge; He puts down one, and exalts another" (Ps. 75:7 NASB). If your role today is small and unrecognized, know that this is God's place for you—now. Establish yourself as a reliable and committed worker, low-level manager, or leader, and in time, you will rise up. The world is looking for great leaders, even if your company isn't.

Can you trust the Great Designer who has placed you firmly in your place, no matter how great or small it seems? The bricks at the top of a wall are no more or less important than those at the bottom, and yet are more easily seen. Were those at the bottom removed, the entire wall would collapse. So it is within every organization, within every military army, and within the Christian church. Alexander conquered a world and found a way to unify each country. To bring unity, one must also be a unifying force—whatever your level of leadership.

Pathway to Creating Unity Within Your Organization

The best example for creating unity among highly diverse people groups is drawn from Alexander's march across the Mediterranean, Middle and Far East. His methods of bringing about national and international unity in his empire could be scaled to organizations, ministries, and companies today. Alexander created unity in six primary ways.

1. He used strategies appropriate to the regions he conquered—in some he was a liberator, while in others he was a conqueror who recognized and paid obeisance to the values and customs of those people.

2. He ensured promotions were based on merit rather than upon birth. This created disunity at one point; nevertheless, he held on to this principle at a time when the class system was the norm.

3. He took time to learn about each conquered group and was careful to tread carefully around their religious and cultural sensitivities.

4. He set and enforced his standards, harshly at times, to ensure loyalty and unity.

5. He was courageous, risking his own position, wealth, and life on numerous occasions. None doubted his competence for leadership, which helped him institute even unpopular policies.

6. Finally, he was an outstanding communicator who was unafraid to go toe-to-toe with friend or foe in arguing his point. He didn't send orders from Greece, but instead, like all great Centurions, he led his battles from the front.

CHAPTER 4

JOAN OF ARC
THE MAID OF LORRAINE—
DELIVERER OF ORLÉANS AND FRANCE

*Ranks and titles don't inspire ordinary people to extraordinary
ends—a pure heart committed to a great cause with unwavering
faith can lead even a nation out of chains into freedom.*

BEFORE YOU READ ABOUT THE LIFE OF THIS CENTURION,
I'd like you to visualize the largest problem you are currently facing
as a leader. When you have this firmly in your mind, consider the
resources available to conquer this challenge—the people, equipment, personal talents, experience, and organizational power to
support you. Now, let's consider the life of a Centurion leader who
also faced what seemed to be an insurmountable mountain.

Begin with me for a moment, halfway through the story, just
outside the city of Orléans in the tent of the French commanders.
In the spring of 1429, they gathered to devise a strategy to rid the
city and surrounding area of the English invaders. Orléans stood on
the dividing line between southern and northern France along the
Loire River. Southern France was loyal to the uncrowned king,
Charles VII. In the north, the Dukes of Burgundy, Normandy, and
Brittany had allied themselves with the English. Orléans had been
under siege for eight months and the people had been starved while
the English controlled the main entry points to the city. France was
weak and divided and led by a fainthearted, vacillating king.

In the commander's tent was the ruler of the city, Dunois, as well as the French captains of war. The English and the obstacles before them were formidable.

As historian Frances Gies noted, "Across the river the French confronted two obstacles between themselves and the Tourelles, the main tower fortress held by the English controlling entrance to the city: the little fortress of St-Jean-le-Blanc to the east, and the forti-fied monastery of the Augustins to the south. The Tourelles itself was . . . surrounded by a moat built by the English to protect the drawbridge."[1]

FRANCE IN 1429
Jeanne d'Arc, Age 17–19

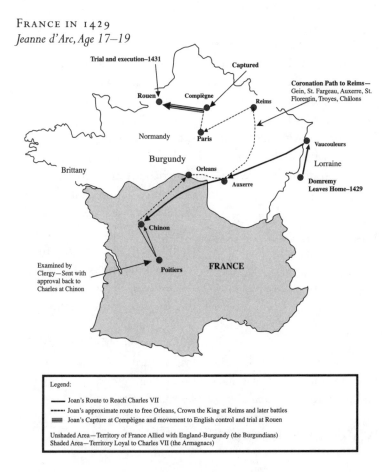

Trial and execution–1431

Captured

Coronation Path to Reims—
Gein, St. Fargeau, Auxerre, St. Florentin, Troyes, Châlons

Rouen   Compiègne

Reims

Vaucouleurs

Normandy   Paris

Burgundy   Lorraine

Brittany   Orleans

Domremy
Leaves Home–1429

Auxerre

Chinon

Examined by
Clergy—Sent with
approval back to
Charles at Chinon

Poitiers   FRANCE

Legend:

——— Joan's Route to Reach Charles VII

----- Joan's approximate route to free Orleans, Crown the King at Reims and later battles

≡≡≡ Joan's Capture at Compègne and movement to English control and trial at Rouen

Unshaded Area—Territory of France Allied with England-Burgundy (the Burgundians)
Shaded Area—Territory Loyal to Charles VII (the Armagnacs)

A teenage girl named Joan had been sent by the Dauphin (the heir apparent), Charles, to assist the French commanders for some dubious morale reasons. It put the commanders in an awkward position. The Dauphin couldn't be ignored, but then what did this girl know of war?

The French leadership decided to delay the attack until their numbers were larger. Joan entered the tent as their meeting was breaking up. Having come from prayer and Mass, she disagreed with their decision to delay: "You have been in your council and I in mine; and believe me, the council of the Lord will be carried out and will endure, and your council will perish."[2]

Grudgingly, the commanders gathered the troops in the morning, and giving a half-hearted effort, soon tired, and decided to withdraw. Gies noted, "Joan reached the Burgundy gate and found Raoul de Gaucourt, second only to Dunois in prestige and authority and told him, 'Like it or not, the soldiers will go out and they will win as they have won before.'"[3] The garrison and town militia rallied to Joan's orders with such enthusiasm that the senior commanders resisting her were threatened by the crowd with bodily harm.

As Joan stood that evening and watched the men returning from the battle, "Dunois and the other captains advised suspending the assault until the next day. Joan would hear none of it. 'In the name of God, you will soon enter the fortress, never doubt it, and the English will have no more strength against you. Rest for a while, eat and drink.' They did as she bade; after which she told them, 'Return to the assault, before God, for the English will have no more will to defend themselves, and their Tourelles *and their ramparts will be taken.*'"[4]

> "All great leaders have one characteristic in common: it was the willingness to confront unequivocally the major anxiety of their people in their time."
>
> JOHN KENNETH GALBRAITH, 1977

Two tries, substantial casualties, and nothing to show for it. Why should the French leaders believe her, the same leaders who had survived the English slaughter of thousands of their best knights just a few years earlier? This Joan was an illiterate and unschooled child of peasant parentage, and all of eighteen years of age.

THE SAD STATE OF FIFTEENTH-CENTURY FRANCE

The French had fallen from the heights of national prestige since the loss of thousands of their best knights facing King Henry V at Agincourt in 1415. The French defeat left the Dukes of Burgundy, Normandy, and Brittany in the north to fend for themselves, and various pacts were arranged to keep their power and lands against a potential English invasion. These pacts protected the dukes but depleted any hope for a united France.

The worst of it all was that in a period of relative sanity, Charles VI "disinherited and banished his son Charles, the dauphin, and named King Henry V of England heir and regent of France."[5] When Charles VI died, his son as dauphin had little hope of ever being crowned king.

FIFTEENTH-CENTURY LIFE

The spiritual influences upon French and English culture in the fifteenth century came from the Catholic Church and those involved in astrology and witchcraft. The Protestant Reformation was still about a century away, and the Catholic Church exercised significant influence all across Europe. The conflict between those involved in witchcraft and those in the Christian faith led the Catholic Church to institute the infamous "Inquisition" to resolve cases of questionable fidelity.

To add to the instability, the plague had spread through Europe just a few years earlier in 1348 and killed twenty-five million people—a third of Europe's population. "It was an unsettling mystery: to people of the Middle Ages who had no way of knowing what caused the disease. They only knew it killed horribly and spread with frightening speed."[6]

The rising interest in spiritual matters was offset by the frightening plague that stymied both civil authorities and clergymen alike. It was a confusing and dark time period during which a peasant child was born in a small village in northeastern France.

DOMREMY—BIRTHPLACE OF JEANNE D'ARC

Joan was born in the region known as Lorraine in the small town of Domremy, most likely in the year of AD 1412. Joan's parents, Isabelle and Jacques d'Arc, were fairly prosperous peasants—meaning they were able to purchase horses to aid them in farming. As a child, she was called Jeanette but was later known by other names. "During her military career and for a century afterward, she was known as Jeanne la Purcelle [pure female or virgin], Joan the Maid, or most frequently 'The Maid.' The first reference to Joan along with her father's surname, d'Arc, came a hundred years later— hence Joan of Arc."[7]

In spite of the fact that Domremy and its sister village to the north, Vaucouleurs, were in a frontier area loyal to the king of France, they were surrounded by the lands and power of the Duke of Burgundy, who had allied himself with the English.

At the time of Joan's birth, the war with England had been superseded by a French civil war between the Burgundians in the north and those supporting the king, the Armagnacs, in the south. The effect on the people of Joan's class was devastating. "English soldiers [in support of their allies, the Burgundians] would march through enemy territory 'burning and destroying all the lands as they pass, both house, grain, vine, and all trees that bear fruit for a man's sustenance.'"[8]

To keep their village from the devastation that was spreading across France and particularly to those loyal to the king, the villagers paid a protection fee to Robert de Baudricourt, the captain of the fortified town in Vaucouleurs, just north of them. It helped little as bands of soldier-brigands continued to pillage at will.

By now, Joan was thirteen, and while little is known of her early life, she had already been baptized in the village church next to her family's home. Other than being recognized by the village priest and some of her playmates as being more pious than most (she would kneel and cross herself at every tolling of the village bell), there was little that set her apart from her peers. Joan's mother noted, "We taught her the Pater Noster, Ave Maria, and Credo, and were very strict with her."[9] Joan spent her early years like most of the village girls actively doing "woman's work, spinning, and household chores" along with "helping her father in the fields harvesting."[10]

But something had happened to her when she was thirteen. In the year that one of the bands of brigands carried off all of the cattle from Domremy, Jeanne d'Arc had her first angelic visitation. In her own words, under questioning she explained:

Joan: When I was thirteen years old, I had a voice from God to help me govern my conduct. And the first time I was very fearful. And came this voice, about the hour of noon, in the summertime, in my father's garden. I had not fasted on the eve preceding that day. I heard the voice on the right-hand side, towards the church; and rarely do I hear it without a brightness. This brightness comes from the same side as the voice is heard. It is usually a great light. When I came to France, often I heard this voice . . . The voice was sent to me by God and, after I had thrice heard this voice, I knew that it was the voice of an angel. This voice has always guarded me well and I have always understood it clearly.

Question: *What sort of help say you that this voice has brought you for the salvation of your soul?*

Joan: It has taught me to conduct myself well, to go habitually to church. It told me that I, Joan, should come in to France and I could not bear to stay where I was. The voice

> told me that I should raise the siege laid to the city of
> Orléans. The voice told me also that I should make my way
> to Robert de Baudricourt in the fortress of Vaucouleurs and
> . . . that he would give me people to go with me. And me, I
> answered it that I was a poor girl who knew not how to ride
> nor lead in war.[11]

Joan in her short years had never traveled beyond her small village of Domremy. There were no means to facilitate her travel
north to Vaucouleurs, nor had she shared her vision and guidance
with anyone, including her village priest. She had no previous contact with Robert de Baudricourt. Moreover, though he was loyal to
the king, he would hardly be disposed to listen to anything a seventeen-year-old peasant girl might have to say. Yet Joan had been
given a vision and her faith, commitment, and courage to pursue
that vision were about to be tested.

HUMILIATION AT VAUCOULEURS

By now, Joan noted that the voices began to speak to her two to
three times a week, telling her she must go to France. She spoke
neither to her parents nor her priest about this, especially after she
overheard what her father said. "He had dreamed that Joan would
go off with the soldiers, and told her brothers, 'If I thought that
such a thing could happen as I have dreamed, I should want you to
drown her; and if you did not, I would drown her myself.'"[12]

Even though she was barely seventeen, she felt she must go to
Robert de Baudricourt at Vaucouleurs. In the spring of 1428 she
left secretly, afraid not only of her parents' reaction but the
Burgundians and soldier-brigands.

In the political realm, after Charles VI died, so did his named
heir apparent, Henry V of England. Charles VII, as the dauphin,
had no spirit to face the English in the north, who took advantage
of the confusion and mounted a fierce assault on the strategic city

of Orléans. Charles VII confined himself to his castle in Chinon, lacking funds, troops, or courage to face the English invaders.

Joan's cousin in Vaucouleurs housed her upon her arrival and requested her husband's assistance in taking her to Robert de Baudricourt. Her insistence, purity, and passionate conviction finally won him over. A knight named Bertrand de Poulengy was present at this short meeting between noble and peasant in May 1428.

"She said that she had come . . . on behalf of her Lord, to ask him to send word to the dauphin that he should hold still and not make war on his enemies, because the Lord would give him help before mid-Lent. Joan also said that the kingdom did not belong to the dauphin, but to her Lord; and that the Lord wanted the dauphin to be made king . . . and that she would lead him to be consecrated. Robert asked her who was her Lord, and she answered: 'The King of Heaven.'"[13] Baudricourt told the knight, "Take her home and have her father box her ears."[14] Upon arriving home, she found nearly every structure in Domremy had been burned to the ground.

The intent of the Burgundians during the summer of 1428 was to capture those cities north of the Loire still loyal to Charles. These included the small, fortified town of Vaucouleurs and the heavily fortified city of Orléans, gateway to the southern kingdom. Things looked increasingly bleak for Charles. The wealthy and titled began to shift their alliances toward the English-Burgundian alliance as a way of ensuring their future survival should the English take Orléans. Having done that, there would be nothing to stop them from marching into the south and capturing Charles and the rest of France.

Joan smarted from her experience with Baudricourt, but six months later, in January of 1429, her voices insisted that she should go again. She went again, lodged with friends for three weeks, and was finally told Baudricourt would not see her.

It was at this moment that one of Baudricourt's knights, Jean de Metz, was in the lodge and overheard this discussion. He asked why she had come.

Jeanne answered, "I have come here to the royal chamber to

speak to Robert de Baudricourt, so that he may take me or have me taken to the king; but he does not care about me or my words; nonetheless, before mid-Lent, I must go to the king, even if I have to walk my feet off to my knees."[15]

It was at this moment that Jeanne made her first convert among the nobility. Jean de Metz promised, with God's help, he would arrange a meeting with Baudricourt. Meanwhile, Jeanne spent every day in the castle chapel praying, where many began to notice the peasant girl wearing a tattered red dress.

Rumors began to spread that a Maid (pure virgin) with supernatural powers was in their region. Believing this, a gravely ill duke called for her and asked her to pray for him. After praying, "she advised him to mend his ways, to stop living with his mistress (by whom he had five children), and take back his wife."[16] She returned to Vaucouleurs disappointed that the duke had no interest in assisting her in her mission or in mending his ways.

> "When a virtuous man is raised, it brings gladness to his friends, grief to his enemies, and glory to his posterity."
>
> BEN JONSON, 1573–1637

She couldn't have been more surprised to find a small miracle awaiting her. Indeed, the rising tide of public opinion regarding the Maid had finally persuaded Robert de Baudricourt of her character and heaven-sent mission. Jean de Metz and five other men-at-arms were sent by Baudricourt to take Joan to see the Dauphin. The record of the meeting concluded:

> Joan came into my house. She was dressed in a woman's garment, red. Later she was dressed in a vest, hose [flexible tweed legging wear] and other clothes proper to a man, and rode on a horse to the Dauphin. I saw them set out all together. When she sought to go, she was asked how she would do it with so many men-at-arms everywhere. She answered that she feared not men-at-arms for . . . she had God, her Lord, who would

clear the way for her to go to the lord Dauphin, and that she had been born to do this.[17]

TO THE DAUPHIN

Joan had a charisma that stemmed from the purity of her character and the cause of her life—that she should fulfill the urging of her heavenly voices to see the Dauphin crowned as king at Reims. Reims was the place where all rightful kings of France were crowned, even though it was now safely in the territory of the Burgundians. The charisma and inner light began to affect all who encountered her.

Her escorts considered her a naïve child for believing she could cover three hundred miles through the heart of enemy Burgundy. "They thought of her as presumptuous and their intention was to put her to the proof . . . They said that in the beginning they wanted to require her to lie with them carnally. But when the moment came to speak to her of this they were so much ashamed that they dared not speak of it to her, nor say a word of it."[18]

Even Jean de Metz wondered at the wisdom of this dangerous and difficult trip. Several times he asked Joan whether she really believed that she could accomplish her task. She opened her heart to him "that she had been sent to do this . . . and that four or five years before, God had told her that she must to go to war to restore the kingdom of France."[19] Her words set a fire in his heart.

They traveled at night, and when they slept, a fully clothed Joan lay apart from her escorts. Her escorts wrote of their fears: "We were eleven days on the road going to the King, then Dauphin. But on the way, we had many anxieties. But Joan repeatedly told us not to be afraid; that once we came to the town of Chinon the noble Dauphin would give us good countenance. She never swore, and I myself was much stimulated by her voices, for it seemed to me that she was sent by God, and I never saw in her any evil, but always was she so virtuous a girl that she seemed a saint. And thus together, without great difficulties we made our way to the place of Chinon."[20]

Over mountains, rivers, and through valleys they crossed more than three hundred miles at night in eleven days through enemy-held territory. The only regret expressed by Joan during the trip was that, because of the danger, they were unable to stop at any church to pray and celebrate Mass. She had convinced most in Vaucouleurs of her character and the high calling of her mission. Could she convince a king?

CHINON—A CASTLE AND KINGDOM IN RUIN

Since the Treaty of Troyes, where his mother cast doubt upon his own legitimacy, Charles "remained sunk in apathy, utterly hopeless, and quite indifferent to the affairs of state . . . leading a miserable existence in the gloomy castle of Chinon."[21] Charles was only twenty-six when seventeen-year-old Joan arrived in February 1429.

In the short history of his reign, Charles had avoided every opportunity to face the English. He much preferred negotiation to shedding blood even when negotiations were to his disadvantage. Adding to his problems was that as his sphere of influence decreased, so did his treasury. As time passed, he could hardly consider going to war because his funds were barely sufficient to sustain his kingdom, much less outfit an army.

Consequently, he spent two years trying to negotiate with the English to relieve the siege at Orléans and sever their tie with the Burgundian dukes. He failed. He had nothing to offer that the wealth of England couldn't match and surpass. The French lacked a sense of national identity and thus removed the strategy of rallying the people to his aid. Such was the state of Charles and his ever-shrinking kingdom when news of a peasant girl on a holy mission reached the king's court.

Upon arriving, Joan sent the king a message stating she had "traveled one hundred and fifty leagues to come to him and bring him aid" and messages for his ears alone.[22] Joan spent two days in prayer and attending Mass waiting for the king's answer. At last she received word that the king would see her. However, when she arrived in the court, she was met instead by his council, who demanded to hear what she would say to the king.

"Joan at first protested that she wanted to speak directly to the king, but under persuasion she informed them that she had come on behalf of the King of Heaven to raise the siege of Orléans and to take the king to Reims for his coronation and consecration."[23] In the end, just as at Vaucouleurs, "Joan's sincerity and invincible confidence in her mission overcame the opposition . . . Her successful journey through territory of the king's enemies, including the almost miraculous crossing of many rivers, impressed the councilors enough to tip the scales, and Joan at last was admitted into the king's presence."[24]

The hall to which she was brought that night was large enough to hold more than three hundred knights standing amid fifty torches along the walls that provided a flickering light. As they watched the illiterate shepherdess enter, the knights must have been inwardly chuckling as they waited for the king's game to be played out. Simon Charles, a merchant, testified twenty years later that "the king deliberately hid himself among the courtiers," while other literature asserted "that the king had a courtier pose in his place."[25] Either way, Joan was to be tested to determine who and what she was.

Walking slowly among the three hundred knights and many other courtiers in that great hall, Joan approached the throne and then turned away, moving through the crowd. Looking into face after face, she finally stopped and knelt down before Charles VII, saying, "Most noble Lord Dauphin, I have come and am sent by God to bring aid to you and your kingdom."[26]

Jean Pasquerel, Joan's subsequent confessor and companion from this moment forward, testified that Joan recognized the king without difficulty, though there were others dressed with greater pomp and richness. "Wherefore, the dauphin answered Joan, 'Not I am the King, Joan.' And, pointing to one of his lords, said, 'There is the King.' To which she replied, 'By God, gentle prince, it is you and none other."[27] She then proclaimed, "The King of Heaven has sent me to see that you are consecrated and crowned in the city of Reims, and you shall be lieutenant of the King of Heaven, who is king of France . . . I tell you *Messire* [sir] that you are the true heir of France and the king's son."[28]

The room was electrified, and the king was joyous. He took Joan aside, they talked a long time, and he grew more elated as time passed. Later testimony, both by Joan and by those who later spoke to the king, said she had relayed to him "a certain secret that nobody knew or could know but God. That is why he had great confidence in her."[29] (What that secret was, was something that Joan and the king never revealed, but has been the subject of much speculation.)

The king put Joan in the company of a noblewoman in the castle and came to visit her several times over the next week. Still, he was beset with doubts and insecurity and counselors who continued to minimize and even vilify Joan's counsel and mission. Ultimately, he decided the only way to settle the matter was to send Joan to Poitiers where clergy, doctors, king's counselors, and those knowledgeable in canon and civil law could examine her.

Those who lead with moral authority, with honesty and integrity, can expect their lives to be examined—particularly by those who don't. A prophecy had been spread for nearly a hundred years that a woman would ruin the kingdom and a virgin from the east, a maid from Lorraine, would restore it. The kingdom lay in ruin. Was Jeanne D'Arc the maid who would restore it? Was she honest, trustworthy, a virgin (as in the prophecy)? Was she on a heaven-sent mission, an agent of the English, or was she something worse?

POITIERS

The examination lasted three weeks and involved more than two dozen individuals from various backgrounds. Joan felt she had little to tell her examiners. "I suppose you have come to question me. But I don't know A from B."[30]

The commission questioned her regarding her visions and angelic visitations that she identified as St. Michael, St. Margaret, and St. Catherine.

> Q: You have said that the voice told you that God wishes to deliver the people of France from their present calamity. If he wants to deliver them, it is not necessary to send soldiers.
>
> Joan: In the name of God, the soldiers will fight and God will give victory.
>
> Q: God could not wish us to believe you without giving us some sign. (The questioner further remarked that they could not advise the king to entrust soldiers to her on her simple assertion, without more assurance.)
>
> Joan: In the name of God, I did not come to Poitiers to give signs; but take me to Orléans, and I will show you the signs for which I was sent.[31]

Joan was questioned at length about her dressing in male attire. They referenced the Bible's admonition against women and men wearing clothing belonging to the other. Joan's answer was that her Lord had called her to war, and that the tunic and clothing she wore were those more of a soldier than a man. Further, it was the Lord who called her to this profession and she must be prepared for the hardships of it, though she would have preferred to stay home tending her parents' animals and helping her mother.

After three weeks of questioning, the first part of the inquiry ended, and "the commission reported that Joan was a good Christian and a true Catholic . . . and a very good person."[32] However, following this verbal examination, Joan was forced to undergo a physical exam to discover, "as Joan's confessor Jean Pasquerel phrased it, 'whether she was a man or woman, wanton or virgin.' A committee of ladies conducted the exam and reported 'they found her . . . a true and complete virgin *(une vraye et entière pucelle).*"[33]

Joan now took the offensive. She told her examiners that she must be given the soldiers she needed and they must let her go to Orléans. "She then prophesied four events: first, the English would be destroyed, the siege of Orléans would be raised, and the city freed; second, the king would be consecrated at Reims; third, the city of Paris would return to the king's obedience; and fourth, the Duke of Orléans would return from captivity in England."[34]

At the end of three weeks of interrogations Joan left her examiners a final word: "There is more in the books of our Lord than in yours."[35]

Of Joan, the committee concluded, "Joan's faith, way of life, and past are irreproachable, there is nothing in her but good, humility, simplicity, virginity and honesty. The ready wisdom of her responses and the sanctity of her life weigh in favor of her mission being a divine one. Therefore, the king's duty is to put the presumption to the proof; if Joan is sent by divine grace and the Holy Spirit, you must not risk rejecting the gift. The sign Joan has promised the commission is the relief of Orléans. For that it is necessary to give her soldiers." The report was adopted unanimously by all of her examiners.

The king accorded Joan the title of *chef de guerre,* or war chief, equal to the captains of war that led the French army. It was a remarkable designation considering the period of history and her lineage as a seventeen-year-old illiterate, peasant girl. She now had to produce the proof that the Dauphin's trust had been rightly placed in her. The only thing standing in the way of that was a very large English army.

ORLÉANS—TURNING POINT OF THE ONE HUNDRED YEARS WAR

Joan now stood "in title" as an equal to the male captains of war. But clearly, titles do not make commanders, nor do they win respect. Our deeds earn that commendation. Joan had been given a title, but that meant little to the other military leaders and even less in the face of the great crisis at Orléans.

The city stood on the north shore of the Loire River. Orléans was connected by a long drawbridge to a twin-towered stone fortress on the southern shore known as the Tourelles. In addition to the Tourelles, the English occupied the monastery of Les Augustins just south of Tourelles. The people of Orléans had managed to cut the drawbridge over the Loire prior to the English crossing it into the city. While that temporarily protected them, it also isolated them. Being situated on the north shore, they were in the territory of the Burgundians, from which precious little help could be expected. From the south, the forces of Charles VII could not reach the city or cross the Loire without encountering the English occupying the fortresses of the Tourelles and Les Augustins.

Of course, there were other places to cross to the north, but there were English fortifications all along that side of the river. Dunois had been pleading for an expedition for some months to relieve the siege. As Joan approached the city, she thought she was part of a relieving army rather than a deliverer sent to feed a starving city. But how to get the food into Orléans? Many attempts had failed at great loss of both supplies and men.

Dunois proposed a plan to build barges and load them upstream on the southern shore, then float them down to the city gates where they could be offloaded by the city's inhabitants. Unfortunately, the wind had been blowing against the current for some time, making the effort futile. Joan was exasperated by all this and wanted to attack the English army immediately. Joan confronted Dunois.

"'Was it you who advised me to come here, on this side of the river, instead of going straight to where Talbot and the English are?' Dunois explained that he and others wiser than he had made the decision. Joan answered, 'In the name of God, the counsel of God is safer and wiser than yours. You thought you had deceived me, and you deceive yourselves more, for I bring you better help than any knight or city, the help of the King of Heaven. It does not come for love of me, but from God Himself who . . . has pity on Orléans and will not suffer that enemies hold both the Lord of Orléans and his city.'"[36]

It was at that very moment, according to Dunois himself, that the winds suddenly shifted in the direction of the current. The boats were loaded and floated downstream, and "Dunois, impressed by Joan and the 'miracle' of the change of wind, now 'had great hopes of her.' He wanted to take her to Orléans where they were most eager to meet her."[37]

Joan, arrayed in full armor, waited until dark to avoid the tumult of people and "rode through the Burgundy gate, fully armed, on a white horse her standard carried before her. Dunois at her side, followed by many other nobles and were surrounded on all sides by a crowd of soldiers and citizens carrying torches, 'as joyful as if they had seen God descending among them.'"[38] The English were completely surprised by her arrival and subsequent relief of the city.

Joan had yet to completely perceive her status. Among the people of France, her arrival was nothing short of a miracle. To the English, "the Maid" was no angel, but as yet, they could not say what she was. They soon found out when Joan dictated a letter to the English commander Talbot.

In very simple language, she demanded the English give up the siege and go home. The English replied that "they would burn her, that she was nothing but a whore, and that she should go back to watching her cows."[39]

It was beyond the comprehension of the English that a woman could live with soldiers without being a prostitute or "camp follower" as such women were known then. They didn't know that Joan had chased the camp followers out of the French camp with a sword and forbid cursing or the taking of God's name in vain. Further, she expected each soldier to confess his sins before every battle. On this she was immovable, and even her captains complied.

Over the next week, she continued to ride within earshot of the English, telling them they should surrender or the number of English lives lost would be grave. They replied with insults. Dunois returned with additional soldiers, and Joan rejoiced that the battle would soon be joined.

Yet even Dunois did not take her role seriously—at least in a military sense. Thus, he led a charge against a fortified English garrison at St. Loup on the southern shore without telling her. Dunois hoped a quick victory over this somewhat isolated stronghold might raise French morale and give them momentum to take on the larger Tourelles. Sadly, it was a disaster.

While Joan was sleeping, she was awakened by an "angelic voice" and sprang out of bed. "In God's name, my Counsel has told me that I must attack the English, but I don't know whether I must go."[40]

She pulled on her armor, mounted her horse, and rode for the eastern Burgundy gate. A great outcry in the city had begun, and as she reached the gate, she was met with the wounded and dead straggling back into the city.

"On catching sight of Joan, the embattled French gave a cheer, renewed their faltering assault, and the English in St. Loup suddenly yielded. Inside the garrison, the *Journal du Siège* reported 114 English lay dead, leaving only 40 to be taken prisoner. The French leveled the garrison from top to bottom."[41]

Joan ordered that since the following day was Ascension Day, the French would not wage war, and that "all soldiers would go to confession and no camp followers should accompany the army since it was for such sins that God would let us lose the war."[42]

Until now, Joan had exercised only moral authority, which she would continue to do. Yet her presence in battle and turning the tide of momentum in that battle convinced the other captains that Joan had greater usefulness. At the following day's strategy session, she was invited to join them.

The next morning Joan confessed to her priest Pasquerel and heard him say Mass, and then joined some four thousand men-at-arms preparing to attack Les Augustins. "An advance party of the French were returning with the bad news that they were not strong enough to take the fort, but Joan cried out to the men with her, 'Let us go boldly in the name of the Lord.'"[43]

By the end of that day, the French had forced the English from

Les Augustins into the Tourelles. There were many casualties and
Joan had been wounded in the foot by a spiked ball, but they had
won the battle. Joan was persuaded to go back into the town while
massive amounts of provisions were now reaching the city.

"She ate supper, and afterward a knight came to tell her that
the captains had decided that, considering their numbers, the victory that God had already granted them, and the fact that the city
was now well supplied, it would be wiser not to fight the following
day. Joan replied with her immortal words: 'You have been in your
council, and I in mine; and believe me, the council of the Lord will
be carried out and will endure, and your council will perish.' She
told her priest, 'Keep close to me, because tomorrow I will have
much to do, more than ever before, and I will be wounded above
the breast.'"[44]

The next morning, the French arose early and bracketed three
sides of the stone fortress. They had to surmount the palisade, the
moat, and the earthworks the English had built around the
Tourelles while the English above them showered them with arrows,
cannonballs, and various missiles. Once they were close enough to
touch the walls and raise their scaling ladders, the English poured
boiling oil on them and then battled them furiously throughout the
day. In the afternoon, as she had predicted, Joan was shot through
her shoulder with an arrow.

She "was afraid and wept and was comforted," Pasquerel noted
as he dressed her wound. Seeing their inspired leader now fallen,
Dunois and the other captains advised against continuing the
assault that day. Many were disheartened as Joan was carried from
the battlefield, her standard fallen. Yet Joan would hear none of
their counsel. She told them firmly, "In the name of God, you will
soon enter the fortress, never doubt it, and the English will have no
more strength against you. Rest for a while, eat and drink." They
did as she bade; after which she told them, "Return to the assault,
before God, for the English will have no more will to defend themselves, and their Tourelles *and their ramparts will be taken.*"[45]

The English, seeing the fall of the Maid, were greatly heartened, and now fought as though they were immortal.[46] The French prepared to renew their attack, while Joan mounted her horse and went off into a nearby vineyard where she prayed for a short time. "She seized her standard and took up her position on the outer edge of the moat, declaring, that when the wind blew her standard toward the rampart, it would be theirs."[47]

Her standard-bearer, exhausted from previous battle, began to fall, and Joan seized it from him as the wind began to blow. The French, seeing her standard raised in her hands, surged forward and stormed the ramparts. The English attempted to retreat within the Tourelles, but the French were closing in from all directions. Simultaneously, as the French ascended the walls and poured over the top, the English attempted to retreat across the drawbridge toward the city. The French had already prepared for this and set fire to a boat and floated it down the river until it rested against the bridge and began to burn. Just two nights before, Joan had come out again to plead with the English to surrender or suffer an evil loss. Now, as the English retreated along the lengthy bridge, it collapsed from the fire and their weight, and four to five hundred English knights and men-at-arms fell into the river and drowned. The remaining handful of English in the Tourelles surrendered.

In Orléans the bells rang. The next morning, the remaining English gathered in battle formation across the river. They stood taunting the French, hoping to entice them to attack, giving the English a chance to snatch "victory out of defeat" just as they had done at Agincourt in 1415. The armies stood facing each other for two hours without moving. Finally, Joan asked for a makeshift altar to be set up where she knelt and prayed. She prayed for nearly an hour, and when she finished, she turned and faced the English. Looking at her, the English army disbanded. Asked what the French should do, she replied, "Our Lord does not want us to fight them today; you will have them another time."[48]

The word spread like a fire all the way to London that a Maid had raised the siege at Orléans—not as a warrior, but through witchcraft. No Burgundian or Englishman would believe that a peasant girl leading a beleaguered French army could have defeated them. Her victory had raised the French from the depths of despair and gave them a glimmer of hope that they might one day dislodge the English from France. "The English feared her as much as a large army [and] more than the rest of the French army, and from that moment on sought to lay hands on her to try her as a witch."[49]

POSTSCRIPT

Following the victory at Orléans, Joan led the king's army in battle through six Burgundian-held towns to bring her sovereign to Reims. On July 17, 1429, with her standard flying, she stood next to Charles VII as he was crowned in the church at Reims—no longer Dauphin, but true king of France. She had fulfilled her vision and commission.

Less than a year later she was captured by the English at Compiegne and taken to Rouen, where she was tried by her captors and burned at the stake in May 1431, at the age of nineteen. While tried by dozens of highly educated clergy, doctors, and lawyers for some seventy-seven crimes, including witchcraft, her answers during a year of inquisition were such that no fault in her character and behavior could be found. Ultimately, the basis for execution was that she wore men's clothes during her soldiering.

Some twenty-five years later Charles had recovered most of the northern French territory as Joan had once promised, and he re-opened her trial at Reims. He invited both English and French to testify, though very few English responded. Those who testified spoke of the many injustices they had observed during the trial and that Joan had been condemned for political rather than religious reasons. The commission found Joan's trial a farce, restored her standing as a Christian, and noted that nearly all who had plotted against her died untimely deaths. Since both England and France were still Catholic, the new finding of Joan's innocence was legitimate in both countries.

THOUGHTS FOR
TODAY'S CENTURIONS

PUTTING ASIDE FOR THE MOMENT ALL ISSUES OF THE SUPERnatural, one of the most remarkable facets of Joan's leadership was the power of purity in her character and its effect on those who followed her.

You might admire and respect Joan, but wonder how her life could possibly benefit your leadership situation. You may not have been visited by an angel, nor had angelic voices giving you guidance along the way, but you have been given something that is common to all men and women. You have been given a conscience—an internal guide to what is good and what is not, what is beneficial to all and what serves mostly your own ends.

Charles Wang, founder of Computer Associates, the largest independent computer software company after Microsoft, IBM, and Oracle, with annual revenue in the billions, makes a powerful argument about life and work: "You should be doing some good, making the world better . . . You have to be pointed in the right direction. You're building a career. You're doing something you really enjoy . . . I always tell everybody, give back, give back. Because if you don't give back, this world is not going to get better. And if you're fortunate enough to do really well, give more."[50] Those are the words, but deeds are what give words power. What are his deeds? Wang's passion is eliminating facial deformities such as cleft palate, and he has established an organization called "Smile Train." His motto? "You are supposed to live by your moral compass and give some back. It's simple."[51] Maybe it is simple, but considering the few who follow this path, it certainly isn't easy.

Some people believe that "moral leadership" and "business ethics" are oxymorons. This has led to widespread feelings that executives, managers, and leaders act only in their self-interest. A survey in 1985 noted "that fifty-five percent of the American public believed the vast majority of corporate executives were dishonest, and fifty-nine percent believed executive white-collar crime occurs on a regular basis. A 1987 *Wall Street Journal* article noted that one-fourth of the 671 executives believed that ethics can impede a successful career."[52]

> But the problem isn't just at the top. "Because of the perceived low ethical standards of the executive class, workers feel justified in responding in kind—through absenteeism, petty theft, indifference, and a generally poor performance on the job. Many workers openly admitted that they spend more than twenty percent (eight hours a week) of their time at work totally goofing off. Almost half of those surveyed admitted to chronic malingering on a regular basis. One in six of the workers surveyed said that he or she drank or used drugs on the job. Three out of four workers reported that their primary reason for working was 'to keep the wolf from the door'; only one in four claimed to give his or her 'best effort' to the job. *The survey concluded that the standards equation of the American workplace is a simple one: American workers are as ethical/dutiful in doing their jobs as their bosses and companies are perceived to be ethical/dutiful in leading and directing them"* (italics mine).[53]

If workers rise up only to the level of expectation of their leaders, then there is a direct correlation between the character of a leader and the organization achieving its mission goals. Long before surveys like the one above, Aristotle suggested in *Nichomachean Ethics* that "morality cannot be learned simply by reading a treatise on virtue. The spirit of morality, said Aristotle, is awakened in the individual only through the witness and conduct of a moral person."[54]

As many modern leaders have descended into the abyss of selfishness and pandering, we lose hope that any other kind of leader could survive in the corruption of the present age. We have so many who have served to lower our expectations that unless things change dramatically, we can only hope for a day when the people will cry out, saying, "Enough! We will have strength *and* honor in our leaders, or we will have new leaders in their place."

Centurions are not averse to taking strong positions based upon integrity, professional competence, and courageous commitment to a vision that eludes lesser leaders. They are not easily blown by the winds of public opinion. They wield a moral power that breaks the chains of many while wounding the ambition, pride, and power of those of lesser nobility. In taking their stand, Centurions create supporters and opponents, friends and enemies. Sadly, lesser leaders, who "stand for nothing" or serve only themselves, create the same divisions without benefiting the organization they serve.

> "The same leader who is charismatic in the eyes of people in distress, for whom salvation lies in change, will be counter-charismatic in the eyes of those who see in change not salvation but ruination."
>
> ROBERT TUCKER, 1918

How high is the mountain that stands before you, and what are the means you possess to ascend and conquer it? Are your circumstances as impoverished as Joan's were? What is going to carry you through the difficult days and weeks ahead? Are you counting on the power of your position and prestige to inspire those you lead to achieve a seemingly impossible goal? If not, what means are you going to use to drive your team to that goal? It is vital to take a moment and examine yourself—look at your inner core—and honestly evaluate how you motivate yourself, your team, and your peers each day. This is one of the defining aspects that identify you either as a manager or as a Centurion.

If you would raise the bar of your leadership, Joan's example is immensely useful, as she had no position, experience, champion, or friend in high places. Are you lacking resources? She had none. Are you lacking skills and expertise? She had none. She did have one thing that you may lack. She had an untouchable moral authority and integrity that won people to her cause little by little. She had an uncompromising faith that she was being called to accomplish something greater than she had the means to achieve. She believed in a *destiny* larger than herself.

In Joan, it pleased the Almighty to prove the great proverb, "God has chosen the foolish things of the world to put to shame the wise, and God has chosen the weak things of the world to put to shame the things which are mighty."[55]

When your people look at you, what do they see you standing up for? Even faith and belief in your cause or calling aren't going to be enough. You must have the courage to commit yourself to your destiny, against whatever odds are before you, and to live out the dream that's been planted in your heart. Sound rare? It is, and that is why there are so few Centurions.

Most leaders lean on their power, their rank, or their title to motivate people to accomplish their goals. In one position I held, my boss was a one-star general. He told me one day, "You'll do as I say because I'm a general and you're a colonel—just made to be abused." At the other end of the spectrum, when I was being prepared to command a flying squadron, a three-star general asked, "Do you know the primary reason why commanders are relieved of their command?" He waited for a moment and then replied, "Arrogance of command." After that, he left the room. Too many leaders today obviously lack a moral compass and don't even know it's missing.

The billionaire New York real estate personality Leona Helmsley was quoted in the *New York Times* as saying, "Only little people pay taxes." Sometime later she stood before a judge who told her, "Your conduct was the product of naked greed, the arrogant belief that you were above the law." Judge John M. Walker, Jr., then sentenced her to four years in prison, seven hundred fifty hours of community service, and $7.1 million in fines for mail fraud and tax evasion.[56] Power has a way of leading us to believe that we should be insulated from being challenged, questioned, or bothered by institutional minutia. The higher we rise in life, in position, and in rank, the more we are tempted to use the blunt force of power to accomplish our goals.

Joan felt she had no better reference for her mission than God Himself, for He had sent His messengers to encourage her to lift a Dauphin to his throne and a nation out of despair. Her conduct and character had never been called into question. Yet that wasn't enough. She was commanded to be examined at Poitiers before the king would entrust himself to her. Later the English would do their best to find her guilty of witchcraft, but stacked as the trial was, they could not.

We must be ready at all times to be called to account for our lives, *especially* if we live them on virtuous grounds. Virtue threatens and angers those whose own lives have been lived under the shadows of expediency and vice.

Joan's pure heart, committed to unselfish ends, led a nation out of despair and crowned a king. Her life still resonates more than five centuries after her death in the flower of her youth. She left us a legacy that while everyone dies, only a few really live. Oh, that more of us would *live!*

PAUSE FOR SPIRITUAL REFLECTION

Take the long view. It is the most important piece of wisdom I can pass to you on your journey as a Centurion. Take the long view. In this world, the focus is upon short-term gains and making as much as you can as fast as you can.

The long view is about seventy years, according to a proverb of King David. "Seventy years are given to us! Some may even reach eighty. But even the best of these years are filled with pain and trouble; soon they disappear, and we are gone."[57] If you want to be a Centurion, you need to base your decisions on something more permanent than the next quarterly report, the next unit inspection, the next promotion, the next . . .

I am always reminded that I will one day meet my Maker. How

will I feel then about my decisions now? That forces me to take the long view. We who lead are reminded that we are responsible to more than earthly authority when we are placed in leadership over others. "Masters, give to your servants that which is just and equal, knowing that you also have a Master in heaven."[58] It is an awesome responsibility that too many take too lightly.

Joan began her journey as a young child by remembering to kneel and pray each time her village bell tolled. This was long before the first angel visited her with a commission. Your journey begins right where you are, wherever you are and in whatever condition your "moral compass" now exists. No person is so far down into the abyss that he cannot begin this journey.

I have "learned" to become *more* of a man of integrity as the years have passed. What I once thought was nothing, now I would not entertain. What I once did without thinking, now I wouldn't even consider. What I once failed to do, now I strive with great passion to accomplish. When I look back, I see the work of God over many years, and it encourages me to keep on pressing closer to Him. Oh, I have a long way to go. The older I get, the more I realize how much farther that distance is. Still, that inspires me to keep pressing ahead rather than succumbing to the pressure of the moment.

We may not all have a destiny as memorable as Joan's. But we can be Centurions who will be remembered by those we led and, most important, by the One who made us.

PATHWAYS TO INTEGRITY-BASED LEADERSHIP

Becoming a Centurion of "strength" seems easy compared to becoming a Centurion of both "strength and honor." When cheating and lying are endemic in a corporate culture, those leaders who resist risk being labeled, marginalized, and even fired. When such behavior is prevalent in the culture as well, the task seems even more daunting. I'm not going to paint a pretty picture here because I've faced those very issues as a leader—and it was painful.

What got me through was this: I believed in a greater destiny than that which ruled by the tyranny of the moment. I began by taking the long view. I knew I was more accountable to a higher power than I was to a petty one. I knew in my gut, in my heart, and in my conscience when I was being asked to cross the line from "honor" into something less. If I couldn't face myself, then how could I face others? And if I couldn't face men, how could I face my Maker?

So how do you start? Take a moment and picture yourself at age seventy, retired and looking back on your life. When you remember your working life, what will be important to you? What will you be most proud of, and what will disappoint you? What are you doing *today* to enlarge those memories that will satisfy your heart about the worth and significance of your life? That is where you begin.

But what about "fear"? *What if I lose my job? What if I lose my house and have to move? What if my reputation is tarnished? The economy is bad; what if I can't get another job? I have a family; I can't afford to take risks.*

You can be driven by fear. Many are. But what if the worst fears above come true? What will you do? You may move. You'll definitely cut back. If you're a Centurion, you'll persevere until you overcome, and your family will watch you set an example they can follow. Most of all, you will still own your honor and self-respect. No one can take your honor from you. Only you can give it away.

I served in the military and rose to the rank of colonel. Most of my bosses couldn't have been more pleased with my work. But I ran across one while I was a colonel in the Pentagon who was never happy with me. Finally, one afternoon he fired me. I was sent packing that day with a box of personal items and his reprimand while he lashed out about me to all my former subordinates and peers. Humiliating? Sure. But I believed then and I believe now, there is a greater power who shapes my destiny.

A week later, the number three man in the air force, the assistant vice chief of staff, called me in to discuss my firing and what they were going to do with me. He had the power to send me anywhere in the world. I refused to bad-mouth my boss, though I felt I had ample room to do so. I said I was going to keep my head high and keep doing my best until I retired the following summer. At the end of that hour-long meeting, he looked at me and said, "Jeff, you can just consider that you're working for me now." He treated me as if he was honored that I was working for him. I was fired by a one-star general and hired by a three-star, and my life improved immeasurably. Some call it "screw-up and move-up," while others call it "failing forward." I believe a Destiny Shaper greater than I guides my steps, even when I'm flat on my back.

Take the small-step approach in constructing your leadership foundation on integrity. Tell those beneath you about it, and then encourage them to give you feedback when you fall short. You will have to be open to this kind of feedback, but it will communicate to everyone how serious you are about your commitment.

When you've talked and walked in the path long enough, your people will know it isn't just a passing fad, but a part of who you are. More importantly, many of them will want to live up to the example you set.

If you believe that a power greater than you shapes your destiny, and you have the persistence to hold on to your honor, integrity, and vision until you see it arrive, someone may write your story five hundred years from now. Heraclitus believed "character is fate." I believe that character reaps destinies.

CHAPTER 5

GEORGE WASHINGTON

FIRST IN WAR, FIRST IN PEACE, FIRST IN THE HEARTS OF HIS COUNTRYMEN

Many are captivated by money, fame, or power while others are content to pick up a paycheck. Motives empower or diminish leadership—what are yours?

WHAT GETS YOU OUT OF BED IN THE MORNING? WHAT comes into your mind when you first wake up? (Other than the morning traffic report announcing, "Ouch. That's gotta hurt. If you're thinking about taking the freeway this morning, turn over and go back to sleep. You're in for a long commute . . .") The question at hand is what gets your juices going—what generates your energy and your enthusiasm about the day ahead?

As a leader, you can be sure that time and circumstances will uncover your motivations. I've always heard that people rise to the occasion. I think it is truer that a person's character doesn't as much *rise* to the occasion as it is *revealed* by the occasion. Throughout our lives we make decisions that form habits and a way of thinking that are unmistakably "us." When we are faced with a fork in the road, the decisive moment arrives. The do-or-die clutch play, the big deal, the key speech, the turning point of the battle—and we are uncovered for who we are—weak or strong, incompetent or able, corrupt or virtuous, cowardly or courageous. It's in the fire that gold is separated from the various worthless elements to which it has been joined for so long.

Sometimes we may be able to avoid the fire, but at some point we're in the middle of it, and if we dissemble or wilt, we must forever endure the stigma of one who cannot or will not suffer the heat. We can be certain that in due time we will be known, and it all begins when the alarm goes off in the morning. Our motives reveal the depth or absence of our character.

The thing that gets you moving in the morning will guide you through your day, reaping opinions about you that will form perceptions and a reputation—and it will be distinctly yours!

In the case of George Washington, his hoped-for life as a landowner on the spacious and cultivated grounds of Mount Vernon was not to be. But why would he exchange that life for an office in a canvas tent leading a hopeless cause without pay or benefits, all the while risking his considerable reputation while Mount Vernon fell into disrepair? And having survived the Revolutionary War, having spurned all requests to lead the new colonies as their "king," what could motivate him to again leave his beloved Mount Vernon, risking a war-won reputation for the crushing headaches as leader of a fledgling nation? The answers to these questions are found in his attitude about work and service and his motives for pursuing each.

> "Though I prize, as I ought, the good opinion of my fellow citizens; yet, if I know myself, I would not seek or retain popularity at the expense of one social duty of moral virtue."
>
> GEORGE WASHINGTON, 1778[1]

This isn't an examination of Washington's battlefield or political exploits. Rather, it's a portrait of a man's decisions and motivations to take command repeatedly, seemingly against his better judgment, and certainly against his wishes. From that discovery, perhaps we might better understand our own motivations about why we work and why we serve as leaders.

ENTRY TO WAR, 1775

By early 1775 the American colonists faced the distasteful future of an ever-increasing tax burden by a king who provided little protection from the frontier Indians who struck at will. The colonists eventually came to understand the English cared little for their welfare and much for their wealth. While many respected the king, few supported the growing tax burden and inconvenience of housing and feeding his troops without compensation. They held no illusions that to obtain their obedience and wealth, the king would shackle every one of them in slavery.

Washington was elected, along with seven others, to represent Virginia at the Continental Congress in August of 1774. The issues of independence and loyalty to their sovereign raged through the long, hot Philadelphia summer. By the following March, unarmed youths on Boston Common threw snowballs, yelled taunts, and swung sticks at the British soldiers who fired upon them, killing five. The ferocity of the anger in the colonies at the unjust deaths crystallized the thinking of many in the Congress. They would have to fight.

Washington reflected on this in May 1775. "The British were fortunate to escape, the initiative and spirit of the minutemen were gratifying, but the outlook was ominous. 'Unhappy it is, though, to reflect that a brother's sword has been sheathed in a brother's breast and that the once happy and peaceful plains of America are either to be drenched in blood or inhabited by slaves. Sad alternative! But can a virtuous man hesitate in his choice?'"[2]

Washington's first reference to embarking upon this course of action—or just participating in the inevitable violence that would follow—was, "Can a virtuous man even hesitate to choose when all he loves will soon be enslaved?" For Washington the cornerstone of his decision was based on motives that flowed from a strong and virtuous character.

Later that summer, the Continental Congress called him to take command not just of the armies of Virginia but of the entire Continental Army in the cause of the national defense. He had already been asked three times and politely declined each time.

There it lay before him—the power to lead an army of an entire continent—to instill loyalty to himself among thousands of soon-to-be well-trained troops. There lay possible glory, rank and title, and a place in history—all the things so many crave. He could exact any amount to finance this cause and ask for and receive wealth for himself as well. In short, the dire circumstances made all of this possible. The question was, *What did George Washington see when he looked in the mirror each day?*

Other nations had faced or would face the same dire circumstances: France had its Napoleon, Germany its Hitler, Russia had Stalin, and each came to rue the day. America had George Washington, who wrote that he faced a dilemma rather than what others would see as an opportunity.

> So far from seeking this appointment, I have used every endeavor in my power to avoid it, not only from my unwillingness to part with you and the family, but from a consciousness of its being a trust too great for my capacity . . . But as it has been a kind of destiny, that has thrown me upon this service, I shall hope that my undertaking it is designed to answer some good purpose . . . It was utterly out of my power to refuse this appointment, without exposing my character to such censures, as would have reflected dishonor upon myself, and given pain to my friends. This, I am sure, could not, and ought not, be pleasing to you, and must have lessened me considerably in my own esteem. I shall rely, therefore, confidently on that Providence, which has heretofore been bountiful and preserved me.[3]

For Washington, his strength and America's safety now lay in his hands. In spite of his reluctance to assume the role and leave his family at Mount Vernon, his sense of honor and duty to his fellow citizens was stronger. As to his financial demands, he wrote:

"I beg leave to assure the Congress that as no pecuniary consideration could have tempted me to have accepted this arduous employment, at the expense of my domestic ease and happiness, I do not wish to make any profit from it: I will keep an exact account of my expenses; those I doubt not you will discharge and that is all I desire."[4]

So having disposed of power and money as motivations, what about glory? This is not as easily disproved because actions and decisions over time are better indicators of the true nature of a heart. But it is interesting that he told a London correspondent a year earlier, "I am now, I believe, fixed in this seat with an agreeable consort for life and hope to find more happiness in retirement than I ever experienced amidst a wide and bustling world."[5] Not exactly the stuff of a glory hunter, but there were greater tests of his character ahead.

THE WAR BEGINS

George Washington took the role of commander of all rebel forces in the colonies, as King George referred to him. He stood a rope's length away from death along with his fellows and defeated an enemy that was superior in training, equipment, and numbers. It was logical, then, that the leaders of the Continental Congress would look to a man of his stature to guide them through the hazards of internal discord in the same wise and valiant way he led them through the fire of war.

The leaders of this emerging nation reached out for a leader—a king—who would benevolently rule them. "Every major nation in the world was then ruled by a king, and royalty had been throughout history almost exclusively the accepted form of government."[6]

Here is one of those times when action, rather than words, best demonstrate the character of Washington. In one moment he would be swept into the lap of luxury, the power of unequalled national office, and the fame that could cause even the humblest heart to quiver with excitement. It only took a single word from his lips, a nod of his chin, a bow of his head, and it was done. But he couldn't do it.

Washington was preoccupied with two other pressing concerns. The first was the treatment of his valiant but weary army, and their growing anger that they would be released to civilian life without recompense of any kind.

Washington understood their well-founded concern as he had yet to be reimbursed for his expenses as promised. His finances were in such deplorable condition that he wrote his overseer, Lund, at Mount Vernon: "I want to know before I come home (as I shall come home with empty pockets whenever peace shall take place) how affairs stand."[7] The answer was not a good one because Lund had not collected rents on the property from various tenants for more than five years. But Washington's concern was far less to his own need than that of the men who served with him. It was not power that possessed his heart, but service.

Throughout the camp of the disgruntled army who had given their years, bodies, and fortunes to defend their fellow colonists, letters began to circulate that they were to be dismissed without pay. The Congress had bluntly notified Washington, "there were no further possibilities of supplying the army."[8] The circulating letters indicated the army had lost faith and confidence in Congress and declared their loyalty to Washington, even should peace be declared. Washington was deeply moved by the condition of the army and the injustice they were facing. He had fought Congress throughout the war for just the barest minimums to keep his army alive and in the fight. Time and again he was stymied by states that had no desire to fund the efforts and men who protected them.

On March 15, 1783, Washington summoned a meeting of his military leaders. The army, now on the edge of rebellion, faced him sternly as he began to speak of his own devoted service and the price he paid for more than twenty years to break English tyranny and bring about freedom. But it was not the kind of freedom they were proposing. The faces before him remained unmoved.

Washington suggested that to ignore the voices of moderation "would mean that 'reason is of no use to us—that freedom of speech may be taken away, and, dumb, and silent, we may be led, like sheep, to the slaughter.' By now, the audience seemed perturbed but the anger and resentment had not been dispelled. Washington then stated that he believed the government would, 'despite the slowness inherent in deliberative bodies,' in the end act justly."[9]

"Washington came to the end of his prepared speech but his audience did not seem truly moved. He clearly had not achieved his end. He pulled a paper from his pocket and something seemed to go wrong. The General seemed confused; he stared at the paper helplessly. The officers leaned forward, their hearts contracting with anxiety. Washington pulled from his pocket something only intimates had seen him wear: a pair of eyeglasses. 'Gentlemen,' he said, 'you will permit me to put on my spectacles, for I have not only grown gray but almost blind in the service of my country.' This homely act and simple statement did what all Washington's arguments had failed to do. The hardened soldiers wept. Washington saved the United States from the tyranny and civil discord that had concluded so many revolutions."[11]

> "His character will remain to all ages a model of human virtue, untarnished with a single vice."
>
> JOHN QUINCY ADAMS[10]

In the end, the peace treaty was signed, but the promises of Congress came to nothing. The army disbanded with only their muskets to take home. Washington's farewell dinner was canceled. He appeared before Congress and graciously resigned his commission and then strode to Fraunces Tavern to say good-bye to the officers who still remained in the service.

"He walked over to the table where a collation (meal) was laid, tried to eat, but failed. He filled a glass of wine and motioned for the decanters to go around. As the officers saw his hand shake and his lip tremble, the bitterness in their hearts was drowned by love. The men who had fought so hard with Washington and suffered so deeply found tears in their eyes. With tears streaming down his own face, Washington embraced each separately, and then he walked out of the room."[12] Washington was now a civilian.

POLITICS OR PASTURES

Washington had served his country and sought to return to the life he enjoyed, the privacy he lacked, and his consort for life who waited for his return. But he was caught, along with the nation, in a terrible dilemma between what had been and what the nation would become. No one in the colonies, either military or civilian, held the esteem and the renown of Washington. And no nation on earth had seen a successful republic develop—a nation of the people, by the people, for the people. Monarchies and tyrants ruled as despots, and few in the colonies wanted the same, even in the form of a strong central government. King George had taught them well to fear such power.

Upon returning to Mount Vernon, Washington faced the monumental task of rebuilding his lands, stables, and tenant farms that had fallen into disrepair over the five years of his absence. His new secretary discovered that Washington had lost some 10,000 pounds (sterling). "He had himself paid not only his own expenses but often those of the whole headquarters operation. At moments of crisis, he advanced money for various other military needs from his own pocket. After he had presented his expense account, Congress being as always short of cash, had met much of what they owed with certificates of indebtedness."[13] Like many others in his day, he sold off his certificates to speculators at greatly reduced prices.

At the end of the war, "one of Washington's aides, Trench Tilghman, was given the honor of carrying the victory report to the Continental Congress in Philadelphia . . . When Tilghman arrived, he asked Congress to give him a draft of money to pay for the expenses of his journey. They couldn't do it. There was not one cent left in the National Treasury so each Congressman contributed a dollar out of his own pocket."[14] Clearly, there was little financial incentive in returning to the government.

Washington diligently pursued planting crops and increasing his stables through innovative breeding techniques. It was a passion that consumed him, and he threw himself into the task with the same vigor he led the Continental Army. His innovations were eminently successful. "American agricultural know-how began with one man, a farmer in Virginia who was the first man in the New World to rotate his crops. He first planted tobacco and wheat: the next year, buckwheat that he plowed under. Then wheat again. And after three years he put the land back in grass and clover. Then he tried corn and potatoes. His harvest of wheat multiplied twenty-five times in five years . . . His coat of arms was changed to add wheat spikes to it as a result of his innovations. No matter his accomplishments of this stage of the nation, George Washington always remained, at heart, a farmer."[15] What he did in farming, he did to a lesser extent in breeding various strains of horses and mules. This wasn't just something to occupy his time while waiting for another political or military opportunity. It was at the heart of what he loved—working the land in the company of his wife and family.

So, it was not glory, fame, wealth, or power that could persuade George Washington to leave Mount Vernon. He had found peace there.

What could possibly pry him out? He knew from the war years the very unpleasant life he would face should he heed the call to lead the fledgling nation: a growing fiscal crisis, Indian uprisings, international political intrigues, foreign government intervention in the colonies, and growing unrest in the population about the unstable state of affairs.

By 1786 the country had begun to come apart at the seams. Rebellions and uprisings were becoming more common (Shays's Rebellion that same year), and Congress had no way of keeping order because it had no money to pay for troops. Washington's health had begun to fail in 1787, with reoccurrences of what was called "the ague," but was most likely malaria. The country was $50 million in debt to foreign governments, yet it wasn't until 1789 that the Continental Congress called a session clearly recognizing the hour was grim. They asked Washington to attend, and though he had steadfastly refused previous invitations to other meetings, he finally agreed. Upon arriving, he discovered that the Congress had unanimously voted him as president—a title they had just devised. What it meant immediately was that the life Washington had loved and known was over. He had again taken, reluctantly, the burden of the nation on his shoulders that he would carry for eight years.

In describing Washington, historian Derric Johnson wrote: "While he was in office, he was one of the most unpopular presidents to ever serve the United States. He was ridiculed in public print, accused of being power mad, and called a tyrant by one leading newspaper editor of the day. Some said he used the office of President just to gain favor and become rich, and critics didn't even like the parties he gave. His Secretary of State resigned in disagreement over foreign policy. Two of his cabinet members quit and formed an opposing political party to fight him. There were riots in the streets, and Congress refused to give him an army to enforce the law. Everyone felt the United States was on the brink of a full-scale civil war. Predictably, scores of newspapers and many American patriots demanded his immediate resignation. He ultimately declared: 'I would rather be in the grave than in the Presidency.'"[16] Those words seemed to reflect more the administration of Lincoln or Nixon rather than the man we consider the father of our country.

Motives empower or diminish leadership. It is the human condition to advance and protect ourselves. Yet it is the unselfish, altruistic, and sacrificial person whom we admire. More than that, we will follow those people into the jaws of death. We see in their unselfishness the character we would have for ourselves. Why look to another when you may possess such qualities? Be the Centurion you were meant to be, and start the battle to conquer the self-centered motives that we cling to for self-preservation. Let self go, and your Destiny Maker will call you in due season to put on the mantle of the role you were born to fulfill.

THOUGHTS FOR TODAY'S CENTURIONS

WHEN THE COUNTRY GOES THROUGH A PERIOD OF ECOnomic stress, most people think a question of "why people work" is irrelevant. The unsophisticated would answer, "People work to pay their bills." But when the country is facing periods of great prosperity, leadership is suddenly sensitive to the reasons their workers are staying or leaving and what they can do to keep their greatest assets. Ultimately, it isn't economics that motivate the best workers—those who produce achievements rather than just results—to stay or go.

Great leaders, who leave lasting achievements, find something deep inside that is being satisfied by what they are doing, giving, producing, or creating. Washington certainly had a paycheck disincentive while at the same time he lacked interest in power, fame, or glory. So, what got him out of Mount Vernon twice, when he was satisfied to work on his estate and develop his ideas of farming and breeding? What caused him to risk the incredible respect and reputation he held among his countrymen after the war, to enter the brutal arena of national politics? The same thing that should motivate all leaders—the same thing that leaders should model and work to instill among their subordinates: *Work is the potential to leave behind something greater than ourselves.*

It is not a right but a privilege—a gift even—to be wise enough, healthy enough, and sought after enough to get up each day and contribute to the world around us. Many are not so blessed. Washington took on the role of commander, later resigned after his work was achieved when he could have personally profited from exploiting it and, finally, left his home and family to suffer the brutal assaults that came with the office of president. He left believing that he was serving a higher cause than his own personal ends—that something greater was at stake than his wealth or personal desires. And so, he rode away from Mount Vernon to enter again what President Teddy Roosevelt so eloquently described as "the arena" some years later:

"It is not the critic who counts, not the man who points out how the strong man stumbled, or where the doer of deeds could have done better. The credit belongs to the man who is actually in the arena; whose face is marred by the dust and sweat and blood; who strives valiantly; who errs and comes short again and again; who knows the great enthusiasms, the great devotions and spends himself in a worthy cause; who at the best, knows in the end the triumph of high achievement, and who, at worst, if he fails, at least fails while daring greatly; so that his place shall never be with those cold and timid souls who know neither victory or defeat."[17]

So where do you stand? Do you feel you are serving greater ends than your own personal prosperity; and is it felt and known among those who work for you? Or do they see a self-serving manager who will do anything to protect his or her own self and position at the expense of all others, company included? Perhaps you fall somewhere in between. Maybe it's time for a second look at the reflection in the mirror after all. You have been given a moment in time and a portion of the power of the Almighty to influence, create, and produce something that could benefit the world around you. Are you living up to that great calling?

Be sure of this: there will come moments in the course of your life when the fires are heated beneath you and all will know what is in your heart. Are you ready for that moment when you must decide whether to leave your Mount Vernon? Are you ready to risk all in the cause of something greater than yourself and your family? Not all are called to such high ends, but all leaders will be called to sacrifice greatly for something greater than themselves.

In the first Gulf War, I watched as many in the UN, who had taken their pay and enjoyed their positions, left Israel and sought the safety of the nearby beaches on the island of Cyprus when the bombs began to fall. They were leaders of small offices, and leaders of stations where dozens of Peacekeepers looked for leadership. When the time came, they were nowhere to be found. Through that experience, I came to believe that character doesn't rise to the occasion, but is revealed by the occasion. It is also in the heat of great personal and national crisis that our motives and our values are tested for their strength and fidelity.

Many who take this approach will not become financially successful. Daniel Boone blazed the trail to the West, cutting his way through the wilderness and opening up the territories to hundreds of thousands who would follow. He believed he was serving a greater cause than himself, yet died penniless. Does that mean he wasn't successful?

Money is a poor measure of success. Just take a quick look at some of the greatest artists, scientists, and creative talents in world history and you'll know this is true—no matter what the culture around you says. Seek to fulfill your calling, the thing that sparks your spirit, and pursue that passion with all the strength you've been given. When you turn back at the end of your days, you will understand the difference between a mundane life spent pursuing money, fame, and power or a magnificent life that served far greater ends.

PATHWAYS TO LEADERSHIP THAT SERVES GREATER ENDS

The greatest leaders were also great risk takers. Stop for a moment and decide if you are willing to become that kind of leader. If not, move on to the next chapter. This risking is costly. If it wasn't, everyone would be doing it. Who wouldn't want to leave a legacy like Washington's behind him?

If you are willing to take the risks, then examine what your current motives are in pursuing your work as a leader. If you understand they are less than noble, then you've found your starting point.

The key to getting beyond the illusions of fame, money, and power is to take the long view. It is paradoxically both simple and difficult. Take the long view—not the quarterly, monthly, or daily view of your business or calling. When you finish your race and look back at the footsteps of your life, what are you going to see, and what are you going to be proud of?

If you take the long view, you will inevitably run up against the fearmongers and the self-serving. You will fight against the tide of those who want to "just get by," and you will have very few joining you as you seek triumph in breakthroughs rather than momentary results. Is it hard? Yes. Is it impossible? No, and George Washington provided an excellent case study in how it can be done.

> "Human happiness and moral duty are inseparably connected."
>
> GEORGE WASHINGTON[18]

As I neared the end of my twenty-two years of military service, I was working in a high-stress job in the Pentagon. At that time, I was approached by a publisher who wondered if I would write a book of inspirational stories from America's history on the battlefield. After a great deal of thought, I decided to take on the project. Every night and weekend for a year, I worked on that book.

Near the end, I was offered the opportunity to continue my service and be promoted to brigadier general within a few years. I politely declined and turned in my papers for retirement at the same time my book was released. This infuriated my superiors, and I was quickly moved from my special status of "golden boy" to untouchable leper. But I believed then, as I do now, that we are created for a destiny greater than accumulating power, money, or fame. (Certainly, being a general could be a high calling for someone if that was his or her destiny. It just wasn't mine.)

Looking back, after the storm passed, I can't say I didn't have regrets about the way things turned out. But I can say that I had no doubts. Washington regretted having taken on the role of president at points, but I also believe that at the end of his life, he had no doubts that he had fulfilled a higher calling than the one he had hoped for in working on Mount Vernon. Before leaving Washington in 1796 after eight years as president, he reflected on his service before Congress:

> The acceptance of, and continuance in the office to which you have twice called me, have been a sacrifice to the opinion of duty, and to a deference for what appeared to be your desire . . . I constantly hoped that it would have been much earlier in my power, consistent with motives, which I was not at liberty to disregard, to return to that retirement, from which I had been reluctantly drawn . . . The strength of my inclination to do this, previous to the last election, had even led to the preparation of an address to declare it to you; but mature reflection on the perplexed and critical posture of our affairs with foreign nations, and the unanimous advice of persons entitled to my confidence, impelled me to abandon the idea. I rejoice, that the state of your concerns, external as well as internal, no longer renders the pursuit of [my] inclination incompatible with the sentiment of duty, or propriety; and am persuaded, whatever partiality may be retained for my services, that, in the present circumstances of our country, you will not disapprove my determination to retire. (Washington's Farewell Address to Congress in 1796 paraphrased for today's language)[19]

What motivates you each morning when the alarm goes off? If you drag yourself from your bed day after day, month after month, year after year, perhaps you have not found your true calling or destiny yet. And if not, isn't it about time you begin the journey you were born for? Isn't it time to start seeking a service that motivates you and energizes you to serve a higher calling each day? If you are courageous enough, you will find that one day you have left more than a memory behind you—you have left a legacy.

CHAPTER 6

ANDREW JACKSON

OLD HICKORY BRINGS THE COMMON MAN TO THE WHITE HOUSE

At times you will lose and you will fail.
It may be unfair—it may be unjust. Press on anyway.
Destiny rewards the persistent!

I CAN ALMOST HEAR THE AUDIBLE GASPS OF LEADERSHIP gurus, "how to make it big" mantra makers, and the plethora of "I have the answer" speakers as I dare speak of failure. I left the Beltway madness of Washington, D.C., this past summer and moved to a sleepy town overlooking a bay. Since arriving, we've been searching for a church, and we wandered into one of those "is it a mall or is it a church?" kind of places this past week.

Toward the end of the service, in which I had been repeatedly told we're all going to be winners, we're all meant to be wealthy and, the best one, "Excuse me, I'm successful," the pastor asked all those under twenty-five to stand up. He looked at them all and said, "I want you to know that we believe in you. Many of you are one day going to . . ." I'm stopping here for a moment to give you the opportunity to think about what a pastor might say to a group of young people at the end of that sentence. I almost fell out of my

seat when he finished it with ". . . start businesses, be very successful, and be champions." I wasn't sure whether I was in a church or
a meeting of investors.

I wondered about how the vast unwashed in the auditorium
responded to his "nothing less than success" message. You know, the
ones who struggle each month just to pay the electric bill and put
food on the table—the ones who make up about half your workforce. Some people face mountains others don't know or want to
believe exist. If you don't want to get down into the trenches with
the people who are giving their blood for you, if you don't want to
help them up when they fall on their faces, if you don't want to share
your own failures and encourage them that tomorrow will be better,
then you have no business in leadership (or pastoring a church).

If you haven't failed or lost at anything and you have no respect
for anyone who does, I will tell you that you have never risked
greatly in your life. You haven't been filled with the spirit of the
explorers who looked at maps that drew a line in the ocean with the
words, "Beyond here lay sea monsters." These were the ones who
believed someone was going to do what was presently impossible,
so why shouldn't it be them? And they passed the boundaries that
had held sailors back for centuries to discover a new world. If
Thomas Edison could fill up a two-story building with burned-out
filaments for two years before he found the right combination of
metals, what does that say about the human condition? It tells me
that for 729 days I am going to be struggling with one problem or
another until I finally find the solution on day 730. And that's only
if I am persistent and courageous enough to struggle until that day
comes.

That is why I think this subject is so vitally important. Because,
like it or not, pain and suffering, failing and falling, are parts of the
human condition. What most people don't realize is that it's not the
beginning and the end of a Dilbert-like existence that seem to afflict
so many. And that is where you as a Centurion come in. If you can
hold on until those sublime moments in life shine through the heart-

break, you will feel a warm glow of finishing, of overcoming and accomplishing what others thought could not be done—or thought you'd never be the one to do! That is your challenge—not only to believe it is possible, but to inject it into those who are looking to you for direction. You can't and shouldn't ignore the pain or the suffering, but you sure can lead people to where they always wanted to go but never knew they could. And that brings us to an uncouth man with muddy boots people called "Andy" Jackson.

Incrementally, almost imperceptibly, the nation had changed. The American states had started on such shaky ground that the natural inclination of most citizens was to look to those who could provide strong and wise guidance. Coming from European stock, George Washington, Thomas Jefferson, Benjamin Franklin, and those of the new American aristocracy were the logical choices as leaders. Indeed, as the decades passed, the wisdom of that deference was seen in the policies and direction they provided—they were the strong rudders on a ship that needed the firm hand of a seasoned captain.

But as the decades passed, the country's makeup also changed. More than a million immigrants a year were landing on the shores of our eastern states and making their way to the outlying territories that had been opened up by men like Daniel Boone. There was land to be had for the hardy and the brave, for the desperate and the persevering, for the honest and the scoundrel. It was a period of unprecedented development of machinery that would lead America into the Industrial Age. Americans began to look more toward leaders who were like themselves, the same hardy stock and attitude—ones who had seen the face of hardship and had survived it.

Of course, the old saying of "Washington is always the last to know" applied back in the early 1800s as much as it does in this new millennium. The common man was looking for a tough and hardy leader who could solve the problems of Indian/settler conflicts, massive land fraud, banking arrogance that foreclosed upon the poor for dubious reasons, and the threat of British intervention in the South at the mouth of the Mississippi. There was a growing distrust in the old aristocracy that appeared to be increasingly out of touch with these mainstream problems.

Andrew Jackson seemed to be a man who matched the tenor of the times. He was born into a poor family in 1767, and his education elevated him enough to be literate and not much more. At age nine, he was chosen to read the new Declaration of Independence in the town square for those who couldn't read the one tacked on the town hall. As a courier during the Revolutionary War, he was captured by the British and held prisoner, later bearing the mark of a British sword on his head for refusing to shine boots.

By sixteen he was orphaned, and having lost what money he inherited in one week of gambling, he swore never to be burdened with debt again. So he took up as a frontier lawyer. Being a lawyer was more about presenting a convincing case than actually knowing the law (with all due respect to Abraham Lincoln). And he was good at it, attracting large crowds to hear his impassioned pleas.

Jackson rose up to assume a judgeship where he was known for telling juries, "Do what is right; that is what the law always means." He was a tough but fair judge and earned that reputation using his pistols when necessary.

> Once, in a village, the local bully, Russell Bean, was brought into court for cutting off the ears of his baby while on a drunken spree. Bean stomped around the court, cursing judge and jury and crowd, and then stomped out of the door. Jackson ordered the sheriff to arrest Bean for contempt of court, and haul him back inside. Mustering some deputies, the nervous sheriff went after Bean but returned empty-handed, announcing Bean had threatened to "shoot the first skunk that comes within ten feet." Jackson rose from the bench, stormed outdoors, and marched up to Bean, a pistol in each hand. "Now," he roared, "surrender, you infernal villain,

this very minute, or I'll blow you through!" Bean stared in Jackson's blazing eyes, then quietly dropped his gun and said, "It's no use, Judge, I give in." He later explained to his friends, "I looked Jackson in the eye, and I saw death; and so I decided to live."[1]

He continued to rise, being elected to the Tennessee Superior Court, the highest court in the state. Later he filled a seat in Congress, and early in 1797, when one of Tennessee's Senate seats fell vacant, he was asked to fill it. Yet Jackson at that time showed little political ambition and did little to distinguish himself in office. He also didn't fit in with Washington's gentry. Thomas Jefferson said of him, "[He] could never speak on account of the rashness of his feelings. I have seen him attempt it repeatedly, and as often choke with rage . . . He is a dangerous man."[2] In fact, he had a hard time spending entire days sitting in session listening to others make long speeches. By April of 1798, he had enough and resigned his Senate seat. His biographer Robert V. Remini wrote, "He had assumed responsibilities far beyond his reach and he virtually made a fool of himself."[3]

Jackson came home and began to build a plantation. He continued to serve as a judge, but it was as a military commander where his name became a household word. He had fallen on his face in the Senate, and yet the year of 1812 was upon the nation. There was a lack of strong American leadership that was apparent to friend and foe as the British hijacked American vessels and crews at will.

Jackson aspired to the post of major general of Tennessee's militia. In an earlier try for the post, he was opposed by the governor. When the post opened again, Jackson offered his services only to find the governor, who could no longer serve another term as governor, wanted the post. The battle was fierce in the political trenches, and an election produced a tie. The new governor, a friend of Jackson's, broke the tie, and at the age of thirty-five, Jackson added major general to his titles. But he was still ill thought of in Washington, owing to his previous misadventures there.

The End of Appeasement, the Rise of Jackson, 1812

President James Madison's policy of compromise and conciliation regarding the growing aggressiveness of British military actions against American interests had failed. By the early months of 1812, the smoldering fire had mushroomed into a transoceanic conflict that would prove whether America was capable of defending itself and its interests against a far superior military and political power.

Congress authorized Madison to call up fifty thousand volunteers in the event of an emergency. The nation itself was hopelessly ill prepared for war. "The six thousand regular infantrymen were scattered from Canada to New Orleans; there were a handful of others—five hundred artillerymen and a few light guns but they were also widely scattered. The available officers were aging generals of the Revolution . . . The US Navy consisted of six frigates and seven sloops [while] Great Britain could blockade the coast with one thousand ships and transport an army of one hundred thousand to reconquer her North American colonies."[4]

While Congress debated the issues of war and peace, Jackson began drilling his seven hundred troops. The war was overwhelmingly opposed in the East with Connecticut, Rhode Island, and Delaware voting unanimously for peace. The representatives of the West and South, known as the "War Hawks" led by Speaker Henry Clay and John C. Calhoun, championed the vote that declared America was at war. Still, it was like waving a fly swatter at a sky full of hornets.

The one redeeming feature for America between 1812 and 1814 was that Europe was also dealing with the conquests of vast territories by Napoleon. In spite of that, Britain displayed an awesome armada of men and ships off the eastern coastline and in the Great Lakes region in the opening months of the war.

The governor of Tennessee offered the services of up to four thousand men under the command of Jackson to serve anywhere needed. The War Department curtly accepted the offer of Tennessee's men, but refused to appoint Jackson to serve as their general.

Meanwhile, the war opened with disasters on the Great Lakes where Detroit was surrendered without a shot. The War Department called two Tennessee regiments to engage there, but left Jackson and his men awaiting a call to arms. Things grew worse when the Indians joined the British and attacked army forts in Indiana (Harrison, Madison, Wayne) and the British navy began blockading North Carolina in the fall. Further setbacks occurred in January 1813, when the British and Indians massacred helpless, wounded Americans in Michigan. That was followed by another British victory at Frenchtown, New Jersey. Finally, by the last week of January, the British extended their blockade to the Chesapeake and Delaware Bays. It was then that Jackson was finally called upon to take his men south to Natchez, Mississippi.

> "Great works are performed not by strength but by perseverance."
>
> SAMUEL JOHNSON, 1759[5]

The call came not from the War Department, but from Governor Blount of Tennessee, who requested Tennessee to assemble fifteen hundred volunteers. More than twenty-five hundred showed up. Blount commissioned Jackson a major general and sent him to serve at New Orleans under James Wilkinson—a man of questionable loyalty to the Union. Jackson said he would gladly serve at sergeant's pay, but as for serving under Wilkinson, "It is a bitter pill . . . but I go in the true spirit of a soldier . . . Should he get troublesome, a way may be found, I think, to deal with him."[6] In any case, he packed his dueling pistols.

Jackson had seen that the men assembled were drilled extensively and were well equipped for whatever they faced. The general spent as much of his own money as the state supplied to outfit, clothe, and feed the troops. Thanks to a law he had written while in office,

Tennessee was not bound, as most states, to remain within its borders when danger arose. Tennesseans could cross at will upon the orders of their senior, and this would become important in action Jackson would very shortly take against the Spanish and Indians.

Meanwhile, Jackson and his infantry pushed off the banks of the Cumberland in flatboats and keelboats. Along with the ice floes in the bitter cold, they floated two thousand miles in thirty-nine days, arriving at Natchez in the middle of February. All of Jackson's troops were riflemen with significant skill; he refused to accept any but those who carried the long-barreled rifles. Because rifle-barreled muskets have a spiral groove inside the barrel, the bullet spins as it leaves the musket, causing it to travel farther and more accurately. Many were capable of hitting targets up to three hundred yards away, and Jackson noted, "Smooth-bore muskets don't carry straight. They may be good enough for Regular Soldiers, but not the Citizen Volunteers of Tennessee."[7]

Upon arriving, Wilkinson ordered Jackson and his troops to remain in Natchez where they could be in a position to strike at the British if they landed in Pensacola, Mobile, or New Orleans. The order made sense, but after two weeks of pacing about his camp, he received the news of the American defeat in Canada and offered the services of his troops to fight the British there. No reply came. Another four weeks passed, and then he received his first order from the new secretary of war, John Armstrong—"disband and turn over your equipment to General Wilkinson." A curt thank-you for your service ended the message.

Armstrong had been in office for two days when he sent the order and most likely wasn't aware of the machinations that lay behind that order. Nevertheless, Jackson was furious at the thought that he should disband his men some eight hundred miles from home. He grimaced at the thought that Washington could be so callous to order his men to walk home to Tennessee without equipment and fend for themselves while traveling through dangerous Indian territory. The men had been unpaid, their shoes were worn out, and so Jackson wrote Wilkinson that if he were not furnished food and wagons to carry his sick,

> I shall dismount the cavalry, carry them on, and provide the means for their support out of my private funds. If that should fail I thank God we have plenty of horses to feed my troops to the Tennessee, where I know my country will meet me with ample supplies. These brave men, at the call of their country, voluntarily rallied . . . They followed me to the field; I shall carefully march them back to their homes.[8]

Thus out of a snub and an aborted mission began a long and memorable journey home. He told his men he would get them home even if they had to eat the horses to do it. "He hired eleven wagons to carry his sick men, obligating himself to pay ten dollars a day for each wagon to and from Tennessee . . . He persuaded Natchez merchants to sell his men clothing on credit. All told he drew drafts for twelve thousand dollars on the quartermaster of the Department of the South, for which he had no authority, and then began the march home."[9]

He gave up his own three horses to carry the sick and walked all the way back to Tennessee. Along the way he ceaselessly walked back and forth among the men, encouraging them, ensuring the sick were taken care of and that all received enough food to keep them going. It wasn't an easy journey, as some roads were too narrow and had to be widened while rivers mandated building temporary bridges. Nevertheless, at some point in the journey, one of his soldiers made an offhand comment that was to stick to Jackson for life. He said, "He's tough—tough as old hickory."[10]

Despite the failure of the expedition, Jackson and his troops were welcomed back in a public ceremony at Nashville. His heroic journey home and the costs he bore made the name "Old Hickory" a common household phrase across the South. However, in Washington, the government auditors refused to honor Jackson's drafts for the transportation of his troops. Members of the state's congressional delegation interceded on Jackson's behalf but got nowhere. Finally, after humble requests to the secretary of war proved useless, the delegation left, saying that the entire state would remember Washington's betrayal of their beloved general at the upcoming election. Two days later, a draft was issued for twelve thousand dollars.

As 1813 passed into 1814, the British navy blockaded the eastern seaboard and around the Gulf of Mexico to the Mississippi and then finally all of the northeastern states. Despite some victories, the U.S. faced a dark future when the British burned Washington in the summer of 1814. Dolley Madison ordered Gilbert Stuart's full-length portrait of George Washington to be taken from its frame and carted away—the only possession to survive the destruction. The president and Congress fled the Capitol while the military torched the ammunition storage facilities in the Navy Yard.

Jackson was sent to Mobile with five hundred regulars just as Washington was burned. James Monroe took over for an exhausted James Madison and sacked the ineffective Secretary of War Armstrong. He called for a vigorous defense of the country. Jackson's relationship with Washington improved immediately as the one general who had fought Indians and the British alike with success. Somehow, Monroe managed to find one hundred thousand dollars to send to Jackson to raise an army to defend the South against the expected British invasion.[11]

In Europe, Britain had finally dispensed with Napoleon, and many of its veteran soldiers and sailors were now available to enlarge their presence in America. Yet the wars had proven costly to England's treasury. Peace talks between the British and Americans had started in Belgium, but no event during three years of war had convinced either side they had yet won or lost.

In the South, the British were enlisting growing numbers of Indians, drilling them and promising them ten dollars for every American scalp. The Spanish territory in Florida was fertile ground for the British. While the Spanish asserted their neutrality in

Washington, they allowed the British and Indian forces to train and grow in strength. An English fleet harbored itself in Pensacola, and all expectations were that they would invade soon somewhere along the Gulf Coast—but where was anyone's guess.

Fresh from defeating the mighty Creek Indian nation that had wreaked havoc and atrocities on a number of occasions, Jackson and his cavalry leader General John Coffee, brought twenty-eight hundred soldiers on horseback. Most were veterans of the recent Indian war, rode their own horses, and carried their own long-range rifles.

Jackson wrote Monroe and warned him he was about to invade Spanish territory: "The safety of this section of the Union depends upon it . . . Pensacola has assumed the character of British Territory. I feel confident that I shall stand justified to my government."[12]

Jackson left Mobile and New Orleans with few defenses and took three thousand men, arriving in Pensacola four days later. While the large British fleet lay off the coast, Jackson made a feint with a few horsemen from the west, but encircled the city and attacked from the east. While the defenses of the city were ill prepared for an offensive attack, they fought throughout the night until the governor came into the street with a white flag. The garrisons of the city capitulated later that day. The Creeks and Seminoles—terrified of the reputation of Jackson—fled into the wilderness, deserting the British. The British fleet destroyed its own Fort Barrancas and put out to sea.

Now the nation's Federalist press cranked out denunciations of Jackson's raid as a gross violation of the territory of a friendly power. Monroe himself was shocked that Jackson had recklessly left New Orleans and Mobile virtually undefended. The Spanish ambassador lodged an official protest. Congress, with little else to do, began an investigation into Jackson's conduct. Failure and career termination seemed to be blowing in the wind, and Jackson had more enemies than friends in Washington. His career careened wildly from failure to victory and then back again.

Jackson's raid raised the morale of his troops as he pressed his men to return to Mobile in three and one-half days. In Tennessee, "young men eagerly paid bonuses of up to fifty dollars for the privilege of becoming substitutes in the militia, on the chance of joining Jackson before the fighting ended."[13]

Jackson placed three regiments of regulars in Mobile and ordered Coffee's troops to Baton Rouge. The general himself rode 170 miles with little rest to New Orleans to raise defenses against the British.

THE BATTLE OF NEW ORLEANS

When he entered New Orleans with a small staff of six, he looked every inch the weary warrior. He was greeted warmly by the French leaders, who held a dinner in his honor. The city gathered outside the residence, and after dinner, General Jackson stood on the iron balcony and spoke while his host translated: "I have come to protect the city. I will drive our enemies into the sea or perish in the effort . . . you must all rally around me, cease all differences and divisions, and join in the patriotic resolve to save this city from dishonor and disaster."[14]

The next few days the city buzzed in a flurry of activity, and then Jackson inspected the assembled troops. The city had raised some fifteen hundred volunteers, including five hundred regulars, some who had fought under Napoleon. But it was a far cry from the forces needed to face the ten thousand British troops that were expected to arrive. Jackson reviewed the troops, congratulated the officers, and said nothing of his disappointment and concern.

Jackson then began vigorously to recruit Louisiana's black freedmen. He offered the same benefits offered to white soldiers—$124 and 160 acres of land—while assuring them: "Due regard will be paid to the feelings of freedmen and soldiers. You will not . . . be exposed to improper comparisons or unjust sarcasm."[15] This, of course, did not set well with many in New Orleans and in the local militia—particularly on the issue of equal pay and benefits. Yet when paymasters began to thwart his will, he stormed into their offices like a hurricane and quickly changed their minds (or at least their behavior) at pistol-point.

But this bluster was far overshadowed by the alliance he would form that most referred to as a "deal with the devil." Even Jackson himself, from the beginning, had no interest in recruiting help from the notorious band of pirates and privateers who had besieged the British and Spanish navies by plundering their ships from Jamaica to New Orleans. He considered them and their leader, Jean Lafitte, a scourge upon humanity and supported their destruction by whatever means available.

The British had no such compunctions about using such men. They sent an emissary to Lafitte, offering him the rank of captain, thirty thousand dollars in cash, land grants for his officers and men, and the release of his brother, Pierre, from jail—once they controlled New Orleans. Lafitte asked for two weeks to consider this offer and present it to his men. Meanwhile, he immediately sent dispatches to his friends in the New Orleans legislature, advising them of the offer, the sailing of the entire British fleet out of Jamaica, and concluded, "Our enemies have endeavored to work on me by a motive which few men would have resisted . . . I offer our efforts in the Defense of the Country . . . I offer myself to defend it . . . I am the Lost Sheep who desires to return to the flock."[16]

> "Failure is but a paragraph in the book of each human life. It is the pages that follow that ultimately define us."

Several influential men approached Jackson about Lafitte, but Jackson wanted nothing to do with what he termed "those wretches," even though the privateers had seasoned naval men, ships with well-armed cannon, and soldiers who were highly skilled. The governor, William Claiborne, sought to change the general's mind without success. Despite this, all actions against the privateers were suspended by the U.S. government, which gave Jean Lafitte an opportunity few men without great courage would have taken. He came to New Orleans to find and face Jackson in person.

> Jean Lafitte faced Jackson on the corner of Rue Royale and Rue St. Philip. We know that Jackson was an impressive figure, but so was Lafitte—over six feet, elegant, well dressed, and fluent in French, English, Spanish, and Italian. There is no record of this exchange, but according to Major Latour [Jackson's chief advisor on the defense of the city], Lafitte offered ammunition, cannon, seasoned gunners to man them, and his maps and knowledge of the country. Jackson liked bold men and bold actions. He accepted, and thus into his army entered some eight hundred seasoned fighting men who knew just about all there was to know about handling big guns.[17]

Lafitte left immediately to gather all of the stores of cannon and ammunition that he had so skillfully hidden in the bayous of Louisiana. Jackson had some three thousand men when the British fleet began to appear in early December, but many were poorly armed and inexperienced. The major challenge facing the British was that the entrance into the city would require shallow draft vessels. While the initial engagements were won by the British and seemed to strike fear into the heart of the city, Jackson knew the test was still to come.

It was miserably cold, and disinformation was spread by Jackson and all in the area that the city's forts were ill prepared and barely defended. The British navy began the enormous task of disembarking most of its sailors into shallow transport vessels and rowing them to land where the major battle would occur—along a narrow tongue of dry land that ran along the Mississippi into New Orleans. Jackson's best opportunity with his limited forces was to prepare an impenetrable defensive line rather than try to intercept and engage the British out in the open. Other troops began to join Jackson now that the British had passed Mobile as the place for the primary battle. General Coffee brought eight hundred mounted riflemen, and the citizens of New Orleans were shocked at the appearances of "Tennesseans with long unkempt hair, unshorn faces, dressed in woolen hunting shirts and homemade trousers wearing wool, raccoon, and fox skin hats."[18]

Seeing the primary route of approach, Jackson ordered breastworks built along Rodriguez Canal—from the swamp to the levee of the Mississippi. Breastworks were aboveground trenches made of earth, rocks, sandbags, masonry, tree trunks, and other available material to construct a wall from seven to eight feet high. In some places breastworks were as high as thirty feet and were usually built above soggy ground where digging trenches was impossible. It was ugly work that thousands in Jackson's polyglot army toiled at around the clock, deepening the canal and throwing black muck inside fallen cypress trees to create a line of defense. "Jackson ransacked the whole city and countryside for tools, carts, wheelbarrows, and wagons for four days and five nights . . . while he remained at the growing wall the entire time without sleeping."[19]

By the time it was finished the wall was eight feet high, twelve feet thick, and eighteen hundred feet long. It was completed none too soon, as the British cannon began to fire on Christmas Day. In spite of this, Jackson had doubts the British would commit themselves against such a formidable defense. When Lafitte arrived, the first thing he did was point out that were he the British commander, he would attack from the end of the line to outflank the breastworks. Jackson heeded his comments and turned all efforts to building an L-shaped breastwork at the end of the line that could be defended should the British strike there.

In Washington, the mood was somber, and the entire country waited nervously. All were aware of what was at stake in New Orleans. The sense in the capital was that Jackson would be overwhelmed by a numerically superior and better-trained adversary.

Sir Edward Pakenham, brother-in-law of the Duke of Wellington himself and a veteran of the Napoleonic Wars, commanded the

British. Altogether, he had more than seven thousand men at his disposal facing Jackson's three thousand. Beyond sheer numbers the British troops were better trained and possessed greater combat experience, nearly unchallenged naval support, and a far more experienced officer corps. Looking at the black mud walls Jackson had erected, Pakenham disdained any other plan except smashing the Americans in the face with an overwhelming and crushing frontal assault. This would be the victory the British needed to force the Americans to their knees and back into servitude to the Crown.

Pakenham unleashed his deadly cannon and artillery on January 7, 1815, bombarding the heavy earthenworks erected by Jackson. Jackson's thirteen batteries, many of which he had removed from his ships and lugged into position, fired in return. The British plan was to throw sugar cane into the canals leading to Jackson's breastworks to support their troops' weight and the ladders they carried to mount the breastworks. However, after hours of bombardment, the British failed to silence the American guns or create a breach in the American lines.

The effect on British morale was significant as the battle dragged on for almost a week. Jackson continued to strengthen his line, and finally, Pakenham committed his infantry to the assault. Ordered to aim at the buckles on the British cross-belts, the American long rifles waited for firing commands, while Jackson's cannons began to tear large holes in the advancing British lines. Now, at a distance of three hundred yards, Jackson's highly skilled marksmen began to pick off large numbers of infantry. Whole British regiments disappeared in the withering and accurate fire. Every mounted British officer was killed or wounded in the first minutes of this final battle.

Pakenham shouted at the now crouching British soldiers, "Shame!

> "I don't measure a man's success by how high he climbs but by how high he bounces when he hits bottom."
>
> GEORGE S. PATTON[20]

Shame! Remember you're British! Forward, gentlemen, forward!"[21] His finest troops of Scotsmen dropped their packs and charged. Moments later, Pakenham himself was shot through the throat. His second, General Gibbs, was told of the disaster and called for the Highlanders—the famed Scotsmen. He asked where they were and was told they had already been decimated as they made their ill-fated charge. He and his remaining leaders charged and were brought down by four bullets. "Commands to reform ranks and attack again were ignored by redcoats whose nerve was broken . . . the battle lasted two hours, with the heart of the attack taking only thirty minutes . . . Jackson lost 13 dead and 39 wounded, 19 missing in action. The British: 291 killed, 1,262 wounded, 484 captured or missing."[22]

Word of a decisive and completely unexpected victory at New Orleans was touched off in Washington as Dolley Madison illuminated her temporary residence, the Octagon House, with scores of candles and the morning newspaper shouted:

Almost Incredible Victory

Glorious News
Rising Glory of the American Republic
Glorious!!
Unparalleled Victory[23]

The news of New Orleans raised the spirit of America out of the ashes in Washington, D.C., and a dozen other places where the British had overwhelmed the poorly organized and undersized American militias. In a period of several weeks this victory made Jackson's name the most celebrated name in the Union. The peace treaty had been signed by the English and Americans in Europe just prior to the battle itself, but the terms weren't solidified and meant precious little until the English navy sailed away in defeat.

PRESIDENT JACKSON? VICTORY, DEFEAT, AND THEN, VICTORY

Jackson arrived home in Tennessee in mid-April to the warm sentiments of his countrymen. He was courted by many to consider running for the presidency, though he demurred at each offer.

Appointed to the governorship of Florida in 1821, Jackson dealt with many issues relating to conflicts, and often in a way that made enemies since he possessed precious little diplomacy. Yet it was this same drive and "never say die" attitude that had become the heartbeat of the new America. Jackson personified the feelings of a growing number of his countrymen that Washington needed a change from the old aristocracy to men who had risen from the soil. But those in the older, established circles of Washington power were ill at the thought of a man like Jackson becoming their president.

In the election of 1824, Jackson won the popular vote and garnered the largest number of electoral votes. He had ninety-nine electoral votes, while John Quincy Adams had eighty-four, William Crawford had forty-one, and Henry Clay had thirty-seven. Because no candidate had a majority of the electoral college, the election was thrown into the House of Representatives.

Crawford, who was seriously ill, was not considered a contender, and the real battle shaped up to be between John Quincy Adams and Andrew Jackson. Henry Clay ultimately turned the election by taking his votes and throwing his support to John Adams—son of the second president. The House voted thirteen states for Adams, seven for Jackson, and four for Crawford. In return (or so it appeared to the public), Adams appointed Henry Clay as his secretary of state and the nation was inflamed by the seeming "stolen presidency"—a familiar echo in this new millennium. Jackson had won the popular vote and the largest number of electoral votes, but still lost the election.

From victory to defeat, Jackson had fallen from opportunity and grace again. Yet, remarkably, his supporters continued to work in Congress during a largely ineffectual Adams administration. "Adams was a brilliant statesman and a poor politician. He failed to win more than a few supporters in Congress. A colorless man, he had no popular appeal and could not rally the country to pressure Congress . . . and Jackson did not wait for the Adams–Clay faction to fall apart."[24]

Jackson just wouldn't quit. He learned from what cost him the first election and built political alliances and continued fighting for the interests of what was termed "the common man." The people were ready for a rough-and-tumble leader who had seen tough times just as they had. By the time of the next presidential election, Adams's party had fallen into the minority in Congress, and Jackson was swept into the office.

Jackson's popularity brought thousands of supporters to the Capitol on Inauguration Day. He let pioneers, backwoodsmen, old soldiers, and immigrants into the newly built White House. "China and glass were smashed in the East Room as people grabbed the cakes, ice cream, and punch from the long beautifully arranged tables. Finally Jackson got away from the wild crowd and escaped through a window. He spent the first night of his Presidency in a hotel."[25] It was the age of the common man and, literally, muddy boots in the White House.

Jackson's persistence saw him successfully through two terms in office in a period of history that was accurately referred to as "the rise of the common man."

THOUGHTS FOR
TODAY'S CENTURIONS

IN THE MOVIE *The American President*, MICHAEL DOUGLAS remarks that "the American people have elected beloved presidents who couldn't put two sentences together." When I think of that comment, it seems to personify perfectly one side of Andrew Jackson. But it doesn't take into account that, in spite of his many shortcomings, his one inarguable strength was his indomitable spirit.

As a rising Centurion, you can love about Jackson that in spite of his imperfections, he was a forerunner of the movie hero Rocky—the guy with all guts and heart and a never-say-die attitude. He just kept rising from the canvas to fight again—and he kept getting smarter each time he fought to overcome another defeat. But Jackson's example isn't a simple one-sided equation. Jackson possessed inner qualities that earned him the love of people around him. A poor diplomat, he honored others who displayed courage and persistence—even when they were his enemies.

Upon defeating the mighty Creek nation, he put out a bounty upon the chief of the Creek people, a warrior named Weatherford who had not just killed men, but more than three hundred women and children.

> A few days afterwards an Indian presented himself to Jackson announcing himself as Weatherford. The American commander expressed astonishment that one whose hands were stained with the inhuman murder of captives, should dare to appear knowing he was being sought so he could be punished. The undaunted chieftain replied, "I am in your power, do with me as you please. I am a warrior. I have done to the white people all the harm I could; I have fought them, and fought them bravely; if I had any warriors left, I would still fight, and contend to the last. But I have none; my people are all gone; and now I can only mourn over the misfortunes of my nation."[26]

Jackson respected Weatherford's persistence in battle and audacity in defeat and allowed this warrior to join the rest of his people rather than executing him.

STUBBORNNESS ISN'T THE SAME
AS PERSISTENCE

A lot of leaders become confused by these two concepts. They believe in sticking to their hide-bound ways as a sign of strength, a symbol of strong leadership in the face of naysayers. Stubbornness is akin to the army still ordering horsewhips in the 1940s and storing them in warehouses. (You never know when you might need a buggy whip.) *Stubborn* is defined as "stiff; unbending; unyielding; persistent; hence, unreasonably obstinate in will or opinion; not yielding to reason or persuasion."[27]

Stubbornness is refusing to listen to anyone who disagrees with you, which is not the same as persistence. Persistence is being willing to give careful consideration to the arguments and analysis of opposing courses of action. It is being willing to have arguments stacked up against your own, allowing your position to be challenged, and if it can stand such scrutiny, staying the course. If you can't defend your course of action with more than bluster, rage, or standing upon your rank or position—you demonstrate the stubbornness of a jackass rather than the persistence of a Centurion. The world is overrun by a herd of the one while the other is as rare as a speechless politician.

PERSISTENCE IS PAINFUL

Don't believe for a moment that the Centurion quality of persistence is going to earn you the admiration and praise of all those below and above you. On the contrary, you will most likely be skewered out of earshot, and you will be the butt of jokes from those afraid to oppose you publicly. Expedience and compromise, especially upon issues touching virtue, honor, and integrity, are the norm and expected behavior for today. Persisting in your principles in a course of action, in a way of conducting your business, or in living out your life is discomforting to those who blow with the wind.

Persistence is best understood when you watch the person or business pay the price for staying the course while everyone else is making what is viewed as the "smart play," or worse, "the safe play."

I've watched a lot of talented people fail because they lacked the quality of persistence. Edison's axiom was that genius is 1 percent inspiration and 99 percent perspiration. You don't perspire the moment you start working—that comes after you've burned a lot of calories and midnight oil on a project.

When I founded Mission of Joy, a nonprofit organization for homeless and orphaned children in India, I started with nothing in a country that was overwhelmed with poverty. In the first three years, a friend and I would send money every month to cover the expenses of running an orphanage for fifteen children and four staff members. As things progressed, our resources were quickly overwhelmed by crushing need. What could we do?

I invested my own money to buy the land and build our first facility—it cost me less than thirty thousand dollars, but it was all the money I had. We built a structure that had a ten-foot retainer wall around the entire property for protection against the high winds. When the next cyclone came, the structure held.

I started by taking in fifteen children and ran out of resources when we grew shortly to fifty. I was a middle-class military officer with a family of five—what more could I do? Persist and keep on persisting. We began to enlist others who had a heart to change the world for these children. So far, our organization, Mission of Joy, has built four more orphanages, a school, twenty churches, and a widows' home. It has paved roads, dug dozens of wells, provided free medical care, and seen hundreds of children come through our doors and survive childhood.

Who are we? No one special. We just believe that if we save one life, that person might just save a million more someday. Most of the time, the work requires us to slog through, putting one foot in front of the other under the worst conditions. It doesn't take great talent to do what we do, but it does take persistence.

There are two primary reasons that most endeavors fail: they aren't begun, or they aren't finished. Centurions certainly begin, and they also understand and remember the vision they had from the beginning, continue to effectively communicate it to their followers, and encourage everyone around them through their personal example, sacrifice, and commitment to that vision. They refuse to be distracted by lesser aims and goals—holding on for the greater prize. It's why we remember the Centurions and forget the "managers."

I return to inspiring examples of persistence to help me remember this when the battle is under way and when the winds of discouragement cause me to want to throw in the towel. Your examples will no doubt be uniquely yours, but these are five of my favorites.

Winston Churchill—Prior to his becoming prime minister, he was asked to address the students of Harrow, his alma mater. All waited in anxious anticipation of his weighty words. He arose and went to the podium. A hush came over the crowd, and in his gravelly voice, he said, "Never, never, never . . . give up." Then he returned to take his seat.

Will Rogers—The man with a quip for everything said, "Even if you're on the right track, you'll get run over if you just sit there."[28]

Bjorn Borg—The great tennis player who won six French Opens and five straight Wimbledon tennis titles was asked the secret of his success. "My greatest point is my persistence. I never give up in a match. However down I am, I fight until the last ball. My list of matches shows that I have turned a great many so-called irretrievable defeats into victories."[29]

Helen Keller—born in 1880, was both blind and deaf. And yet, through the persistence of herself and her great teacher, Annie Sullivan, Helen Keller learned to speak through sign language, wrote eight books, and eventually graduated from Radcliffe College.

Raoul Wallenberg—In 1944 Wallenberg sought and was granted, by the Swedish foreign minister, the assignment to go to Budapest "in an attempt to save the Jewish community there—the last left in Europe." Wallenberg began to make Swedish passports for as many

Hungarian Jews as possible. "Future congressman Tom Lantos accompanied him to the German trains, where Jews were being packed together like animals for their journey to certain death. He helped the Swede pull people off." Lantos wrote that Wallenberg "bluffed his way through. He had no official authorization. His only authority was his own courage. Any officer could have shot him to death. But he feared nothing for himself and committed himself totally."[30]

Yes, Wallenberg was captured by the Russians in the fall of 2000, and after years of denial President Putin commissioned a study group that concluded Wallenberg was shot in Lubyanka Prison shortly after capture. Everyone dies, yet few really ever live. Raoul Wallenberg lives on today, and so do more than one hundred thousand Jews whose parents received Wallenberg passports.

Make your own list, and open it up when the winds of discouragement and impossibility blow in your face. When everyone around you tells you that you're a fool for persisting, don't be afraid to re-evaluate what you are doing. If your work, dreams, goals, and visions can't stand the winds of a good argument, you probably should listen harder or adjust your sails. But if in the face of all of those doubting Thomases, you can still say, "I am committed to this course, and will pay the price, because I believe in my heart I am doing the right and best thing," press forward. Destiny has a way of rewarding the persistent.

PATHWAYS OF THE PERSISTENT CENTURION

Persistence means valuing your purpose more than caring about who values you. That takes character. Have you spent any time developing the qualities of Centurion honor—the kind where you risk everything, persisting to the end because you know what you are doing is right?

Persistence means you live according to the destiny you have been called to rather than the expediency of short-term profit. It means you know that you have limited years and while you can make more money, you cannot buy more years. They are fixed and in the hands of almighty God. When you turn around and you've retired from your career that seemed so consuming, you won't look with regret upon the life you led. Rather, you'll be content no matter how thick or thin your wallet may be. That is light-years ahead of what most people settle for today—the thing many refer to as "success."

Persistence means you have a vision, have been given a vision, or have developed a vision that consumes your waking moments. Without a vision, what is there to persist for? A paycheck? An illusion of fame? A momentary seat at the table of power? Life is more than those three combined or anything they define.

Finally, persistence means you are capable of enduring suffering and doubt and derision and even hate. People who are persistent threaten those whose character is too weak to develop this Centurion quality. Consequently, they react with the only tools they have—and they are most unpleasant. The Centurion, in persisting, must expect this to be his lot—and still be able to press forward. If you become someone like this, you will be a world shaper, a culture changer, a destiny maker, and maybe even a mountain mover. With Centurions, you can never tell.

CHAPTER 7

GEORGE B. MCCLELLAN
COMMANDING GENERAL OF THE ARMY OF THE POTOMAC

There will never be enough—money, resources, people, time, or information—make the decision anyway.

IN THE MOVIE SATIRE ON CORPORATE SURVIVAL *Head Office*, a mid-level executive mentors a brand-new protégé on the rules for surviving among the sharks while rising up in their cutthroat business. He tells him, "Rule number 1, *never* make a decision. You can only get into trouble making decisions." In a nearby office, a harried executive who apparently violated this rule stammers and sweats as he explains to his boss, "I didn't *make* that decision; I only *approved* that decision. There's a big difference. I know better than to make a decision like that."

One of the most frustrating things about watching a sporting event is when it is poorly officiated. When everyone in the stands can see the fouls and penalties better than the referees standing right next to the offender, it makes you want to stand up and yell, "MAKE THE CALL, REF! MAKE THE DECISION!" (OK, I'm sitting back down now.)

139

For those depending upon a decision, it is the ultimate frustration to hear "*that* person is out and she is the only one who can make that decision," or "there is a backlog in that area, and it will be thirty to sixty or ninety days before we can render a decision on your request." It is at the bottom line where businesses and organizations feel it most, and many corporations have feedback tools that lag long after a disastrous decision or "no decision" has been made. In the military, as in highly competitive markets, those who delay are effectively standing still, because the result is the same— they are surpassed, become irrelevant, and are ultimately absorbed by their fast-moving opponents.

While war has a way of clarifying abilities and the tolerance for failure is small, power is often just as ambiguous as it is in the civilian sector. Decision making is a key element of success and should be integral to evaluating leaders for increased responsibility and promotion. While most leaders develop along the way, there are tendencies, traits, and habits that seem to solidify in individuals across the spectrum and are revealing precursors to both success and failure. This was certainly the case in the person of George B. McClellan. Even his beginnings were auspicious as he began his journey in the cradle of West Point, then later commanded the Army of the Potomac and some two hundred thousand men in 1861 and 1862.

PREPARATION FOR LEADERSHIP— WEST POINT TO MEXICO

George McClellan had many outstanding qualities that made him the golden boy of his superiors. Yet from the beginning, making decisions wasn't one of them. Self-doubts plagued McClellan, and he responded by assigning blame for failure to subordinate and superior alike. What he could not grasp, for all of his outstanding leadership qualities, was that indecision, delayed decisions, and no decisions *are* decisions. Their consequences are as powerful, either for good or for bad, as the decisions we make.

McClellan was only fifteen and a half when he arrived at the Point, one of the youngest to join the class of 1842. While age certainly shouldn't be the only consideration for leadership, it is a strikingly appropriate factor, considering he would later command the Army of the Potomac at age thirty-four—an age even his superiors felt was too junior to have adequately absorbed the lessons of success and failure.

Our first insight into the young man's character and personality suggests a vacancy in relationships—a sense of alienation that would follow him throughout his life. In a letter to his sister he noted, "I am as much alone as if in a boat in the middle of the Atlantic, not a soul here cares for, or thinks of me—not one here would lift a finger to help me . . . I am entirely dependent on myself . . . and take the blame of all my mistakes."[1] His instructors would note that McClellan was very bright, especially when he applied himself to his subjects, but his performance was only average when he was uninterested—even when he possessed above-average intelligence in those areas. McClellan arrived at West Point with 133 other cadets, of whom 83 survived their freshman year. By the end of that first year, McClellan ranked in the Top 10 while his classmate Thomas J. "Stonewall" Jackson would struggle to find his way into the Top 60.

As head of the Dialectic Society, he was given the honor of presenting the graduation address, and he talked of war as a "great game" that man plays, officers bearing the essential part. He quoted Napoleon extensively, and was soon referred to as "the young Napoleon." Even though he graduated second in his class, it was a situation he found difficult to swallow, and he wrote his family, "I must confess I have malice enough to want to show them that if I did not graduate head of my class, I can nevertheless do *something*."[2] It was a harbinger of a ghost rider that seemed to accompany him his whole life, whispering, "You've been mistreated again; will you ever measure up?" Leaving West Point, he was given his choice of assignments, and because engineers were considered the best of assignments, he chose that specialization.

Meanwhile, the U.S. was engaged in a heated war with Mexico. The army general in chief, Winfield Scott, towered over this endeavor figuratively, as he did literally over most men at six feet five inches and weighing two hundred fifty pounds. He had won his reputation in various campaigns including the War of 1812 and was on the march to Vera Cruz and then to Mexico City itself. Using divisions of volunteers (referred to as "Mustangs") and regular army West Pointers, Scott made his way over four hundred miles to Tampico without delay. McClellan had joined the army as a young lieutenant in a company of engineer soldiers. His opinion of the volunteers was one that many of his peers shared—they were inept and unreliable. This impression stayed with him throughout his military career.

His attitude about the war was much as he'd expressed it in his graduation address: he saw it as an activity of grand adventure. He wrote his mother, "I could live such a life for years and years without becoming tired of it. . . You never saw such a merry set as we are—no care, no trouble—we criticize the Generals—laugh and swear at the mustangs and volunteers, smoke our cigars and drink our brandy, when we have any . . . We are living on the fat of the land—game, oysters . . . Champagne, warm baths when we want them."[4]

> "A President who doesn't know how to decentralize will be weighed down with details and won't have time to deal with the big issues."
>
> DWIGHT D. EISENHOWER[3]

McClellan demonstrated considerable courage in the campaigns of Mexico and earned a brevet (temporary) promotion to captain by the time Mexico City fell to General Scott's army. He served with many officers who would become renowned during the Civil War. In spite of McClellan's accomplishments, senior officers noted Robert E. Lee's daring during dangerous reconnaissance missions he led again and again that brought vital intelligence to the headquarters. Interestingly enough, while McClellan also admired Lee's daring, he later noted a year into the Civil War, that in spite of Lee's personal bravery, he was "'too cautious and weak' when faced with responsibility."[5]

What he learned and the lessons he took with him were as important as the actions he demonstrated on the field. He was neither shy nor prudent with his declarations. Instead of sharing them with his peers within the safe confines of the campfire, he penned them to a U.S. senator. His letter seemed pernicious rather than constructive as he

- protested the awarding of a commission and promotion to a "soon to be famous" scout called Kit Carson;
- berated all volunteers as incompetent and undeserving of any significant rank compared to graduates of West Point; and
- concluded his missive with harsh indictments of political generals, Patterson and Pillow, both of whom he served under.[6]

He learned the value of a siege versus frontal assault and later the importance of turning movements (to quickly shift a large number of men to face a new direction) under General Scott (whom he also felt beneath recognition) at the battle of Vera Cruz. However, there were lessons that he could have learned, but didn't, while in the field with General Scott.

General Scott displayed considerable courage in his willingness to throw out the military manual when necessary. He used joint operations with the navy to provide covering artillery support; he used speed to surprise and strike the enemy before they could form lines of defense; he mastered the use of reconnaissance and trusted the intelligence he gathered from it; and he struck when the iron was hot rather than perfected—refusing to let shortages of manpower and supplies become impediments unless they were extreme. All of these were important lessons. And all failed to register with Brevet Captain McClellan.

FROM LIMBO TO METEORIC RISE

Like most officers after the war, McClellan resigned himself to a banal existence and dull postings until his time of service was complete. During the interim years between 1847 and the resignation of his army commission in 1857, McClellan returned to his permanent rank of second lieutenant. There is a saying in the military that movers move, and shakers shake. McClellan was a little too junior to be a shaker, though he tried mightily. Yet he did move—ten assignments in nine years meant his name came to the attention of many across that decade of service.

He was reassigned to West Point for what appeared to be routine duty. Yet he again displayed his temper and willfulness against his superiors when he was called to explain his absence from mandatory chapel, required of both faculty and students. After resolving that conflict, he clashed with the commander of engineers over the location of a storage shed of all things. He had little taste for compromise, though he was loath to admit it. He often defended himself by explaining disputes as a difference of opinion, a distaste for incompetent leadership, or an insult to his honor and superior competence. He was fond of saying that he didn't care for anyone's opinion as long as he was right—though right was surely in the eye of the beholder. All this shaped McClellan's actions as a young second lieutenant while at the Point. It was time to move on.

"Randomness rules less in those willing to steer."

He managed to escape West Point and began a series of expeditions for the army, which had assumed the task of searching out a route for a continental railway passage across the Rockies. He led one of these expeditions with some sixty men and more than 150 horses. He tried several passages and decided nearly all would be unsuitable because his Indian guides told him they were blocked by snow at least twenty feet deep.

He found only two passes he considered suitable, both close to the joining of the Naches and Yakima rivers—in mid-western Washington. Yet he took what Indian guides told him as fact about the suitability of these passages without traveling there to see them for himself. He disliked the assignment anyway, and if he ended up failing to find a suitable passage, it was hardly worth the risk to his reputation. He settled on "indecision" and said there wasn't a suitable passage. When told by Isaac Stevens, the governor of Illinois, to *find* a way through, he considered that a political order and disregarded it. When he met

"Delayed decisions and no decisions have consequences as powerful as decisions we make."

with the governor at the Canadian border, they argued. Governor Stevens then dispatched his own team from the Puget Sound area of eastern Washington, and they cut a way through, encountering only six-foot, not twenty-foot, snows. In his final report, McClellan blamed a dry winter and a fluke that allowed the other party to find a way through. Meanwhile, later explorations found a pass ultimately used to build the railroad to the Pacific Northwest—one within five miles of where McClellan had explored.

He was finally called to return to Washington and shortly after given an assignment in Kansas keeping the peace between "free staters and slave staters." He considered this a disgusting prospect, especially since he would have to serve under a volunteer colonel with some arrogance of his own—an appalling condition McClellan could not stomach. By this point, he had been promoted to regular captain, but resigned his commission after being offered a post in the Illinois Central Railroad.

Timing was everything, and he took up his position with a sense of freedom to make decisions without having them constantly reviewed by superiors. He was an excellent administrator and was promoted to vice president within a year. His salary was nearly four times what he made in the army, but late that year the economy suffered a financial downturn. It affected all sectors, and "cuts" were the only thing he was asked to make. He made the initial cuts, and then true to his nature, he began to fight with his superiors over every instruction they gave him. Admirably, he offered to give up his salary until things improved. It didn't help as the railroad was one step short of bankruptcy. Within several weeks, the entire economy began an upswing that saw the Illinois Central out of the red. Nevertheless, he was still unhappy in his position, and he looked for and found another opportunity at the Ohio and Mississippi Railroad. Within a year he became its president.

By the time Fort Sumter was fired upon, George McClellan was already actively pursuing an opportunity to command troops. President-elect Lincoln would not take office for ten more weeks but was putting out a call for officers. He, along with most, considered McClellan as one of the bright stars and considered him for command as a brigadier general. McClellan was politically well connected and knew of Lincoln's intentions. However, he was also being courted by the governors of Ohio, Pennsylvania, and New York to command their troops. These commands would make him a major general of the state volunteers. Ultimately, New York came late to the negotiations, and Pennsylvania's telegram offering him command was misrouted. So, he began his Civil War service as major general of Ohio's volunteer army in the western theater of operations. He was thirty-four years old. The choice gave him the highest possible rank, even though he was forced to lead "volunteers."

McClellan's Star Engages Afterburners

While there were no aircraft in the Civil War, save the few balloons that were used for reconnaissance, it is an apt description—afterburners—to describe a man who within one month of the beginning of the war rose from shadows into the limelight as a major general of both army volunteers and regulars. He was only outranked by the general in chief himself, Winfield Scott.

With such auspicious beginnings, we would—like most of Washington at that time—expect nothing less than auspicious ends. Indeed McClellan was well thought of by his troops from the outset, even when things went poorly at the Union position at Malvern Hill in eastern Virginia. "An entire division, underfed for days, deserted the sputtering campfires where in a gloomy rain it was cooking the first hot meal of the week, in order to splash through the mud and hurrah as he galloped down the road."[7]

Start off well he did. Lincoln initially called for seventy-five thousand troops nationwide, making Ohio's share ten thousand troops. Allotted three million dollars by the Ohio legislature, McClellan saw this as a mere down payment on what he desired—thirty thousand men from Ohio alone, which would require three times his budget. He was a prodigious worker and rode from one camp to another as he roused all involved in the training of his twenty-two Ohio regiments. Yet the same problems evident earlier beset him once again.

While the war raged in the eastern theater, he insisted that his area was critical and in crisis as he demanded more of everything. He offered to cross Ohio with twenty, thirty, or forty thousand men to help in the East, yet in his first battle engagements in eastern Tennessee, his movements were tentative and his orders vague. While he managed to gain the upper hand, the confusion so evident in the execution of his battle plan led him to write Washington, saying, "In heaven's name give me some general officers who understand their profession. I give orders and find some who cannot execute them unless I stand by them. Unless I command every picket and lead every column I cannot be sure of success."[8] In the end, he pinned all the blame for his first less-than-stellar Civil War engagement upon one of his subordinate commanders.

Things grew even worse in the eastern theater following the rout of the Union Army at Bull Run in June 1861. The saying that "even good things can come out of a train wreck" was no less true then. The entire North reconsidered all of its previous assumptions about the length and cost of the war, and leadership questions were added to the debate. McClellan was recalled to the East and assigned to command the division of the Potomac, which encompassed both General Irvin McDowell's army and the defenses around Washington.

In keeping with his pattern, he threw himself into his work, personally supervising everything, trusting no one else to measure up to his expectations. Within a few months, he again came to loggerheads with his superior. He courted the press and was an impressive figure and persuasive speaker. The press, as it is wont to do, made a quick judgment as to the new general's ability. The *New York World* wrote, "It is evident that General McClellan has done more in ten days towards organizing the advance than Scott did in ten weeks."[9] Considering that the war was to last more than four years, it is clear that assessment was, at best, premature. Nevertheless, the die was cast in the public's eye, and McClellan used it to his benefit.

He wrote and spoke to everyone who would listen that General Scott had no cohesive strategy and he alone could lead the army in a grand sweep across the South to crush the rebels and seize Richmond. He stated he could do all this if only he could get three hundred thousand men and six hundred artillery pieces. He said his enemy already outnumbered him two-to-one and asked that every command be placed under his control, for none other could be trusted.

> "It is only our deeds that reveal who we are."
>
> CARL JUNG, 1934[10]

Even though his numbers bore no semblance to reality, the young Napoleon had shouted loud and long enough to be heard. The North was desperately seeking someone to pull its army out of the mud of Bull Run, and McClellan seemed confident enough to do it. Scott tried hard to present the obvious—that the South had thirty-five thousand at Bull Run and could not have tripled their forces in the three weeks since McClellan assumed command. Still, McClellan cried, "Crisis," stating he was heavily outnumbered (now four-to-one) and that he must be reinforced no matter the cost to any other region (Ohio's problems were no longer his, and their needs were now irrelevant).

McClellan had stirred so much public sentiment that Lincoln was convinced that a change was needed, and Scott, ever the gentleman, offered his resignation. On November 1, 1861, McClellan was designated by the president to command the entire Army of the North. It was everything he ever wanted, yet his title was a reflection of possibility rather than power—as he would soon learn.

SHINING STAR TO TARNISHING STAR— INDECISION, INACTION, AND WASTE

From the beginning, Lincoln had quietly commented that should "he accede to General McClellan's newest call for one hundred thousand fresh troops, the general would come back the next day with the news that the enemy now numbered four hundred thousand troops and he could not advance without reinforcements."[11] It was a stunning prediction of what would occur over the next seventeen months of McClellan's command.

McClellan, as usual, threw himself into the new tasks that confronted him, asked for patience from the press and public while asking for more equipment and men from his superior. He continued his habit of creating a black cloud of doubt while escaping his own culpability and letting his superiors take the blame. This time, however, it was only him and the president—a very different situation than he had ever faced when dealing with military superiors.

As the months passed, one opportunity after another slipped through his grasp as he failed to make a dent in Lee's army. From inactivity to an occasional battle, he hesitated to throw himself into the grand strategy that he had once proposed under General Scott. There was always something that prevented him from being able to achieve his ends—and the blame always lay elsewhere.

Lincoln's approach to McClellan was to often ride into his camp and sit and talk with him face-to-face. His orders to McClellan, as were his orders to all his senior generals, were given with an uncharacteristic humility in superiors. He showed deference to his subordinate's authority.

> *To Halleck* (19 Sept 1863): "I hope you will consider it . . ."
> *To Burnside* (27 Sept 1863): "It was suggested to you, not ordered . . ."
> *To McClellan* (13 Oct 1863): "This letter is in no sense an order."
> *To Banks* (13 Jan 1864): "Frame orders, and fix times and places, for this, and that, according to your own judgment."
> *To Grant* (30 Apr 1864): "If there is anything wanting which is within my power to give, do not fail to let me know it."[12]

As the months passed, pressure on McClellan began to mount from all sides. Soldiers, once counted upon to give him their steadfast support, began to refer to him as "Macpoleon." When McClellan would pass by, his subordinate commanders would now have to order their troops to be ready to provide appropriate "hurrahs."

Lincoln tried every way imaginable to get his general to take the offensive. In spite of Lincoln's diplomatic approach, McClellan's tender sensibilities were easily offended, and he attacked his superior for all the failings that were most certainly his own. He began to write, as was his habit, to any who would listen or print his diatribes:

> *16 August 1861*, "The President is an idiot . . ."
> *11 October 1861*, "The President is nothing more than a well meaning baboon."
> *17 Nov 1861*, "I went to the White House shortly after tea where I found 'the original gorilla,' about as intelligent as ever. What a specimen to be at the head of our affairs now."
> *8 Apr 1862*, "The President coolly telegraphed me yesterday that he thought I had better break the enemy's lines at

once! I was much tempted to reply that he had better come and do it himself."

29 Oct 1862, "If you could know the mean and dirty character of the dispatches I receive you would boil over with anger . . . But the good of the country requires me to submit to this from men whom I know to be greatly my inferiors socially, intellectually, and morally! There never was a truer epithet applied to a certain individual than that of the 'Gorilla.'"[13]

As Lady Macbeth continually washed her hands, never quite getting the stains off, so McClellan nursed his wounds in disdain, spite, and blame, never quite finding these salves sufficient to remove the doubts that nagged him. Still, he was in the "game" as he called it, and he fought as well as he could in spite of the ever present self-doubt he exhibited over his problems and seeming injustices.

By mid-September 1862, McClellan had recovered from his defeats at Manassas and Chantilly, and he blocked Lee from moving into Maryland. Lee's army needed to forage for supplies, and the South was becoming barren from overuse and the destruction of war. Lincoln's prodding had finally hit home, and McClellan moved out cautiously to face his wily nemesis.

Last Chance, Lost Opportunity—
Antietam, September 1862

If Lee had anticipated McClellan's quick recovery, he would not have found himself on the defensive. Even so, in contrast to McClellan, Lee spent no time bemoaning his fate of being outnumbered. He immediately redeployed his army defensively in the area of Sharpsburg, Virginia, to await the arrival of his right arm, Stonewall Jackson. McClellan arrived in force on September 15, 1862, putting Lee's back against the Potomac. Yet being ever cautious, he spent another day and a half arranging his troops and getting all in "perfect" order. "This was a grievous error, as it gave Lee time to gather up all his troops and establish a formidable line."[14]

Lee ably used the time to choose his position of defense. While he could do little about the Potomac, he pulled his forces just behind Antietam Creek, forcing the North to cross one of three bridges to get at him. This put the Union Army in very deadly and narrow fields of fire.

September 15 came and went. On September 16 McClellan noted that he would fight the enemy that day using his grand "design." What that "design" was has always been a question, but from the generals beneath him, the initial consensus was that McClellan wanted to attack both Lee's left and right at the same time, essentially putting them in a vise. Strangely, General Burnside on the left had no knowledge of this. In fact, McClellan had removed half of Burnside's resources on September 15 and moved them to the right—a strong message that he had little confidence in Burnside and McClellan's expectation that those forces would be better used on the left. The result meant that General Joe Hooker would be the one to attack on the right and Burnside would serve as a distraction rather than as the second half of the vise to crush the rebels.

As September 16 wore on no orders came from HQ, and McClellan continued with administrative tasks and personally supervising the placement of troops—clearly demoralizing his senior commanders. He held no staff meetings for his senior commanders, and McClellan's vague communications left commanders wondering about their responsibilities. McClellan spoke of a great victory pushing Lee into the Potomac, yet all his troop movements were made with defense in mind, hoping to avoid defeat rather than pursuing that ever-elusive phantom called "victory."

The extra day allowed three of Jackson's divisions to arrive at Antietam. Delaying the battle until sunrise on September 17 allowed two more of Jackson's divisions to arrive ready to fight. By 9:00 A.M., his last division arrived and marched into position. Lee now had about forty thousand troops divided between General Walker on the right, D. H. Hill in the center, and Hood holding the left.

The day and a half of delay cost McClellan his only chance to hit Lee while his army was divided. Though he faced an enemy just over half the size of his seventy-five thousand men, McClellan believed he was fighting an army of almost one hundred twenty thousand. He wired Washington he would do his best even though he was grossly undermanned, this while his entire Sixth Corps (some twenty thousand men) stood in reserve and never saw battle at Antietam.

Before sunrise on September 17, Jackson discerned the movements of the Federal troops and, instead of staying in reserve, positioned his divisions as they arrived on the left where he expected Hooker to pose the greatest danger. As sun broke over the waters of the Potomac, an observer described the beginning of the largest clashing of forces to date between North and South, in which 115,000 men fought in what proved to be the bloodiest single day of the war.

> The advance of the Federal Army was a brilliant spectacle. As the troops descended the more gentle slopes of the mountain on the Antietam side, the morning sunlight was reflected by the muskets of the infantry, their regimental colors fluttering gracefully in the cool autumn breeze . . . For miles in advance the glitter of steel could be discerned and the sight of these long columns of troops was thrilling and inspiring.[15]

Hooker launched the battle on Lee's left, at dawn on September 17, while his boss McClellan stayed in bed for two hours, believing the noise to be the rebels withdrawing across the Potomac.

Hooker's advance brought about a furious response, and McClellan, now up and in action, ordered him reinforced. The reinforcements under General Sumner took two hours to arrive, and McClellan's plan was now apparent as Hooker crossed the Antietam, followed by Mansfield and, later that night, Sumner.

Jackson moved all of his forces to intercept this large attack against Lee's left. Hooker's artillery and musketry cut up much of Jackson's forces and looked to accomplish accidentally what was not well-planned intentionally.

> Scarcely had this taken place when Jackson reformed his line, and fell with furious rage upon Hooker. The combat that ensued was of the most awful description, for the men loaded and discharged their muskets at less than one hundred yards range, the carnage being terrific. There stood the two lines, neither giving way, but each withering under the deadly storm of bullets. Hooker finally requested assistance, but his reinforcements were cut to pieces trying to cross a wide corn-field trying to reach him. Then the Fourth Alabama and First Texas made a heroic charge against Hooker but were driven back after desperate hand-to-hand combat.[16]

That day, every Federal action was fought in uncoordinated movements. Since there was no planned offensive (other than Hooker attacking Lee's left while Burnside created a diversion on Lee's right), the only thing troops and commanders could do was react to what was happening in front of them.

"It is not so much that weaknesses bring downfall; rather it's refusing to over-come them that results in repairable errors ballooning into colossal disasters."

In the center, things were even worse. Lee had positioned his troops under D. H. Hill along a long and very old road that was below the sur-rounding terrain and was aptly named "Sunken Road." D. H. Hill strengthened that road with a breastwork of fencing and posts to pro-tect his troops. The North couldn't see Hill's position until they had ascended a hill and were within seventy-five yards of the rebels. Northern casualties were severe, the first division to arrive losing 40 percent, the second losing 30 percent of their troops.

By now, all attention had shifted to the center where Northern troops were being cut down like wheat before a scythe. Finally, General Richardson's four thousand veterans went into the breach, acting independently, like every other Union commander that day. His first attack failed to reach Sunken Road, suffering horrific casualties. Then, without reason, the South began to evacuate this strong position.

Richardson exploited this confusion in the Southern ranks by pushing forward into the breach. Lee now barely held his center with just a scant number of artillery. The opportunity to cut Lee's army in half was at hand when Richardson was mortally wounded. His replacement arrived from McClellan's headquarters with orders to stand fast and hold the position. The Union's chance to exploit the advantage was soon lost as Lee quickly reinforced his center.

On the right Hooker had suffered very high casualties while the center suffered the same. Jackson had lost thousands as well. In four charges and countercharges, the ground was nearly invisible as bodies littered the field and troops walked over them to get at each other.

Meanwhile, McClellan had lost track of Jeb Stuart's cavalry. General Stuart made a complete circle around the Union lines, penetrating into Pennsylvania, crossing the Potomac, and returning by way of Leesburg, Virginia. He collected desperately needed supplies and destroyed railroad trains and tracks, machine shops, and a great deal of property by setting it on fire. The daring raid infuriated all in Washington, and it was a disappointing epitaph to the costliest day of battle.

McClellan felt they had done well and extracted in blood at least as many men as he himself had lost. He sent a victory telegram enumerating all of the captured men and armaments he had garnered while not losing a single gun or battle color to the enemy. It fell on deaf ears. While the South had fourteen thousand casualties, three thousand killed in action, the North suffered nearly twelve thousand casualties, two thousand killed in action. It was a greater blow to the South to lose so many men, but it was a moral victory to have survived while being outgunned and outnumbered—a fact not lost on Lincoln. McClellan was ordered to advance, but he delayed two days and in that interval, Lee and all of his troops vanished. McClellan fell back to reorganize, retrain, and call for more troops and supplies.

Six weeks later, General in Chief Halleck wired McClellan to press the attack rather than lose the good weather that remained. Increasingly, McClellan seemed to see a world ruled by randomness, lifting up men like Lincoln, while debilitating and destabilizing men like himself. An opaque cloud of malaise and growing depression seemed to cover him. He tried to move, ever so slowly, but his long delay after Antietam was the last straw. Lincoln sent a telegram on November 5, 1862, relieving him of his command. It seemed to be a respite rather than a humiliation as the cloud lifted and the whispers of his ghost rider were lost in the wind of the news.

In amazing spirits, he left his command in a manner that was recalled by many who witnessed it. McClellan climbed upon his horse, placed his hat on his head, and rode briskly through the ranks of his assembled men. Astride his horse, he spoke sincerely and affectionately to all of them, and men responded by cheering him roundly. The response seemed to rekindle his old magnetism that had been lost along the way. "Whole regiments dropped their muskets from the position of salute, to cheer their general, none of the colonels seeking to control the enthusiasm of their men, or compel the decorum of emotion on seeing it displayed by his soldiers . . . His final words to the soldiers gathered around him were simply, 'Boys, I want you to stand by General Burnside as you have stood by me. Good bye.'"[18] Except for his memoirs years later, which allocated blame to many others, it was over.

> "A decision is the action an executive must take when he has information so incomplete that the answer does not suggest itself."
>
> ADMIRAL ARTHUR RADFORD[17]

THOUGHTS FOR TODAY'S CENTURIONS

THERE ARE PROBABLY A DOZEN OR MORE LEGITIMATE reasons why an executive won't make a decision. Yet there are just as many other circumstances where leaders were capable and faced a situation requiring a key decision that they didn't or couldn't make.

Most indecisive executives don't even know they lack the ability to pull the decision trigger. Rather than be decisive, they heed the call of the "five sirens of delay" present in nearly every circumstance and every sector. The sirens call out hoping to capture another victim yielding to their deadly voices and are too often rewarded as both the leader and those below them suffer the pain and penalty of procrastination. The five siren songs play to our primordial instinct for safety and fears, ever reminding leaders that their decision risks their own safety, success, and future as well as those who work for them. The five deadly songs tell us:

1. "You're risking too much; you'll end in disaster."—Leaders who fall prey to this call are more afraid of making the wrong decision than no decision, believing no decision is much safer than a bad decision. They fear a bad decision will bring about unpleasant reprisals, and so they choose apparent safety versus unknown risk. The result of this choice is an organization that remains stationary waiting for perfect battlefield conditions rather than seeking out opportunities and exploiting them.

2. "You don't have enough authority."—Often a leader has the authority, but is afraid to exercise it. In those cases, leaders will send the decision up-channel to a supervisor. Risk-averse executives view this as preferable to making a decision that goes south and causes those above them to question their competency. Authority is often implied or assumed in business as it is in war. Consequently, this

excuse can be valid, yet relied on regularly, it prevents any organizational forward momentum.

3. "You don't have enough information."—Most leaders understand rightly that with more time comes more information and better information provides the basis for a better decision. But some leaders fall into the habit of waiting indefinitely for more information so that the "correct" decision will be more obvious. However, the passage of time also commonly changes the circumstances, which puts a decision maker right back where he started— waiting for the "fog of war" to lift. He becomes like one of Samuel Beckett's characters, always waiting for Godot.

4. "You don't have enough time."—Many leaders are comfortable making decisions at a certain pace. They look for a minimum amount of time to evaluate a problem and make a decision. When they are forced to decide without that minimum time, they may freeze like a deer looking into the headlights. These leaders seem to be standing still as battle and business swiftly evolve. With the competitive nature of business, politics, and war, the decision-making cycle has seen a frightening acceleration—in many cases necessitating an instant decision or instant failure. It is a cycle that never slows down or retreats—you play or pay.

5. "You don't have enough resources."—Making a decision to move forward requires resources—there is no contesting this law of physics. You cannot create motion without energy, and you cannot produce energy without resources. Yet the question is more complex than this. Human beings can achieve greater ends than they realize. With even a modest amount of resources and the right kind of leadership, organizations have accomplished what was previously believed impossible. Those who succumb to this siren song find that they *never* seem to have enough. They go on to overestimate their competition or enemy, believing the worst case about their own potential and the best case about their opponent. ("I have too little, they have too much—I need more to ensure success.") The uncertainties of business and war mean that often our opponents

are facing the same kinds of problems that we are. The difference might just come down to this: one side faced its shortcomings and built a bridge over its fears while its opponent did not.

There are five sirens calling out "delay, defer, but don't make a decision." It takes a clear understanding of the burden of leadership to act because you must, even in the absence of the things leaders want most—more money, people, resources, time, and information.

Every leader has weaknesses. Few leaders are self-aware enough to know their own while even fewer surround themselves with people who can offset those weaknesses. Finally, only very few leaders actually listen to those people when they tell them the things they'd rather not hear.

Who are your counselors, and do they provide you with stimulating insight? Do you ask for their counsel if it isn't offered, and do you listen to it when it is? No leader has all the answers. It is "in the counsel of many that even a fool can become wise" and where leaders become Centurions. Centurions know that all wisdom cannot (and does not) reside in one. Our experiences, education, and inborn gifts bring varying levels of wisdom to the decision-making table.

In the end, though, the decision will rest with you. You can delegate it at your peril, but you cannot delegate your responsibility. As Harry Truman so succinctly and dryly noted, "The buck stops here." *Delayed decisions and no decisions have consequences as powerful as rendered decisions.* A "no decision," at the end of the day, is still a decision.

> "When the decision is up before you—and on my desk I have a motto which says, 'The buck stops here'—the decision has to be made."
>
> HARRY S. TRUMAN, 1952[19]

That's why they pay you the big bucks—and even if your compensation is small, no leader can remove the bull's-eye from his back until he removes the mantle of leadership from his shoulders. Knowing that controversy or even failure will one day knock on your door, isn't it better to have chosen the path yourself rather than be driven into the ditch by others? Randomness rules less in those willing to steer. The destiny to lead well, like the decisions you make, rests in your hands.

Pathways to Centurion Decision Making

I spent more time with the character study of George McClellan than with the others believing "success teaches a few lessons while failure teaches a thousand." In the case of McClellan, in his rise and subsequent fall, there appears to be an undercurrent of failure tugging at his feet even though his head is ever lifted up to the lofty heights of power. The undercurrent is fed by self-doubt, indecision, and blame shifting. To recognize solvable problems is the beginning of reaching the means to overcome them. The keys rest in dealing with the five sirens of delay that call out to and resonate with our fear of failure, our thirst for promotion, and the associated desire for safety.

The Centurion understands that we cannot land among the stars unless we shoot for the moon. No person ever accomplished great feats without great risks or great sacrifice. The risks we perceive as so great may, in fact, be the ordinary stepping-stones that lead across previously impassable and troubled waters. That few others have crossed only reinforces the need for calculated risk and temporarily letting go of our desire for safety.

It is in those moments when we risk that the Centurion is separated from the fool. It is always a difficult dilemma and one that will be second-guessed by those who stand smugly along the sidelines. Command and true leadership always involve risky decisions that pit the need to achieve a goal against the risks to ourselves and those who follow us. When you suffer losses along the way, and suffer them you shall, you will experience the discomfort of reviewing your actions and living with the results.

In the hours between dusk and dawn, you will replay your decisions over and over—the ones that even you second-guess. The weight of the mantle you wear seems heaviest during the night. As a Centurion, you are called to both risk and achieve—both key ingredients to final success. You can deny them, you can ignore them, but you will never overcome great obstacles without coming to grips with them.

Come also to grips with the very human desire for power, self-importance, and fame. They are the spurs that many leaders overuse, the spurs that wound their employees—the horses that will carry them to the finish line. In the end, they alone feel the thrill of victory when it comes, while the horse hopes for a better rider—one that knows an encouraging word can accomplish as much as a sharp spur. There are surely moments when the spur is called for, but far less than is commonly thought. When victory comes, all can share in the joy of accomplishment that was reached only with the complete dedication of the entire team.

The last four sirens—lack of authority, information, time, and resources—all boil down to excuses we use to delay or neglect the necessity of a decision. They are but different facets of the same opaque and tarnished image of a manager—one who manages the situation rather than leads the willing. Those who use these crutches have failed their position for reasons that may be peculiar to them, but common to all is the ill effect they bring to their units and organizations. With a bit of articulation and persistence, and with enough wise counselors around them, most leaders can overcome the lack of authority, information, time, or resources.

It is sure that authority is ambiguous, even in a rank-driven system such as the military. If a corporal is able to win a medal of honor, how much more can his superiors achieve? We suffer today, not so much from a lack of information, but from an overabundance of useless, unfocused information that isn't pertinent to the current crisis. Find the means to cull the useless from the relevant and you will find yourself head and shoulders above the situation. It is no easy task, yet it is a critical task in this rapidly developing information age. It is a certainty that you will never have all the

time you desire to produce a perfect solution to a gripping problem. Why not focus on putting out a workable solution today while
the battle is raging, rather than a perfect solution that will be
wholly irrelevant tomorrow? Finally, realize that you will always
lack enough resources to do the job perfectly. I found while supervising flight operations involving three thousand people, that with
enough imagination, I could take a miserly quantity of resources
and bend and stretch them until we covered the minimum requirements to attain our goals. Isn't it true that "necessity is the mother
of invention"? Find yourself in want, and you'll find out what you
and your people are capable of producing. You'll never know what
you can do until you are stretched.

The melody of these sirens' songs is a tune that resonates and
calls out not to our strengths, but to our weaknesses. It is a wise
leader who knows not to listen to the counsel of the sirens of fear.
Decisiveness is the bedrock foundation of an energized and aggres-
sive organization. When leaders can't or won't *make the tough call,*
or are incapable of making it, they take the steam out of the engine
of their company's progress.

Clearly, this means leaders face the danger of failure every time
they make decisions. The successful ones learn to build an organization of people willing to climb mountains because their leaders
will blaze the trail, shoulder the blame, and help them achieve their
sleeping dreams. When you can do this, you will no longer be their
manager—you will be their Centurion.

CHAPTER 8

GENERAL ROBERT E. LEE

GENERAL OF THE ARMY OF NORTHERN VIRGINIA

Are you in a position of weakness? Weakness is only one side of a coin—strength the other. Turn the coin over and be BOLD!

SOME MAY BE SURPRISED BY THE INCLUSION OF ROBERT E. Lee among the great Centurions in history. We may look back at a period of history and with perfect hindsight judge something differently from the way it was judged at the time. Cultures change and power changes hands while nations rise and fall. It is never easy to look back and fully understand the reasons why people, nations, and cultures behaved the way they did. It helps to read about our Centurions as seen by their contemporaries.

It may seem strange to learn that there was scarce dissent about the character of Robert E. Lee following the bloodiest war in this nation's history. His chaplain summed up the nation's feelings on Lee after the war: "He was a foe without hate; a friend without treachery; a private citizen without wrong; a neighbor without reproach; a Christian without hypocrisy, and a man without guilt. He was a Caesar without his ambition; a Frederick without his tyranny; a Napoleon without his selfishness; and a Washington without his reward."[1]

Lee's genealogy can be traced all the way back to Richard the Lionhearted. His family arrived on the shores of Virginia in 1641, and he is honored today with a statue alongside George Washington in the U.S. Capitol rotunda. Both are represented as well by statues in the Virginia State Capitol Building. In speaking of Lee, two other presidents noted:

> We use the word "great" indiscriminately, but we reserve the word "noble" carefully for those whose greatness is not spent in their own interest—that was the characteristic of General Lee's life. (President Woodrow Wilson)

> He will undoubtedly rank as without any exception the greatest of all the great captains that the English-speaking people have brought forth . . . As a mere military man, Washington himself cannot rank with the wonderful war-chief who for four years led the Army of Northern Virginia. (President Theodore Roosevelt)

Although many are unaware of it, Robert E. Lee was Lincoln's first choice to lead the Northern Army against the rising tide of states seceding from the Union. It was with sadness that Lee wrote, "With all my devotion to the Union, and the feeling of loyalty and duty as an American citizen, I have not been able to make up my mind to raise my hand against my relatives, my children, and my home. I shall return to my native state, and share the miseries of my people, and, save in defense, will draw my sword on none."[2]

In a country that was barely seventy years old, it isn't surprising there was little nationalist fervor. In many ways, nationalism was as reviled then as it is today, but for somewhat different reasons. Fleeing the oppressiveness of monarchical tyranny, few thought that a central government would care as much about a state's needs as those living within the state. Hence, in the Civil War, most units were designated by the state they hailed from (e.g., the Twentieth Maine, the Fourteenth New York, etc.). Today, nationalism seems to offend the sensibilities of those who believe we should care more about the world's problems than our own, the world's poor rather than our own poor. Ironically, nationalism is equated today with arrogance of nations, while in the 1800s it was equated with arrogance of the central government.

In a world in search of Centurions, we are hard pressed to find a better example than Lee of the quality of boldness—particularly among leaders who, from a position of weakness, are capable of exhibiting a strength that renders their adversaries impotent again and again. Few like Lee could get inside the mind of his adversary, bluff repeatedly and successfully, strike and then move massive numbers of troops in minimum time, strike again, and all while being outnumbered between two-to-one and four-to-one.

Maybe you're not Ford in the 1930s, a defense contractor in the 1940s, J. C. Penney in the 1950s, Philip Morris in the 1960s, Exxon in the 1970s, IBM in the 1980s, or Microsoft in the 1990s. Good, then this will mean more to you—because you are going to be like most of your peers and competitors—outgunned and underequipped for the job you have to accomplish. Boldness under such circumstances may seem almost foolish, yet boldness may be the one advantage you have over a larger and less agile opponent. Unlike Lee and those who lead in battle, your life may not be on the line—but jobs, your employees' welfare, and their families' welfare may be. You may have less muscle, so you will need more brains. You have to reorient your thinking, behavior, and strategy. Pull off the sunglasses of pride and arrogance, and drop them into the nearest trash receptacle—you'll see the path ahead and the obstacles more clearly without them.

> "The 'fog of war' works both ways. The enemy is as much in the dark as you are. BE BOLD!!!"
>
> GEORGE S. PATTON JR.[3]

Beyond Initial Bravado—Setting the Stage for Lee's Command

It is almost inconsequential to discuss "bold" moves at the beginning of an endeavor. Many can "talk the talk," and both sides in the Civil War had plenty of "leaders" thundering threats, breathing smoke, and spewing fire. It is useless to judge anyone by the boldness of his plans. It is more instructive to wait until enough time has brought about both the blush of victory and the disappointment of defeat to evaluate the quality of boldness within the heart of a Centurion. Boldness is not about impetuous words or actions in a vacuum. Rather *boldness is the courage to risk greatly in spite of the odds, understanding the consequences and gravity of defeat at the hands of a capable and committed opponent.*

By the summer of 1862, both sides in the war were in real trouble for very different reasons. Enough blood had already been spilled, and more than a year had passed since the hotheads and blowhards on each side had predicted a quick victory and a longer victory party. Such is the confidence of those who never experience the sound and fury of battle or know the suffering that follows it. So outspoken was the bluster that Lee remarked, "We appointed all the worst generals to command the army and all our best generals to edit the newspapers."[4] It was the same on both sides then and, ironically, remains just as true today.

Over the Precipice—The North and the South to Battle

Within three months of Lincoln's election seven states seceded from the Union, and six more would follow. Lincoln called for seventy-five thousand troops to put down the insurrection. General McDowell was given command of the Union Army and ordered to take Richmond, the seat of the newly formed Confederate government. In July 1861, McDowell assembled nearly thirty thousand men at Manassas, while he left a sizable number twenty-five miles away guarding the capital.

He was more efficiently organized than the South, having four divisions of thirty thousand men, while the Confederate Army under General Johnston fielded two separate armies with thirteen independent brigades. The South also lacked a clear command hierarchy that would tie together these many individual units.

On July 21, McDowell ordered the Union Army into battle by making an initial feint in one direction and then heavily attacking from another at a place near Manassas Junction, Virginia, known as Bull Run. By midday, it looked as though the North was going to win its first engagement against the Southern rebels. But in spite of poor organization, the Confederates re-formed several times and put up a valiant resistance against McDowell's troops. Yet the numbers against them began to tell until late in the afternoon when General Tom Jackson arrived with six thousand troops. Jackson formed a solid line joined by retreating Confederates, causing them to regain heart and turn the tide of the battle. With renewed energy, they unleashed a furious assault against the previously impervious Union lines. After a brief resistance, the Union troops broke and ran, stumbling through a sea of well-dressed, Washington onlookers who had come to enjoy the show. While the first significant battle of the Civil War ended in a Northern defeat, it was more symbolic than substantive. There were less than fifteen hundred Union soldiers killed—a far cry from the bloody battles that lay ahead, but it served to awaken the Union to the determination and capability of its Southern foes.

To this point, President Jefferson Davis kept General Lee at his side, planning the war from Richmond. Lee's desire not to raise swords against the North was slowly receding into the past as the North attacked the area around his very home in Arlington.

After the embarrassment at Bull Run, Abraham Lincoln replaced McDowell with General George McClellan to head the Army of the Potomac (see Chapter 7). The thirty-four-year-old

McClellan was well liked by the troops and insisted that his army should not undertake any new offensives until his men were fully trained. He also demanded two hundred thousand more troops. He spent a number of months gathering and training troops. It seemed reasonable in light of the disaster at Bull Run the previous summer.

But by the spring of 1862, the Northern press was beating Lincoln and McClellan mercilessly for what appeared to be a lack-luster effort to finish the war. The one positive achievement for the North came during the late winter; General Grant had taken his army along the Tennessee River with a flotilla of gunboats and cap-tured Fort Henry, forcing General J. H. Johnston to retreat with his troops to Nashville. McClellan's inaction in the East resulted in Lincoln placing General John Pope in charge of all Northern forces assigned to the Army of Virginia.

McClellan, after much prodding, finally unglued his army from Washington and began a march to Richmond where his aim was to surround and lay siege to its inhabitants and finish off the South by capturing its capital. Once word of McClellan's armies reached Johnston's ears, he rushed troops into posi-tion to stem the growing numerical superi-ority of the North. In the first battle at Shiloh, the North lost about thirteen thou-sand while the South lost ten thousand. But it looked good for the North as the South was forced to evacuate many of its troops from Tennessee.

"Boldness sharpens the sword."

ANCIENT SAYING[5]

Things continued to improve for the North in May as McClellan moved 150,000 troops into the Shenandoah Valley and surrounded Stonewall Jackson's 17,000 men. But Jackson attacked first one and then another of McClellan's subordinate generals and then broke through to join up with General Johnston's troops. With 41,000 troops, Johnston counterattacked McClellan in a place ironically known as Fair Oaks. Both sides suffered equal casu-alties, but Johnston was lost to the South after being severely wounded. President Jefferson Davis could no longer afford to have Robert E. Lee as his senior strategist and war planner sitting in Richmond. He sent him to take over command of the Army of Northern Virginia.

Lee first ordered all his forces to retreat and re-form around the outskirts of Richmond. From there he directed efforts to strengthen the city's defenses, streamlined the organization of the Southern command structure, and replenished his troops with supplies and weapons. Lee was well aware of the vast advantage in manpower McClellan held over him. He knew with enough time, McClellan would wear his troops down if they continued to tighten the ring around Richmond. Lee wasted no time after fortifying Richmond. He gathered his commanders, drew up offensive battle plans, assigned responsibilities, and attacked. Though McClellan never believed it, he outnumbered Lee by more than two-to-one with his 120,000-man army facing Lee's forty thousand.

On the first day in what would be called the Seven Days Battle (June 25–July 1, 1862) things did not go well for Lee. The South lost a battle at Mechanicsville, but surprisingly, McClellan decided to retreat to a safer position at Gaines Mill. The second day was more evenly matched in losses, but McClellan gave up his supply base and retreated even farther to the James River. He wrote to his superiors in Washington that night insisting he had preserved the honor of the army but had lost the battle because his forces were too small. Strangely, McClellan had over 20,000 troops that were held in reserve during this battle.

From the James River, McClellan withdrew across the Virginia Peninsula for additional safety. Lee attacked again at Savage Station on June 29, at Glendale on June 30, and finally at Malvern Hill in a heroic, but vain, attempt to destroy the Union Army on July 1. The Seven Days Battle was costly for the South with fifteen thousand killed and wounded compared to the North's eight thousand. Still the battle was seen in the North and South as a Southern victory.

Richmond was no longer threatened; the North had fallen back each day until the troops were bottled up at Harrison's Landing (southeast of Richmond between the James and York rivers) and morale drained away with every mile the Union Army retreated. The notoriously wicked habit of playing "not to lose" plagued General McClellan in what would be seen as the first quarter of the Civil War.

THE SECOND BATTLE OF MANASSAS—LEE CALCULATES AND CHOOSES "BOLDNESS"

Having driven McClellan's army from the outskirts of Richmond and into a bottleneck at Harrison's Landing, Lee now faced General Pope, the new leader of the Army of the Potomac. In the Seven Days Battle, Lee's strategy was to remain on the offensive as much as possible and dictate rather than let the battle come to him.

It may seem premature to judge a leader after only two months in the seat of command. Yet war has a way of quickly defining both the small and the great and accelerates the refining process to reveal an individual's inner core at a pace that peacetime rarely discloses. The remaining Civil War years only served to reinforce what was shown during Lee's first six-month tenure as commander of the Army of Northern Virginia. It is always under pressure that Centurions are revealed and pretenders are unmasked.

General John Pope, commanding the Northern forces, and General Lee were about to see their two opposing forces meet. Each needed to instill boldness into his troops. General Pope's method was fiery rhetoric to his assembled troops.

> I have come to you from the West, where we have always seen the backs of our enemies; from an army whose business it has been to seek the adversary and to beat him when he was found; whose policy has been attack and not defense . . . I presume that I have been called here to pursue the same sys-

tem and to lead you against the enemy . . . Meantime I desire
you to dismiss from your minds certain phrases . . . I hear
constantly of "taking strong positions and holding them," of
"lines of retreat," and of "bases of supplies." Let us discard
such ideas . . . Let us study the probable lines of retreat of our
opponents, and leave our own to take care of themselves.[6]

Pope's words seem to echo Lee's, except that Pope had a fondness
for words and issuing of General Orders that seemed to abuse the
civilians as well as the army. (For example, all Southern males in
territory captured by Pope were subject to arrest; all supplies could
be seized from anyone for the price of a paper voucher; women as
well as men could be executed for attempting to communicate with
their family members should they have family in the Southern
army, etc.) His remark "[we will] leave our own to take care of
themselves" was badly interpreted among his troops as meaning he
would not care for the wounded. When he remarked that "from
this day forward headquarters would be in the saddle," his troops
sarcastically laughed and said, "Pope's hindquarters are in the saddle and his headquarters are nowhere."[7]

Lee said little to his troops, but wrote to Jefferson Davis, "We
cannot afford to be idle, and though weaker than our opponents in
men and military equipment, we must endeavor to harass, if we
cannot destroy them. I am aware that movement is attended with
much risk, yet I do not consider success impossible."[8]

Lee had settled on General Jackson and General Longstreet as
his two "go-to" leaders, giving Longstreet the bulk of the army and
using Jackson as his foot cavalry. Jackson had performed somewhat
sluggishly in the Seven Days Battle, yet Lee believed that Jackson
would live up to his nickname (earned at the battle of Manassas)
"Stonewall" and redeem himself.

Consequently, he sent word to Jackson not to await opportunity,
but to seek it out—not to expect detailed orders, but to initiate and
attack wherever the moment presented itself. Finally, he urged

Jackson to guard against stragglers—a clear sign to Jackson that he was to take the offensive actively against Pope. His approach was to instill boldness in his senior leaders by giving them sufficient latitude for independent action—and the expectation that they would take it.

Within a few days of these instructions, Jackson took Pope's supply depot at Manassas and burned it, while Jeb Stuart, Lee's cavalry commander, raided Pope's camp itself. Jackson had also fought off Pope's attempt to take Gordonsville, the only railroad connection between the Shenandoah Valley and Richmond, while awaiting reinforcements from Lee. For some reason, Pope believed that all the signs demonstrated that Jackson was in retreat, and he ordered his subordinate General McDowell to lead the pursuit. He wrote Washington, saying he thought he "had finally bagged the slippery Jackson. I see no possibility of his escape."[10]

> "In battle the greatest danger always threatens those who show the greatest fear. Boldness is a bulwark."
>
> CATILINE, 108 BC[9]

In truth, Pope had formed his army on the hills in a semicircle, with Bull Run River and Washington behind him in the east. To the west and south lay Jackson's army stretched out in a fairly straight line. On August 28, General Longstreet arrived in force and took up a position to the right of Jackson, such that their forces formed an L shape around Pope on the hills above. Assessing the situation, Lee realized that Pope could field more men than he could, but Lee had observed the Union Army had shown an aversion to risk and the current situation "rendered risks unavoidable."[11] He would try to use that to his advantage.

General Pope's subordinates had discovered Lee's formations and rode in to inform Pope that Longstreet had arrived with significant forces. General Pope would hear none of it, believing these reports were excuses for inactivity rather than informed assessments of the enemy's position and strength.

On the morning of August 30, Generals Porter and Hatch, under Pope, began a furious and sustained attack against Jackson. Longstreet, as was his habit, continued to position his men and artillery that morning in a methodical way, even though Lee pressed him to begin a flanking attack against Pope's position. By 4:00 P.M., General A. P. Hill, under Jackson, had repulsed the Union attacks a number of times and appeared to be nearing the end of his resources.

He sent word to Jackson of his dire circumstances.

"'Tell him,' said Jackson, 'if they attack again, he must beat them! A staff officer from Hill later reported to Jackson, 'General Hill presents his compliments and says the attack of the enemy has been repulsed.' Jackson grinned and replied, 'Tell him I knew he would do it!'"[12]

Jackson noted, "[My] entire line was engaged in a fierce struggle. As one line was repulsed, another took its place and pressed forward, as if determined, by force of numbers and fury of assault, to drive us from our positions. So impetuous and well-sustained were these onsets as to induce me to send to the Commanding General for reinforcements."[13]

Longstreet was ordered by Lee to provide reinforcements, but instead opted to finally open up a full offensive against Pope with his large artillery batteries. This lifted the pressure that had been on Jackson and made Pope realize that he was facing a larger and more determined force than he had expected. The initial reports he discounted proved painfully true.

Though McDowell had been charged to pursue Jackson, by noon he realized Jackson hadn't moved. Instead, he "devoted himself entirely to the defense of the turnpike against an attack coming from the South or Southwest. And General Pope, now seeing his danger, was prompted to take such steps as were yet available to ward off disaster."[14]

Too little, too late. Lee ordered Jackson and Longstreet's fifty-five thousand men to move forward in an L shape against Pope's seventy-five thousand men who had been on the offensive all day against only Jackson. Longstreet's surprise and Jackson's resilience had now put the North on their heels. Pope railed against McClellan for not sending him reinforcements while the rebel yell filled the battlefield and Longstreet began to roll up the flanks of Pope's army. The North initially began an orderly retreat, but at some point discipline broke down and a full flight ensued. It wasn't until Pope's army reached Washington that McClellan's reinforcements were seen. There was enough blame to go around for everyone to share—but Pope bore the brunt of it.

Lee's army feat was even more remarkable considering the state of his soldiers. When asked why he didn't pursue Pope all the way to Washington, Lee replied, "Because my men had nothing to eat. I couldn't tell my men to take a fort when they had nothing to eat for three days. I [had to] go to Maryland to feed my army."[15]

The North had lost almost fifteen thousand and the South nearly ten thousand in the second battle of Bull Run. As Pope approached Washington, he met McClellan who was now (again) appointed to lead the Union Army. "Pope asked if the new field commander would object if he rode on to Washington. 'Not at all,' said McClellan—but he himself would ride to the sound of firing. Pope rode off and the troops behind him shouted 'Boys, McClellan is in command of the Army again! Three cheers!'"[16]

> "The wicked flee when no one pursues, but the righteous are bold as a lion."
>
> PROVERBS 28:1

In truth, it would be nearly two more years before Lincoln "could find his Lee" among the generals in the Union Army. At Richmond, upon assuming command, Lee could have set up a defensive perimeter and tried to hold out against the North. He didn't. He set up defenses and then launched a bold offensive. At the second battle of Bull Run, Lee was outnumbered and outmaneuvered. Instead of retreating or setting up a quick defense, Lee ordered Longstreet and Jackson to take the offensive against the numerically superior Pope. Lee's actions were irrational according to his opponent, General John Pope. He expected his enemy, Lee, to begin to retreat. Again and again, Lee would use audacity and boldness while holding a weaker hand. It was the kind of leadership Lincoln continued to search for until he found General U.S. Grant.

THOUGHTS FOR TODAY'S CENTURIONS

FOR SOME, BOLDNESS MAY APPEAR SYNONYMOUS WITH QUALITIES that are ironically antithetical to the very principles that are the heart and soul of a Centurion. Some think boldness is nothing more than coming up with a good line to use on a member of the opposite sex. In business, some view boldness as exuding an external bravado while believing something quite different inside. Perhaps for those whose tendency is to rule arbitrarily and by authority of their rank or position, it might be illuminating to explain what boldness is not.

- Boldness is not the same as mule-headed obstreperousness— loud, noisily defiant, or aggressively boisterous words or actions.
- Bold leadership is not the same as foolhardiness, irrational brashness, swaggering bravado, or frenzied activity.
- Boldness is not the same as rudeness.
- Boldness is not "forget the facts, damn the torpedoes, and full speed ahead."
- Boldness is not "shoot now and let God sort them out."

Again, Centurion boldness is the courage to risk greatly in spite of the odds, understanding the consequences and gravity of defeat at the hands of a capable and committed opponent.

BOLDNESS REQUIRES TRUST

Boldness requires something few leaders either desire or acquire. It requires vertical and horizontal trust. Those above you must have the stomach to allow you to pursue your vision to accomplish their ends. And those with you and serving you must be willing to follow you because they respect you and believe in you. You must build their confidence in you through sustained performance that demonstrates five concrete fundamentals of trust—concrete character qualities that inspire organizational boldness:

> "Be bold, Be bold, and everywhere, Be bold."
>
> EDMUND SPENSER, 1590[17]

1. That you will give them the vision and the means to achieve it—a vision they may not believe possible unless you walk the point and take the lead;

2. That there are no sacrifices you won't make on their behalf to help them achieve the goals and objectives you and your leaders have set for them;

3. That you care less for your own well-being than for theirs;

4. That you are take full responsibility for whatever mistakes and failures occur and that you accord them all the credit when victory is achieved; and

5. That when they fail you, as people surely do, you will deal with them personally and professionally, remembering they are human beings, worthy of your respect even in failure.

If you do these things, you may find you have the reins of stallions that must be steered rather than motivated. The need for boldness is never as apparent as when the risk is greatest; and at that time, the leader's survival depends upon trust he either previously created or neglected.

Boldness Does Not Require Perfection

In the late 1980s the military fell victim to a new philosophy called "zero tolerance—zero defects." The purpose was to encourage—even demand—that its leaders would expect perfection in performance and hold people accountable for their performance. Fast forward a decade and we find "customer in-service training," TQM programs, ISO 9000 achievements, and Baldridge Awards as the marks of a career on the fast track—all new leadership philosophies invented and implemented with varying degrees of success.

Yet to use a medical analogy, when you go in for surgery, you don't thank the doctor for not screwing up—success is expected. What you really need in difficult circumstances are innovative thinking, cutting-edge approaches, and doctors who are keeping up with the latest techniques in their field. A zero-defect mentality just doesn't cut it in a competitive environment. In the military, second place isn't an option—second place is death and defeat. You've got to have bold people who risk failure to achieve victory where none thought it possible. In most organizations, defeat and death may not come with the same lightning speed as in war, but in a risk-averse corporate culture they will come soon enough.

Zero-defect warriors aren't incompetent, but they are dangerous because they assume reaching zero defects for a defined period is the pinnacle of performance. A company today could perfectly replicate an iron lung used earlier in this century to treat the respiratory failure that accompanies polio. Yet polio is rarely encountered today, and those needing respiratory assistance would hardly want an iron lung when ventilators are more efficient, effective, and safe. Mike Armstrong, CEO of the "reinvigorated" AT&T, insists, "I don't expect anyone to be perfect. It's not human nature. What I do expect is that they will take risks, correct mistakes, and learn from both."[18]

In the military, the maxim is, "it's a one mistake air force/army, etc." That kind of comment from the rank and file speaks of a top-down philosophy that perfection is the standard. It also says to those below, boldness isn't required—just don't screw up what we've told you to do. If you or your leaders are in the habit of conveying an attitude that says, "If I wanted your opinion, I'd ask for it," expect to get very little feedback. Even if your ship is sinking, your team may go down in silence while desperately seeking the nearest exit.

BOLDNESS REQUIRES WILLINGNESS TO RISK GREATLY BY BREAKING THE MOLD

When I say "break the mold," I'm not saying "break all the rules." Boldness in business and battle is much deeper and more difficult than just breaking rules. It's knowing when and where to break the rules, and where and when to enforce them with an iron will. That's why boldness isn't a sword fresh from the smelter but one that has been tempered until it is more durable, sharper, and more refined than untried steel. It has a sharpness wielded with purpose rather than used as a mindless instrument of destruction.

America is a nation that loves coffee. But Starbucks took a good thing and turned it into a mega-successful business. They did it by breaking some rules, adopting different models, and providing something lacking in America's coffee-drinking experience—a social ambience.

After spending time in Europe, especially in Italy, Howard Schultz was immensely fascinated with the culture of the coffee bars that were everywhere. Anyone who travels in Europe finds social gathering places; in Spain it's the tascas, in Ireland and England, the pubs, and in Germany, the beer gardens. Schultz knew there was no comparable environment in America.

America's culture never seemed conducive to building these "gathering places" for conversation and a warm drink—particularly one brand or one franchised conglomerate. We are a people who drive hard, play hard, and don't take much time for social amenities. In many parts of the world, business rarely begins until an extended set of social events are completed.

When Schultz returned from Europe, he attempted to convince his bosses of the efficacy of the idea of creating this in America. In the early 1980s, he opened his own stores, *Il Giornale*. They were successful enough for him to line up investors to buy out the four Seattle Starbucks stores and begin to expand out of the Pacific Northwest. From there he began to build on his vision of what Starbucks could become—more than just a coffee shop, a social gathering place—a comfortable ambience with a variety of excellent coffees. In the end it became much more than that, particularly for the people who worked for him.

The single biggest cost in the fast food industry is employee turnover and training. Schultz decided on a bold approach to make a change in an industry that averages a 250 percent annual turnover rate. The first thing he had to do was change the perception of Starbucks as a company set apart from all others. To do this he had to put his money on the table.

He decided to offer a benefits package to part-time employees normally reserved for full-time staff. The benefit package called "Bean Stock" provided part-timers with health insurance and stock options. This wasn't a management package or a full-time employee package; it was a package for part-time employees.

Fascinated by this imaginative approach, I sat down with Gretchen Denzer, a full-time college student in Seattle, and part-time Starbucks employee for the past year.

Q. What caused you to want to work for Starbucks?

A. As a Spanish major, I've spent a lot of time overseas, and I've really enjoyed some of the European coffee shops I visited. I think it is really great that Starbucks took that ambience and transplanted it here. I was really attracted to the benefits that Starbucks offered even their part-time employees—especially the stock offered part-timers as a way of someday helping to pay off my college bills.

Q. What has kept you with Starbucks?

A. I was also looking for a long-term opportunity rather than just a part-time job. After a year of working part-time, I was moved up to shift supervisor. Then my manager began to talk to me about the opportunities available to move up within the retail store and later to my ultimate goal—being a coffee buyer.

Q. It sounds like you've found a home. Do you think you represent many of your coworkers?

A. Well, of course, everyone has their reasons for working here. But we have stacks and stacks of applications of people who would like to work here, which I think says something. Also, what I think is unusual is that I can transfer anywhere in the country. So when I graduate next spring, I'm applying for Starbucks Retail Management Team program. I'd like to relocate to Arizona and be an assistant manager. As long as things go well there, I hope to use my Spanish skills to move into the corporate level and develop international marketing skills by becoming a coffee buyer in South America.

Q. When you started working at Starbucks, did you have these kinds of dreams?

A. Not really. Of course, I liked the benefits, the environment, and the way the employees were treated. But what kept me here was that they encouraged my desires for a long-term career and showed me ways my skills could benefit the company and vice versa. In the end, it was a win-win situation. Most of my college peers are very unsure about where they are going to end up and what they'll do—especially those with liberal arts degrees. I feel blessed to have a solid plan for where I'm going when I graduate. When I tell my friends about the benefits of Starbucks, most of them begin to ask specific questions about how they can apply. I think that sums it up.

Getting everyone onboard with Schultz's vision was the real test. "Schultz concedes that offering these benefits did not make him wildly popular with his shareholders—at first. 'When we made the decision to give equity to part-timers—we were the first company in America to do it by the way—we had to stand up to the shareholders and say this was going to be dilutive. But we told them if we do it right it will be accretive, because it would lower attrition and increase performance. It was a difficult thing for them to decide to agree with me on.'"[19] The proof is in the output, and Starbucks reaped the reward. Since adding part-time employees to its company health benefits and stock program, turnover dropped below 60 percent.

FIND YOUR STONEWALLS!

At the heart of boldness are strength and commitment—both vertically and horizontally. First, are the people in key positions below and above you strong enough to lead with integrity? You can charge every hill as a bold leader, or you can inspire your organization to do the same thing. If you can multiply boldness, you will multiply every other measurement of success.

Used in the right way, boldness becomes a multiplier of the forces and resources available to a leader or commander. In the end, it preserves rather than wastes assets while infusing a fighting spirit among employees and warriors that can't be replicated by money, power, or any award we can bestow. At its best, boldness becomes a living energy within the heart of the organization that is no longer leader-driven, but is possessed and demonstrated by each individual with fire and perseverance.

In an age of declining virtue in government, business, and culture, Ace Greenburg took the bold move of building a financial investment company founded upon principles—Bear Stearns. In light of all the corporate scandals in recent years, under his leadership Bear Stearns escaped such notoriety. (Note: in 2003, under a new CEO, however, that emphasis changed.) "Once hired, Bear Stearns employees are expected to work hard, and above all, be ethical. How do you make sure that those ethical standards are upheld? By making sure ethics are everybody's responsibility and reward people—immediately and with cash—when they identify lapses."[20]

Yes, he took a lot of hits from within and without his organization for creating a culture of so-called informants. His response? "You don't want to rely on an internal audit committee where it takes years to find something . . . We're very much in favor of whistle blowers. We encourage it and pay them five percent of whatever error they uncover . . . I have written checks as large as fifty thousand dollars."[21]

This bold approach in a business where "money" *is* the business benefited both employees and shareholders. The compensation packages for senior managers are strictly based upon how well the company does—no options, no bonuses, no *nothing* if the company doesn't profit. And yet insisting that all decisions be founded upon ethics, both legal and moral, has been a boon to their bottom line. What did he use as his example? "Well, the Naval Academy, West Point, and the Air Force have a policy—and some colleges do too—that if you don't turn people in you get in trouble. If it's good enough for them, why isn't it good enough for us? If somebody is trying to put us out of business, what's wrong with having somebody tell us he is trying to break us?"[22]

Think that was bold? He took it a step farther. "All the senior managing directors, three hundred of them, are required to give away four percent of their total gross income to charity every year. Most of them give much more. We don't care what they give it to, but we audit them to make sure they do."[23] Why? He insisted upon this because he believed we were lucky to live in America and that we owed something to those less fortunate.

It was as simple as that and as hard as that. He was bold enough to stake the bottom line on the belief that you could build an ethical company with ethical leadership and still make a profit in, of all businesses, securities and investment banking. If you want any significant change in your organization, you are going to have to lead it with boldness, and then infuse it in your senior managers and those in the next level below.

CONCLUSION

At Chancellorsville in 1863, Lee faced General Hooker and was outnumbered four-to-one. The safe strategy was to keep whatever forces he had together. However, he had purposively put bold leaders into key positions, and Stonewall Jackson was his boldest. So Lee asked his opinion, and Jackson said he would take twenty-six thousand men (leaving Lee with seventeen thousand to face Hooker) and, shielded by a forest, outflank Hooker's right. "In the words of Lee biographer Emory Thomas, 'this was audacity to the point of madness.'"[24]

Lee's only words to Jackson were, "Well, go on." Jackson took his troops largely through very narrow roads, through thickets for nearly twelve miles to get astride Hooker's army. When he had arrived, he assembled eleven brigades stretching nearly two miles long and launched his attack. Hooker, hunkered down defensively waiting for reinforcements, was taken by surprise and suffered some seventeen thousand casualties and a demoralizing loss. While the South suffered thirteen thousand casualties, the generalship of Lee and Jackson (who was mortally wounded at Chancellorsville) was seen as superior in the North and the South alike. Hooker was soon replaced, and Lee, having pushed every Northern general from the field while outmanned and outgunned, believed he could take the war to the North and sue for peace. Such was the result of Hooker's blind spot, Jackson's boldness, and the loss of so many more soldiers toward the end of the Civil War.

Lee would later say of Jackson, "Such an executive officer the sun never shone on. I have but to show him my design, and I know that if it can be done it will be done."[25] The key then is to find your

Stonewall—and not just one—but many. Then infuse them with the spirit that, even if outnumbered and under-resourced, gives them the courage to say, "We can find a way," and the integrity and boldness to do it.

As for Lee, he was a man of honor in victory as he was in defeat. He had hoped that the advance into Pennsylvania would force the North to begin peace talks. His loss and narrow escape sealed the South's fate. There would be no peace talks; there would only be victor and vanquished. As he went to Appomattox Court House to sign the terms of surrender, he described his journey as harder than dying "a thousand deaths." Even so, he admonished his fellow Southerners to refuse the path of bitterness and "abandon all your animosities and make all your sons Americans."[26] When anger, division, and bitterness were spreading like infection, he was bold enough to admonish reconciliation and peace. Even his final adversary, Ulysses S. Grant, honored Lee after Grant was elected president. He restored Lee's citizenship, which had been denied him, and encouraged the divided nation, saying, "If the South follows the example of Lee, eventually all will be well with the country."[27]

CHAPTER 9

GENERAL ULYSSES S. GRANT

GENERAL OF THE ARMIES OF THE POTOMAC

*Stand up for your people and care for them—
they will take care of your mission.*

GRANT SURVEYED THE CONFEDERATE FORCES STRETCHING more than seven miles before him. Behind them lay the town of Vicksburg, where famine stalked the residents and whose defenders had been reduced to one meal a day. The mules and dogs in the area were being eaten as quickly as they could be found.[1] Time and again Grant peered across the blistered terrain looking for a sign of surrender.

General Grant was both tenacious and patient as he unleashed a terrible fusillade of some six thousand mortar shots every twenty-four hours upon the rebel positions. Confederate General John Pemberton and his men fought bravely, and the toll on both sides was enormous. More than nine thousand Union casualties and ten thousand Confederate casualties filled the hills and valleys, hospitals, and makeshift medical camps within and without Vicksburg.[2] The fusillade destroyed nearly every structure standing and forced

185

Pemberton and his staff to take shelter in a cave beneath his head-quarters.[3] After nearly forty days of battle, the South raised the white flag of surrender on July 4, 1863, and the American flag was hoisted over the courthouse in Vicksburg. As Grant watched the gaunt apparitions of the Vicksburg defenders lay down their arms, he ordered his quartermaster to distribute rations to them.[4]

The news of the victory at Vicksburg caused an embattled President Lincoln to take notice of the short, heavily bearded Union general with a cigar in his mouth. There were too few messengers bringing good news from the front. Lincoln thought of Grant as "the quietest little fellow you ever saw . . . The only evidence you have that he's in any place is that he makes things git! Wherever he is, things move."[5] The more he thought of it, the more he realized that was exactly what had been missing—someone to make things "git."

Lincoln promoted Grant to general of the Union Armies in March of 1864. Grant had established himself as a hero of the Union Army three and a half years into the Civil War—a war that was costing the United States a million and a half dollars, four hundred men killed, and another four hundred wounded each day.[6] He understood the urgency of the hour and knew he needed to establish himself quickly and change the course of war fast.

Grant was a well-liked but modest man who eschewed even the cheers of his own men as he rode past their positions. "To those who were near him, Grant was kind and considerate, and the fact that his staff officers clung to him through all the grades he attained, while they could have earned higher rank by more direct duty in the line, is proof of his disposition."[7]

In addition to a highly motivated and superbly led opposing force, Grant faced a competition for resources to defend Washington. General Lee had moved at will against the Union Army in the past; consequently, both Lincoln and Secretary of War Edwin Stanton held a well-grounded belief that a strong capital defense was paramount to Union survival. This defense, however, stripped previous field commanders of the very resources needed to take the offensive.

Following the disaster at Bull Run in 1861, McClellan took over and focused on turning raw recruits into an effective fighting force. He was successful and effective in restoring the spirit of the army. However, after coming up on the losing end against General Lee on several occasions, he felt inadequate resources were the root of his troubles. Unfortunately, his lack of battlefield success didn't give him credibility when he complained to Secretary Stanton following the Seven Days Battle in 1862:

> I know that a few thousand more men would have changed this battle from a defeat to victory. As it is the government must not and cannot hold me responsible for the result. I have seen too many dead and wounded comrades to feel otherwise than that the government has not sustained this army. If I save this army now, I tell you plainly that I owe no thanks to you or to any other persons in Washington. You have done your best to sacrifice this army."[8]

There were more problems for McClellan than a lack of support from Washington, as they developed from his continued angry epistles about his superiors (Chapter 7). His desire to fight an almost set-piece battle—to magnify his problems while underestimating those of his enemy—meant he rarely found the conditions suitable to take the offensive. His strategy could be compared to the football team with a small lead. In an effort not to lose it they implement a "prevent defense" long before the fourth quarter is over. In playing it safe against an enemy risking all to win, McClellan gave up the offensive to the South.

Following the bloodiest day of the war at Antietam, Lincoln relieved McClellan and replaced him with Burnside. Four months later, following another disappointment against the South's smaller numbers at Fredericksburg, Lincoln replaced Burnside with

Hooker. Hooker lasted a year and a half until the Union Army was defeated while holding a three-to-one advantage at Chancellorsville. It was at this point that Lincoln pinned his hopes upon Grant. Within the first month, Grant found himself not only fighting the South, but fighting for the men and munitions needed to strengthen his field armies.

Grant's battle for resources wasn't just a battle to attain personal power or to build an empire. General Meade was facing the bulk of Lee's army in May of 1864 in the area of Spotsylvania, Virginia. "During the first day at Spotsylvania the Federals lost ten thousand men, while the Confederate loss was very near nine thousand."[9] Meade needed whatever he could get to keep from being annihilated by a determined and extremely well-led Southern army, and Grant was determined to supply Meade in any way possible.

To stand up for the men who would face battle without adequate resources, Grant decided to confront his leadership. Believing that it was easier to ask for forgiveness than ask for permission, he boldly took action and then faced the consequences. This was borne out in a confrontation that took place a month after assuming command of all armies in the field.

"Well, General, are you ready for a move?" asked Stanton. [Secretary of War]

"Yes, I think so. The roads will soon be dry enough for wagon and artillery. Then the army will march," said Grant.

"Of course, you have taken proper care that the defences [*sic*] of Washington are all right?" continued the Secretary.

"Oh, yes. There will be enough troops in the Alexandria forts to meet any emergency," replied Grant, quietly.

"That's right. You know we must have the forts completely garrisoned. That was why we organized those regiments of heavy artillery, so that they could not be taken from the fortifications. It was my own idea. Our experience has been that that confounded rebel general, Lee, has generally contrived to threaten the national capital no matter how the Army of the Potomac moved against him."

"Well," replied Grant, very dryly, "when I once begin fighting Lee, he will have something else to think of. He will have no time to threaten Washington, so I have taken some of your heavy artillery to strengthen Meade."

"Have you?" exclaimed Stanton, thoroughly startled. "How many have you taken?"

"About thirty thousand up to the present time."

"Thirty thousand! Oh, see here, General Grant, this won't do. And I will not have it. We must feel perfectly safe while you are fighting in those Virginia woods beyond the Rapidan. I am Secretary of War, you know, and I shall insist on those heavy artillery regiments being sent back."

"I am very sorry," responded Grant, "but the men are needed, and they will stay where they are. As for the questions of authority, I supposed when Congress made me a Lieutenant General, to command all the United States armies, the rank carried some power. In fact, I rather think I outrank the Secretary of War when it comes to disposing of the troops."

"I don't want to quarrel with you, General," said Stanton; "but this question must be settled at once. Let us go and see the President."

The Secretary of War and the General walked over to the White House where they were admitted into the presence of the President. Upon seeing the grave expressions on their faces, he exclaimed, "What has happened?"

"Well, Mr. President," replied Stanton, "the fact is, the Lieutenant-General has, without my sanction, taken away nearly all the garrisons from the Alexandria forts, and I have protested. You know we must protect Washington."

"Have you, indeed, taken the Alexandria garrisons?" inquired the President, turning to the heavy-bearded Lieutenant General.

"Yes, Mr. President," replied Grant. "About half of them."

"And do you realize that this city may be in danger if not protected?" continued Mr. Lincoln.

"I have already told the Secretary of War that when the Army of the Potomac begins hostilities, the Confederates will not have any time to threaten Washington."

Mr. Lincoln remained silent for a minute of two, and then said:

"Well, Mr. Secretary of War, when the people of the United States selected Mr. Grant, as Mrs. Grant persists in calling the General, to take the chief command of all the United States armies, they and their Congress evidently intended that he should have some power. You and I have been trying for three years to run this war, and we don't seem to have made a very good job of it. Now, suppose we let the Lieutenant General try his hand. He has to shoulder all the responsibility if he fails."[10]

That settled the issue, and later when Grant recalled another fifteen thousand men from the garrisons of Alexandria, they came without further objection.

Grant faced a quandary all leaders face at some point: protect yourself and personal needs, take care of your people even at personal cost, or find a Solomon-like solution. Unfortunately, Solomon-like resolutions aren't always possible, and a choice between yourself and your people is necessary. Grant's answer was to subjugate his personal risk, confront his superiors, and stand up for the sake of the men who served him. In this case, his superior was able to see the wisdom of giving his new general the latitude and resources needed to fulfill his responsibilities.

General Grant was in a very difficult position having to follow six failed Union generals. His beginning wasn't auspicious. During the terrible war of attrition with the South, he earned ample opportunity for his men to despise him for his losses. In a period of five weeks in the spring of 1864, Grant fought three major battles at the battle of the Wilderness, Spotsylvania, and Cold Harbor, losing fifty-five thousand men in the process.[11]

In spite of this discouraging beginning his men rightly felt his care for their well-being. He measured out the lives of his men carefully, "suffering, at Vicksburg and Chattanooga, fewer losses than Lee's troops at Gettysburg. He was far more frugal with human life than his leading Confederate counterpart . . . preferring to take prisoners than to slay foes."[12] He felt the loss of his men keenly and later wrote in his own memoirs, "I have always regretted that the last assault at Cold Harbor was ever made . . . no advantage whatever was gained to compensate for the heavy loss we sustained."[14]

> "After the battle, the scenes are distressing, and one is naturally disposed to do as much to alleviate the suffering of an enemy as a friend."
>
> ULYSSES S. GRANT[13]

General Grant's concern for the welfare of those around him extended even to those of his enemy. During the battle of Spotsylvania, "the general encountered wounded men at a farmhouse in the area. In one room, he found a Confederate corporal who had been wounded in the right cheek. The general secured medical assistance for the soldier, then moved on . . . By the time he returned to the headquarters that night, he was covered in mud."[15] It was quintessential Grant who bore the weight of a war that would cost five hundred thousand lives and still take time to reach out to a solitary wounded soldier. Even on the final day of the war, Grant demonstrated concern for the foot soldiers in the Southern army. As the surrender document was signed inside the small courthouse at Appomattox, Lee remarked he needed to exchange a few Union prisoners as soon as possible. He went on to say, "I have no provisions for them; indeed, I have none for my own men."

Grant thought for a moment, and he asked, "Suppose I send over twenty-five thousand rations. Do you think that would be a sufficient supply?"[16]

Grant's humanity never compromised his ability to carry out his mission. Rather, it enhanced his standing in both the South and the North as a tough, honorable, and resourceful commander. In seeking the mission at any cost, many leaders today believe that jettisoning their "humanity" is the first requirement in being competitive. On the contrary, there is great power in a moral leader who has time for even a wounded enemy.

THOUGHTS FOR TODAY'S CENTURIONS

IT MAY SEEM PASSÉ OR ANACHRONISTIC TO READ SUCH descriptions of those who put service, subordinates, and even their competition or enemy before themselves. Many organizations and leaders today seem to believe they don't owe anything to their people beyond a paycheck. They not only don't stand up for their people; they stand up *against* their people. Shuffling blame for poor performance and expecting subordinates to give up everything else but their work and then abusing them at work have become too commonplace in today's culture.

While in London on business, I picked up *The Daily Telegraph* and read about the attempt of a CEO to motivate his management staff. His motivational method helped his company's stock slide 22 percent inside of a week. He sent an e-mail that minced few words:

> We are getting less than forty hours of work from a large number of our EMPLOYEES. The parking lot is sparsely used at 8:00 A.M.; likewise at 5:00 P.M. As managers, you either do not know what your employees are doing or you do not CARE. In either case, you have a problem and you will fix it or I will replace you.

NEVER in my career have I allowed a team which worked for me to think they had a forty-hour job. I have allowed YOU to create a culture which is permitting this. NO LONGER . . . Also, no more discussions on employee benefits. Hell will freeze over before I increase them . . . I want to see the parking lot full by 7:30 A.M. and half full on weekends. You have two weeks. Tick, Tock.[17]

There is no example like a bad example, and this one's a gem. Business seems to have only recently discovered that "people" are a precious resource and must be treated with dignity and respect to be retained. However, Christ long ago counseled, "In this world the kings and great men order their people around, and yet they are called 'friends of the people.' But among you, those who are the greatest should take the lowest rank, and the leader should be like a servant."[18]

The value of a simple word of praise, a note to an ill employee, or consideration for a subordinate in time of need cannot be underestimated. The examples of leaders failing woefully in the area of "people care" are legion.

One corporate manager wrote, "My sister passed away and her funeral was scheduled for Monday. When I told my boss, he said that she died just so I would have the day off on the busiest day of the year. He asked if we could change her burial to the next Friday and then added, 'That would really be better for me.'"[19]

A coworker of mine, having recently separated from his wife, faced the most difficult challenge of his life. Each day he went to work with a terrible weight upon his shoulders while he wrestled with the choices before him. His boss, noticing his demeanor during this difficult period, called him in to discuss it. Instead of words of support and encouragement he was told, "Make a decision. Either divorce her or get back together, but get over it." The air force promoted the supervisor to brigadier general.

About a year before I retired from the air force I became very ill.

Twenty years of good health, and I finally couldn't shake an illness. It went on for many months while the doctors tested and tested to find the source of my abdominal pain. Finally, they told me that I needed exploratory surgery.

After talking with my doctors, I went back to work. At a meeting that Thursday afternoon, my boss assigned a project to me due on Monday. Another weekend of work, normally not an unusual situation. But not now.

"Boss, I need to talk to you about something."

"What is it?" he asked warily.

"Well, I've got to go in for exploratory surgery on Monday."

He thought about that for a few seconds, then asked, "Well, are they going to use local anesthesia?"

"No, boss, it's general anesthesia, and I may be in the hospital a few days. If they discover what they think I have, I'm going to have a long follow-up treatment."

At this point he asked others to leave the room save myself and his deputy. When the room cleared, he pulled up his chair and said, "Jeff, you know we're really behind on our officer personnel reports. I need you to make sure all of yours are on my desk before they open you up on Monday."

That was the last thing I expected to hear come out of his mouth. I had served three command tours and led others in times of conflict. I tried to keep my face from showing what was inside of me.

"Don't worry, boss, my division has all ours completed."

"Oh, OK." Then he got up and went back to his desk. Our conversation was over. The last I heard, the air force promoted him and gave him a second star.

He never called my house when I went into the hospital, sent a card, or inquired of my well-being until he saw me some weeks later. It was a blind spot and very damaging to his leadership, though he never knew it.

I have also been privileged to observe senior leaders who know what it means to "take care of their own." When I was a young captain assigned to Headquarters Strategic Air Command, General John T. Chain took over as commander in chief (CINCSAC). Until that time, there had been an unwritten policy at the headquarters called "Loyalty Saturdays." To anyone who wanted to get ahead, it meant being at his desk until noon on Saturdays. When General Chain took command, he noticed the parking lots were full on Saturdays and asked his senior staff for an explanation. Most of them were surprised by the question and responded by saying there was a lot to do. He decided that this was a poor way to run the headquarters when the nation wasn't at war. So he told them to pass the word that this wasn't expected or required. Changing an organizational culture, however, doesn't happen overnight, and this situation was no exception. The word may have been passed, but people either didn't believe it or were afraid of being marked as "non-team players."

General Chain then told the security troops who guarded the building to start taking names of everyone who came in on Saturday. He told them he expected to see their list on Monday morning when he walked through the door. Within a month, the parking lots around HQ SAC on Saturdays were depleted. All of us in the staff were given back two full days a week to enjoy a more balanced work and family life.

> "He trained his men and looked out for them . . . [and] 'when my father saw the wounded at Vicksburg, his eyes filled with tears.'"
>
> FRED GRANT,
> SON OF ULYSSES S. GRANT[20]

Taking care of your people, what the military calls "care and feeding," is crucial to the success of any organization. Too many leaders, grateful for the opportunity to take over their new position, quickly seek the favor of their benefactors to the detriment of those they lead. What is not well understood is a lesson I learned as a young officer and never forgot. Most of the time, it is not your boss but those who work for you who determine your success. They're the ones that truly get you promoted. If you take care of your people, *they* will accomplish the mission.

A Pause for a Spiritual Reflection

As was the case of Grant, sometimes taking care of your people requires you to stand up to those above you. I saw this occur while attending a church in Costa Mesa, California, in the early 1970s. It was a church made up chiefly of young people coming out of the hippie and drug culture of the 1960s. Many young folks came to this church as a last desperate act, hoping to find some meaning to their existence. Pastor Chuck Smith had constructed a large circus tent in a field where services were held. As the years passed, music groups sprang up from this church, and a more diverse group of worshipers filled the church. As folks with long and short hair fellowshipped together, money was raised to construct a building. After many months of building and years in the old tent, the church moved into its three-thousand-seat sanctuary.

As people came into the sanctuary on that first Sunday, ushers in suits greeted and steered guests toward empty seats. However, what was common in the old tent suddenly wasn't acceptable in the new church. Many young folks wore California casual clothing, and a number came in bare feet. The ushers, under instruction to keep the sanctuary looking nice, made the barefoot attendees feel unwelcome. It was quite a shift from entering the old tent with a canvas floor. No one minded what one wore or didn't wear on his feet there. When Pastor Smith discovered what had happened, he called for a meeting of the board.

As the board gathered before him, Pastor Smith said, "Either we are going to allow people to attend this church, shoes or not, or we're going to tear out the carpet so they can." That settled the issue that night. The carpet stayed and so could anyone who came, shoes or not. Billy Graham noted, "When a brave man takes a stand, the spines of others are often stiffened."[21] Life in the church, business, and military worlds are not so very different on this issue.

It is critical to let your superiors know where you stand and what your team must have in order to succeed. Each situation and organization is unique, but there is no better time to do this than on day one. It is a comforting "fiction" to tell yourself that once you get the position or are more firmly established, you'll stand up for yourself, stand up for your people, or stand up for your values. Some leaders work in "ethically challenged" organizations and must define the line of integrity they refuse to cross. Others work in "management challenged" organizations and must stand up for their people each day to get the things they require.

Pathways of a Servant Leader

Considerations for aspiring Centurion servant leaders:

- Are you a ruler or a servant of those under your responsibility? Do you know the names and faces of those who work for you?
- When was the last time you asked about the personal needs of someone who works for you?
- When was the last time you met the needs of an employee beyond the workplace?
- Do you mentor employees to assume greater responsibility or is it too time intensive or does it threaten the security of others in leadership?
- What kind of working climate have you established for your employees? Are people seen as a means to the end, or are they seen as the catalysts who will help you reach your end if treated as valued resources?
- When you pass away, how will you be remembered where people were concerned: as one who cared about himself, or as one who cared about everyone else?

In a period of war, General Grant sought to care for the needs of his men and even his enemies. How is it that so many are so lacking in such care and concern in peacetime leadership? It is a question that points to a lack—a lack of Centurion strength and honor. It

points to a self-absorbed, careless nature that has yet to wear the caring, empathetic leadership mantle worn by Centurions. In Grant,
even his enemies knew and respected him, as his later election to
the presidency demonstrated.

Are our businesses, ministries, or careers so hurried and so
important that we cannot take time along the way for the inter-
ruptions of those who depend upon us and maybe those who don't?
I think a Confederate soldier with a wounded cheek never forgot
the Union general who stooped to give him aid. When was the last
time you walked through your division, sat with your employees,
or sent a note of personal encouragement?

As the end of the war drew near, Grant received one of the most
unusual displays of honor ever recorded. As was his habit, Grant
placed his dusty hat on his head, mounted his horse, and started off
at a steady canter. The recorded account noted:

> [As] Grant rode along his line he heard a Federal picket sen-
> tinel [guard] call out, "Turn out the guard for the command-
> ing general." Grant as usual replied, "Never mind the guard."
> To his astonishment the Confederate sentinel, on the oppo-
> site bank of the creek, then shouted, "Turn out the guard for
> General Grant." The entire Confederate picket line, instantly
> fell in, faced the Federal general and presented arms. General
> Grant returned the unexpected salute, and rode on.[22]

An honorable man is always respected, whatever the color of his
uniform, the stripes on his sleeve, or the title on his business card.

CHAPTER 10

ABRAHAM LINCOLN
BY THE PEOPLE, FOR THE PEOPLE, *with* THE PEOPLE

*Centurions have Contact Charisma. They know
their people, not just their functions.*

ABRAHAM LINCOLN WAS A MASTER OF USING STORIES TO
illustrate his points. If he were to be talking about the topic of *out-of-touch* leaders today, this story would capture his fancy.

BIRMINGHAM, UK: *January 21, 2001*

Bosses of a publishing firm are trying to find out why no one noticed one of their employees had been sitting dead at his desk for FIVE DAYS before anyone asked if he was feeling okay.

George Turklebaum, 51, who had been employed as a proofreader at a New York firm for 30 years, had a heart attack in the open-plan office he shared with 23 other workers. He quietly passed away on Monday, but nobody noticed until Saturday morning when an office cleaner asked why he was still working during the weekend.

His boss, Elliot Wachiaski, said, "George was always the first guy in each morning and the last to leave at night, so no one found it unusual that he was in the same position all that time and didn't say anything. He was always absorbed in his work and kept much to himself."

A post-mortem examination revealed that he had been dead for five days after suffering a coronary. Ironically, George was proofreading manuscripts of medical textbooks when he died. You may want to give your co-workers a nudge occasionally.[1]

The story about George was first published in England and then in the United States before someone began to check the facts. After trying to track down the source without success, the story was retracted as an "urban legend"—a hoax. What is most telling is not that it was a hoax, but that many in the corporate world so readily believed it. This story seemed to resonate with readers as they poured out their own stories of how insulated and out of touch their bosses really were.

Ever worked at a place where you rarely saw the boss and he saw you even less? I once had a boss I could barely get an appointment with, even though I oversaw and managed more than a billion dollars of his assets. You may wonder if your boss knows your name or if it even matters to him. Can leaders be any different in an age where information is moving from machine to machine in milliseconds and decisions are requested at nearly the same speed? It's possible, but you can accomplish a great deal if you're willing to mix your competence with sincerely enjoying being with your people.

In business, political, religious, and military organizations, leaders must interface with a stunning variety of people to be successful. A Centurion must find the way to achieve Contact Charisma with many entities to survive the difficult periods each organization inevitably faces.

Lincoln's leadership style is the gold standard in what I call "Contact Charisma." Contact Charisma is a connection between a leader and another that leaves the other ready to follow the leader no matter what the cost. It is developed by leaders who genuinely care about their employees and spend time finding out about the conditions and challenges their people face. To differentiate between Lincoln and some recent charismatic leaders, his purpose wasn't to wow you so he could take advantage of or deceive you. Lincoln was looking to connect with you so he could understand your point of view, and you his. To really understand his approach to others, we need to look at his contemporaries during the mid-1800s.

Beginnings—Encouragement for Leaders Without Looks and Means

The traditional biography of Lincoln begins with his humble birth in a log cabin. What is more important here is that he was a man known for his humble nature. His closest friend, Joshua Speed, a general store merchant, met him when he arrived at his store in Springfield, Illinois, in 1837.

> "In times of our trouble Abraham Lincoln has had his turn of being the best abused man of our nation."
>
> Harriet Beecher Stowe, 1864[2]

When he walked in, he asked to buy a bed on credit, explaining that he was just a beginning lawyer and that, if he failed, he might never be able to repay the debt. "As I looked up at him I thought then, and think now, that I never saw a sadder face."[3] Speed knew that Lincoln had no clients. Instead of selling him a bed, Speed offered to share his small room with him above the dry goods store. "Beaming with pleasure, Lincoln exclaimed, 'Well, Speed, I am moved!'" Mr. Lincoln was then twenty-seven years old—a lawyer without a client, no money, and all his worldly wealth could be summed up in the clothes on his back and the few items in his saddlebags.[4]

And so he began his career. A lawyer's office in this period was often just the edge of a sidewalk on the sunny side of the courthouse, and accommodations for circuit-riding lawyers were sparse. Typically, up to eight would sleep two-to-a-bed in whatever housing accommodations the town provided. Once the town's legal issues had been argued and concluded, the judge along with the lawyers would ride onto the next town. The pay, as might be expected, was meager.

> "Don't socialize with them. Don't get too close . . . Talk about teamwork and say such things as: 'we are like a family here!' Talk about your people as your 'greatest assets' . . . At the same time—without any sense of incongruence—'downsize' the organization laying off your 'empowered' . . . 'greatest assets' and 'family members.'"
>
> THE CLUELESS MANAGERS[5]

Most of his life, including those years in the White House, Lincoln gave little thought to his appearance. It was said that his shoes never knew black polish and his clothes never saw a whisk broom. Once he got into the White House, to get him to dress up, the staff would announce that it was necessary because the event was "official." This would motivate him to polish his appearance because, more than most things, Lincoln wanted to live up to the trust that others had placed in him.

Beyond his clothes, he was not an attractive man in the sight of his contemporaries. His friend, Speed, echoed one of the kinder portrayals when he described him as "a long, gawky, ugly, shapeless, man."[6] His enemies painted him in even more disparaging terms, comparing him to various animals.

Lincoln often laughed at his own looks with a story claiming that a stranger came up to him one day and handed him a pocket-knife. "I was astonished and told the stranger that the knife was not mine. But the stranger told me, 'This knife was placed in my hands some years ago, with the injunction that I was to keep it until I found a man uglier than myself. I have carried it from that time to this. Allow me now to say, sir that I think you are fairly entitled to the property.'"[7]

He lived in an era that did not appreciate plainness any more than today. Lincoln depended upon an inexorable logic and belief that some truths cannot be hidden by even the clumsiest speaker or an unsightly appearance. Lincoln had a legendary ability of using stories to make his most important points.

"One might meet him in the company of the most distinguished men, of various pursuits and professions, but after listening for two or three hours, on separating, it was what Lincoln had said that would be remembered. His were the ideas and illustrations that would not be forgotten. Men often called upon him for the pleasure of listening to him."[8]

As a law student, his fellows remarked about his ability to "bone down" to hard work—to devote himself completely to the case with focused concentration. John Littlefield, a fellow law student, wrote about this serious nature but also noted: "Lincoln always manifested interest in everybody with whom he associated . . . He struck you as the sort of man who would go out of his way to serve you . . . In his freedom of intercourse with people he would seem to put himself on par with everybody; and yet, there was within him a sort of reserved power, a quiet dignity which prevented people from presuming on him."[9]

As a lawyer, Lincoln had a habit of surprising his peers who were unfamiliar with his methodology and charisma. Often, his gangly appearance, backwoods Kentucky accent, and folksy stories caused them to believe him a less than apt attorney. He further disarmed them by often agreeing to many of their arguments after they had presented their case. But they underestimated him to their own ruin. One of his courtroom opponents, Leonard Swett, stated:

"He was as wise as a serpent in the trial of a cause, but I have had too many scars from his blows to certify that he was harmless as a dove. When the whole thing was unraveled, the adversary would begin to see that what he was so blandly giving away was simply what he couldn't get and keep. By giving away six points and carrying the seventh he carried his case, and the whole case hanging on the seventh . . . Any man who took Lincoln for a simple-minded man would very soon wake up with his back in a ditch."[10]

His ability to see his opponents' point of view became part of his charisma. Even though the disagreement remained, they knew he had considered their request or opinion fairly while persuasively presenting his own. Surprisingly, he was apt at putting aside personal feelings about an individual, opponent, or enemy, which lent added weight to his appeal. "He never judged men by his like or dislike for them. If any given act was to be performed, he could understand that his enemy could do it just as well as anyone."[11] Later he would employ and keep even his outspoken enemies in his administration.

INTO POLITICS—CHARISMA OF A COMMON MAN WITH UNCOMMON CHARACTER

When the political powers look for a candidate to back, they are looking for a winner: someone with ability, background, charisma, and track record (and today, money) to take their party into power. If you were looking at the resumes of the presidential candidates in 1859, Lincoln's would seem more suited for the outhouse rather than the White House. In brief, here is his less-than-stellar track record in his often quoted dismal resume of success and multiple failures.

> 1832—Lost his job and was defeated for state legislature
>   company captain of the Illinois militia in the Black
>   Hawk War
> 1833—Failed in business
>   Appointed postmaster of New Salem, Illinois
> 1834—Elected Illinois State Legislature
> 1835—Sweetheart died
> 1836—Re-elected to Illinois State Legislature
>   Had a nervous breakdown
> 1838—Defeated for speaker of the Illinois House

1839—Admitted to practice law in U.S. Circuit Court
1840—Argued first case before Illinois Supreme Court
1842—Admitted to practice law in U.S. District Court
1843—Defeated for nomination to Congress
1846—Elected to Congress
1848—Lost renomination to Congress
1849—Rejected for post of land officer
      Admitted to practice law in U.S. Supreme Court
1854—Defeated for U.S. Senate
      Elected to Illinois State Legislature
1856—Defeated for nomination for vice president
1858—Defeated for U.S. Senate[12]

If anything, Lincoln's record would seem to be one to overcome rather than to propel him into office. His potential for office was panned during his seven debates in 1858 with Stephen Douglas, who faced him as a U.S. Senate candidate. "It was Abe Lincoln's rival, the little Giant from Illinois, the smooth, self-assured Stephen A. Douglas who was the resplendent figure in the Lincoln-Douglas debates."[13] A New York journalist wrote, "Two men presenting wider contrasts could hardly be found: . . . [Douglas], a short, thick-set, burly man . . . proud, defiant, arrogant, audacious, [and Lincoln] the opposite . . . tall, slender and angular, awkward even, in gait and attitude."[14]

Lincoln lost the election to Douglas but was remembered, though not loved, for his frank assessment that "a house divided against itself cannot stand. I believe this government cannot endure permanently half slave and half free." Though it proved prophetic, it was badly received. "[It was] not a welcome message to bring as the house caves in on its occupants, who to the last want to believe that this, too, will blow over, and all will be as it was before—that another shoddy compromise with a moral evil will hold it all together."[15]

So what was it about Lincoln that caused the nation to turn to him in 1860 over three other candidates including Douglas?

"Electioneering in the nineteenth century was as much a social time as it was a political affair. In order to create enthusiasm for their ticket, party leaders organized huge parades, rallies, barbecues, pole-raisings, flag-raisings, banner-raisings, and other community-wide festivities. All of these campaign events were very participatory, including the stump speeches, during which people unreservedly shouted out questions or comments. Such combined political and social gatherings were especially welcomed in the countryside as a break from the isolation of farm life."[16]

This was where Lincoln was at his best. His folksy stories struck a chord with many, and he knew his constituency as well as the issues facing the nation. His reputation of honesty was surprisingly untainted in spite of many attacks by political foes, who conceded his integrity while arguing, "Yes, but that is all you can say in his favor."[17] His charisma was communicated person-to-person and in small group interactions along the campaign trail through storytelling, winning many through his wit as well as his wisdom.

> "Technical skills are not enough to make outstanding leaders, what is needed is emotional intelligence. The ability to touch the people they lead on an emotional plane, and not technical brilliance alone, sets good leaders apart from their average counterparts."
>
> THE NEW LEADERS[18]

Douglas, in trying to win Southern support and maintain Northern as well, was caught on the horns of a dilemma. He couldn't argue for Federal sovereignty without alienating his Southern supporters, and he couldn't come out strong for states' rights and slavery without alienating the North. Lincoln had made his position well known during his losing Senate race, so he stood firm whatever the consequences. During the presidential debates, Lincoln used this dilemma against Douglas by continuing to ask him questions that he couldn't answer without alienating his followers.

Lincoln made his points with metaphors the voters remembered.

"Slavery is doomed, and that within a few years. Even Judge Douglas admits it to be an evil, and an evil can't stand discussion. In discussing it we have taught a great many thousands of people to hate it who have never given it a thought before. What kills the skunk is the publicity it gives itself. What a skunk wants to do is keep snug under the barn in the daytime, when men are around with shotguns."[19]

Following these debates, voters for the Democratic ticket split their support between Douglas and two others, while Lincoln took the Republican Party to the White House. He won the election garnering only 40 percent of the popular vote but the majority in the Electoral College. Before he took the oath of office, the South, state by state, began to secede. It was an election victory that was even more contentious than the presidential election of 2000.

Abe in "The People's House"

The path to office in modern politics seems to be "say or do anything in the campaign, then do whatever you want when you get into office." If a candidate seems particularly persuasive, charismatic, or genuine, the false façade is soon discarded once the prize is in his hands. It is a sad testimony reflecting Lincoln's own well-turned phrase, "You may fool all the people some of the time; you can even fool some of the people all the time; but you can't fool all the people all the time." If Lincoln's common-man charisma was a political ploy or a means to an end, it would end once he was sworn in as the sixteenth president of the now divided United States.

If any president had reason to separate himself from his constituents and spend his time on a crisis, it was Lincoln. With a rival government set up in power, troops being called to duty on each side, and radical politics fanning the flames of war, he faced the worst emergency since the nation's founding. But as I argued earlier, character doesn't rise to the occasion so much as it is revealed by the occasion. It is in the fire that the true character of a human being is revealed—and it was no different for President Lincoln—still "Abe" to the core.

French journalist Ernest Hauranne visited America in 1864 and wrote of his amazement regarding the access Americans had to their leader in the White House:

"He receives petitions from his people . . . I have been taught discretion by our customs to the point where I wouldn't dare go past the door's threshold without a guide or special invitation . . . Yet, its doors stand open to every American: like a church, it is everybody's house. At all hours of the day, you will find curious or idle people milling about in the great reception room where the President holds his popular audiences."[20]

Another journalist continued the story of these daily meetings:

"Is the petitioner a poor widow who wants a [job] in one of the departments? The President reads her credentials and asks a question or two in his quiet but shrewd way. He writes a note on the card to be given to the cabinet minister . . . The next act may be to receive a distinguished foreign diplomat; or it may be a brigadier general wanting a promotion, an inventor after a contract, a curiosity hunter with an autograph book . . . No man but Mr. Lincoln ever knew how great was the load of care which he bore, nor the amount of mental labor which he daily accomplished."[22]

> "My former boss . . . had a habit of snapping fingers to summon support staff; or, if in search of a secretary, would bang on the women's restroom door calling out names until someone responded."
>
> E-MAIL TO NPR.ORG[21]

Lincoln's answer to a question about seeing so many "seekers" showed a keen understanding of his fellow creatures: "I ought not blame the aggregate, for each abstract man or woman thinks his or her case is a peculiar one, and must be attended to, though all others be left out; but I can see this thing growing every day."[23] He would sum up his dilemma with a story about his children: "My neighbor saw me carrying my two sons, one under each arm. The boys were both crying. He asked me what was wrong and I replied 'Just what's the matter with the whole world. I've got three walnuts, and each wants two.'"[24]

Lincoln never lost his openness to the public even up to the day of his death. To him the White House was the people's house, and he wouldn't bar the door to keep them out.

FIRSTHAND KNOWLEDGE ISN'T EASY TO GET, BUT IT'S IMPOSSIBLE TO BEAT

Contact Charisma ignites a flame when leaders care enough to leave their office to breathe the air their subordinates must endure. In recent years, the leadership term for staying in touch with your people was called "Management By Walking Around," or MBWA, which was coined by Tom Peters and Robert Waterman in their book *In Search of Excellence*. Yet a concept is just a concept, difficult to imagine until you see it demonstrated by an apt model.

In Lincoln resided a persistent curiosity that began as a boy who digested every book he could lay his hands upon. As president, he understood his decisions guiding the war effort were completely dependent upon his knowledge of the army's progress in the field. To get this, he could rely on reports from various agents, journalists, and military messengers, or he could find out for himself—by getting out of the White House.

For Lincoln, wandering was a way of life, having spent much of his life stumping for office, or traveling the circuit as a young attorney. Getting firsthand information provided the margin between winning and losing his case in court. He sought the same as president.

In 1861, Lincoln replaced General Fremont chiefly for being so out of touch with his command. In explaining his reasoning, he wrote, "He is losing the confidence of men near him, whose support any man in his position must have to be successful. His cardinal mistake is that he isolates himself, and allows nobody to see him; and by which he does not know what is going on in the very matter he is dealing with."[25]

Lincoln's presence at the office of Secretary of War Stanton was legendary. He was a frequent resident of the telegraph office inside the Department of War waiting for news of the latest battle, the latest enemy movement, or the latest request from his field generals. "Sometimes during crucial battles Lincoln made the trek (from the White House to the Department of War) two or three times a day, and once in a while he spent the night in the telegraph office waiting for dispatches from the field."[26]

In his first year in the White House, Lincoln averaged thirteen to fifteen days a month out of the office. He would often show up unannounced at his senior generals' camp to get a firsthand account—from McClellan to Grant. In 1862, he averaged ten days out of the office, and by the end of the war, "Lincoln spent half of the month of March [1865] and the first fourteen days of April doing little else than visiting his troops in the field . . . When the Civil War ended, President Lincoln was still in the field and . . . was one of the last people in Washington to hear of Lee's surrender to Grant at Appomattox."[27]

Lincoln wanted his senior leaders to know what was expected of them. Rather than just put it in writing or even in a conversation, Lincoln often illustrated his most important directions with a relevant story. General Grant related how Lincoln explained his most important concern to him upon assuming command of the Army of the Potomac.

> Just after receiving my commission as Lieutenant General the President called me aside to speak to me privately. After a brief reference to the military situation, he said he thought he could illustrate what he wanted to say by a story. So he explained, "At one time there was a great war among the animals, and one side had great difficulty in getting a com-

mander who had sufficient confidence in himself. Finally they found a monkey by the name of Jocko, who said he thought he could command their army if his tail could be made a little longer. So they got more tail and spliced it on to his caudal appendage. He looked at it admiringly, and then said he thought he ought to have still more tail. This was added, and again he called for more. The splicing process was repeated many times until they had coiled Jocko's tail around the room, filling all the space.

"Still he called for more tail, and, there being no other place to coil it, they began wrapping it around his shoulders. He continued his call for more, and they kept on winding the additional tail around him until its weight broke him down." I saw the point, and, rising from my chair, replied, "Mr. President, I will not call for any more assistance unless I find it impossible to do with what I already have."[28]

Lincoln's leadership quality of leaving his memory and his stories implanted in the people he met, the people he worked with, and the people who worked for him is quintessential Contact Charisma. What is remarkable is that his willingness to leave the White House occurred during years of an intractable war. If ever he could have had a reason to stay close to home, it would have been during this national crisis. Instead, he focused upon his need to know what was going on in the field and find out the quality of his commanders. For him, there was no substitute for seeing things with his own eyes—hearing things with his own ears. For those who served under him, seeing the president out and about the Union camps was a great morale booster. Establishing Contact Charisma requires both—you need to know what is going on, and your people need to know that you care enough to get firsthand information from them. Lincoln was one of the few Centurions who did this with aplomb.

THOUGHTS FOR
TODAY'S CENTURIONS

A RECENT STUDY INVOLVING MORE THAN SIX HUNDRED CEOs and one thousand middle to senior managers in the *2003 Workplace Reality* survey revealed the following astounding facts:

- 95 percent of CEOs believe their managers are happy, while only 56 percent actually are.
- Discontented managers increased from 38 percent to 44 percent over the previous year.
- 71 percent of CEOs thought that only 10 percent of their managers would leave in the next six to twelve months, while 53 percent of their managers were planning to do so.
- 62 percent of managers said they were staying because of the present economic climate, while only 5 percent of CEOs realized this. (68 percent thought their managers stayed with the company because they loved the work.)
- And, despite all the memos, personal letters, open-door policies, departmental and company meetings, many managers did not think the boss communicated that well. Only 19 percent of the managers felt their bosses communicated effectively, while 21 percent said the boss was hopeless at communication.[29]

In academia this lack of awareness is sometimes referred to as being in the "ivory tower," in Washington it's called "being captured by the bureaucracy," while most people just call it being "office bound." Whatever the name, it is costly to the leader, the subordinates, and the organizations alike. Lincoln's example, according to his secretaries, was that he spent about 75 percent of his time meeting with people. While his military guard and staff protected his person and time, "Lincoln complained about the well-meaning protection saying, 'It is important that the people know I come among them without fear.'"[30]

Each leader has to discover the method that works best for him. I had one general that I worked for who would come right into my office space, pull up a chair, and tell me to get him a cup of coffee. After I fetched the coffee, we would sit and talk about a wide range of topics until he was satisfied he understood what was going on—and this at a time when I was a mid-level manager—a captain with about seven years of experience.

Another leader remembered a unique approach his CEO used years earlier. "One of my manager heroes was Pete Gillespie. Pete was president and CEO of a Chicago paper merchant, buying paper from paper mills and selling it to users. I knew Pete when I had a summer job in his warehouse. Pete had a spare office next to his work office and it contained a barber chair and hair cutting supplies. One way Pete kept in touch with the men in his company was to give them free haircuts. He was a good barber, though he apparently never learned to cut women's hair. Everyone—managers, sales personnel, hourly workers, and even the summer-time warehouse help would make appointments to have their hair cut by the CEO. And during the haircut, Pete Gillespie chatted and got to know his people."[31] The lesson here is not that managers should become barbers, but that managers should find ways—appropriate to them—to keep in touch with their people.

"But I can't find the time—I don't have the resources—I have too much paperwork—I have others who are supposed to take care of that—I have to keep my boss happy" are excuses used by managers uncomfortable developing Contact Charisma. I worked for a boss whose office was two floors below me. Over a two-year period, I invited him repeatedly into our workspace to hear from the people who were accomplishing the work that made him successful. He set foot on my floor twice in that time for a total of two briefings, even though I had twenty-five different programs and more than a billion dollars of his money at stake. I mentioned this to other division chiefs, some who worked in office space only fifty feet away from our mutual boss. They astonished me when they told me he had never visited their offices.

To be successful you have to feel the texture, fly the skies, walk in the trenches, or breathe the air of the environment where your people will make or break your business. For some, that means extending your comfort zone from the controlled environment you call your office. It's true that you can call everyone into your office, the same as Lincoln could have ordered General McClellan to report to the White House each week to update his progress. But when you get out and smell the air where your people are living and sometimes dying, you get an inimitable assessment far superior to any report the best briefer can provide. The commercial goes, "Porsche—there is no substitute." There is also no substitute for "being there"—a person of the people, by the people, and *with* the people.

PAUSE FOR SPIRITUAL REFLECTION

There just couldn't be a better example of "being there" than Jesus Christ. We were poor in spirit, and He came into the world in the poorest of circumstances. We were lost, and He left His heavenly office to live among us and lead us into the path of life. We were unproductive, inefficient, and self-centered at best. He taught and demonstrated a better way to lead lives of fulfillment; to benefit those above as well as those below us in responsibility.

Jesus went to where His future disciples were living and work-ing—mending nets by the sea. Like Lincoln, He used stories to illus-trate the kind of work He was calling them to perform. He led by personal example for nearly three years through daily contact with His followers. He had no office, but He made every meeting with others an opportunity to communicate His message through the wis-dom of His words and deeds. He never wrote His instructions down, and yet His words and charisma were so powerful that many remem-bered His teachings word for word years after He walked this earth.

He had no system of "getting the word out" through mass e-mails, mailings, telephone messages, or shareholder meetings. Yet His words burned into the hearts of those who heard about Him, and they came to hear Him in droves. He was the antithesis of most leaders, and so we find His example somewhat disconcerting and uncomfortable. Frankly, I find Lincoln's example uncomfortable because I have had to force myself out of the office when it would have been more comfortable to stay inside.

Jesus didn't aim to please everyone, and He obviously made enemies along the way. Every life of integrity will create controversy because it makes people uncomfortable. In the presence of your quiet, honest leadership, and the benefits that accrue from it, are people uncomfortable around you, perhaps even so angered by you that they border on the irrational? When people are moved out of their comfort zones, we can expect resistance and even strong emotions. Yet these reactions didn't keep Jesus from going where He was needed—even when He knew the reaction would be unpleasant. He wasn't afraid to confront those who claimed to be part of His organization (the Pharisees and Sadducees in particular), and went right into their workspaces to do it.

He never had many of the modern methods of reaching the masses that are available in our society today; yet more people know the details of His life and words than any other person who ever lived. Clearly, His charisma was the result of far more than just being in contact with the people who followed Him in His day. His method of training twelve key individuals, while not neglecting the majority of His other followers, serves as a powerful example to integrate into our method of communicating guidance and vision to our organizations today.

Pathways to Contact Charisma Leadership

Charisma is an elusive and nearly indefinable concept, and yet it is an irresistible kind of magnetism that draws people to you—that makes others want to follow you and even be like you. You might look at yourself and shake your head in disbelief wondering how anyone could cultivate that kind of loyalty. Of course, if you have little interest in people beyond their capacity as a cog in the company's great wheel, you may not be ready to grasp this unusual and nearly irresistible force.

People with charisma have a strong sense of who they are—of their self-worth. That doesn't mean they are self-centered egomaniacs, but it does mean they have enough confidence that they are willing to be more transparent than most of their peers. Many others, though technically brilliant, have but a small capacity to connect with their people.

Can this kind of charisma be developed? To a great degree, the answer in most cases is "yes." That's the good news. The bad news is that for some of us, it is going to take more effort and sacrifice than we've ever made before. That is why developing Contact Charisma is the first step toward developing your ability to garner the support of people who will help you fulfill your planned missions. You don't need to start scheduling and attending numerous parties to show your face. This kind of charisma isn't "spun" or "marketed" or "staged as a publicity event." It does mean you need to be a professional in whatever endeavor you pursue—and pursue it with all your heart.

For a writer, Contact Charisma is also achieved through written words and occasional speeches. To do that, the writer must be completely versed in his profession and able to communicate in word and speech.

The following personal example may not be perfectly apt, yet it will get you closer to your destination. While I was writing the portrait of Joan of Arc, I was completely lost in the fifteenth century. When I wrote her chapter, I spent six weeks reading everything I could find about her. But I wanted more. I wanted a copy of the original trial record from AD 1429. I learned that original manuscripts were in various French universities, and in addition to being carefully protected and nonremovable, they were all in French. Then my search led me to a man who had translated the trial some seventy-five years ago. I found a single copy of his work in one rare bookstore in England encased in a cardboard slipcover and shrink-wrapped. I bargained with the owner and finally agreed to terms. What I opened was a treasure of questions and answers, but also drawings and notes of the trial that shed light on the partiality of the proceedings.

I read it cover to cover and got a much better understanding of the nature of this incredible woman. After reading the original transcripts, I can tell others her unknown stories in speeches that inspire and mesmerize. For most leaders, their business or ministry means their charisma is shaped and strengthened in one-on-one and one-on-many personal contact events.

When it comes to painting the portraits of leaders, I use words as brush and paints to convey qualities of the characters I write about. I'm ultimately interested in *them!* I want to know the details of their lives, of their strengths and their failings because I care deeply about the nature of who they were and the lessons they might teach us. My feelings about their strengths and weaknesses can be somewhat masked, but not to most perceptive readers. They can tell if I'm faking it.

> "Leadership is not so much about technique and methods as it is about opening the heart. Leadership is about inspiration—of oneself and of others. Great leadership is about human experiences, not processes."
>
> LANCE SECRETAN

Are you willing to be that interested in the people who will make or break you? Or are they really just nothing more than tools, cogs, or stepping-stones on your road to success? Are you willing to invest yourself and your time in them? If you honestly think that it isn't that important or it's too much trouble, you can go through the motions, but your efforts will be seen for what they are. People are intuitive and more so as time passes. On the other hand, if they really matter, they will sense that and will follow you into the deepest valley and climb the tallest mountain to achieve the goals you have jointly set.

HERE ARE SOME IDEAS TO START
YOU ON THE PATH

1. Instruct your secretary to schedule time out of your office every day—at least one hour. Find one lower-level worker the first day and visit him in his workspace. Find out about what kinds of challenges he is facing and what he has been doing. Then find a lower-level supervisor and do the same thing the next day. Work your way along until you've met and spent time with every member of your organization. It will be the best bargain you ever made—a small amount of your time for a tidal wave of pertinent information.

2. Get reports from the source whenever possible. If that means taking a trip, walking up the stairs, or having them come to you (as the lesser alternative), then do that. You'll be surprised by how much clarity you'll gain when you speak face-to-face with someone.

3. Invite people to question your ideas and directions during the formulation stage. If you can't respond with clear and convincing answers, then take a step back and rethink your position. An idea that can't stand the light of an argument is not one that should see the light of day.

4. Take the long view. I've said this before in this book, and I'm saying it again now because it is a cornerstone of building Centurion leadership. You're not going to impress your bosses immediately with this strategy. What you are going to do is develop incredible loyalty and a work ethic among your team or organization that ultimately will impress not just your bosses but theirs as well. Moreover, you'll build an organization that is powerful because you always stay a step ahead of your competitors by looking into the future.

5. Be patient with yourself. It's going to take time, effort, and practice. No one becomes charismatic with the snap of his fingers. Watch others who possess this and learn from them. Never stop watching and learning from those who are more successful at this than you are. It's not a weakness to admit your limitations; it is a weakness not to improve them.

CHAPTER 11

THE ROMAN CENTURION

NO DEADLIER OCCUPATION, NO WARMER HEART

Moral accountability is the foundation, either solid
or crumbling, upon which our legacies stand.

THERE WAS ONCE A GREAT ROMAN CENTURION. HE BORE the scars on his body of countless brushes with death, of numerous moments of sadness when he held his own soldiers as they blew their last breath in his face. He knew both victory and defeat and the elation and grief that came with each. At the end of many years he came home. After thousands of days of forced marches into hostile territory, he returned home a weary man. In his home, his family waited, hoping for the day when he might survive and come home at last. As he stepped through the door, he was met with the stares of a family who thought they had seen a ghost. He was home; he was finally home. Of the tens of thousands who went off to war, barely a third would return, sometimes far fewer depending on the competency of the consuls who led them. But this Centurion had survived.

Looking around at his family, he rejoiced to see each of them: children who were no longer children but young men and women;

a wife who had grown older but more beautiful with age. And for this Centurion, his servants held a special place in his heart large enough to love even the lowest born. Yet in this house, one of his most devoted servants was sick, and sick enough to be at death's door. The Centurion had seen it many times before—the gray pallor, the shallow breath, the cold skin. All were signs that death was in the room. So what was that to him? He had traveled a thousand miles to finally rest his weary feet and war-torn mind. Looking at his servant, though, he knew his work wasn't finished.

This man wasn't just a boss. He wasn't a supervisor, and he wasn't a manager. He was a Centurion, and that meant something. He was powerful and strong, a wily survivor of a hundred battles, and yet even with all that, he was impotent in the face of death. He was helpless against the inexorable power of this invisible foe. Yet like most living in Israel then, he had heard the strange stories of someone who healed the sick and even raised the dead. This Jesus was a man that death feared rather than the other way around. If he could get to this man, perhaps he might yet save his servant. One thing he had learned along the way was that pride had little use in the face of death—some died heroes, more died cowards, and the rest just died. If he were called a coward for seeking out a Jewish teacher for help, then so be it if this Jesus could save His beloved servant.

"The character of a leader isn't readily visible at the bottom line. But look at what happens to companies whose leaders are morally vacant reckoning comes without warning."

He had traveled a thousand miles to kill for Rome; what was a dozen miles more to try to save a man as dear as his own son? And so he went to see Jesus, the One who held sway over the foe he could not touch, much less defeat. He went because he cared about all who served and counted upon him. He cared because he was a Centurion. The Bible recorded this short but remarkable incident:

When Jesus entered Capernaum, a centurion came to Him, imploring Him, and saying, "Lord, my servant is lying paralyzed at home, fearfully tormented."

Jesus said to him, "I will come and heal him."

But the centurion said, "Lord, I am not worthy for You to come under my roof, but just say the word, and my servant will be healed. For I also am a man under authority, with soldiers under me; and I say to this one, 'Go!' and he goes, and to another, 'Come!' and he comes, and to my slave, 'Do this!' and he does it."

Now when Jesus heard this, He marveled and said to those who were following, "Truly I say to you, I have not found such great faith with anyone in Israel . . ."

And Jesus said to the centurion, "Go; it shall be done for you as you have believed." And the servant was healed at that very moment. (Matt. 8:5–13 NASB)

We've come to the heart of it. The foundation of all principles lies here. It is something that few give any attention to because the foundation is hidden beneath the beauty of the structure above. The foundation must be poured into solid ground that can hold both the weight of the concrete and the building above it. The right amounts of cement and stone must go into what will harden and ultimately support tons of weight.

The cement crews normally do their work in the early hours before other workers arrive onsite. The cement crew receives a preliminary evaluation after pouring, but doesn't receive its final grade until well after the building is finished. As time passes, both the ground and the building settle, and it is then that the true test of workmanship is known.

We may overlook or take for granted that our nation's businesses, military organizations, and the leaders who run them have a solid foundation of integrity upon which we depend. We may not even know we depend upon their "good word" until we find large cracks in the foundation, large potholes undermining our freeways, or large gaps in accountability that undermine our confidence in public institutions. It's not just "the economy, stupid." It is so much more than that; or as Eisenhower counseled, if we give up our principles for our privileges, we will ultimately lose both.

It is fashionable to belittle the value of such things as moral character. Virtue is seen as a commodity that can be bought and sold like shares of common stock. But the day comes when like dominoes, one after another, the leaders fall and company after company is "weighed in the balance and found wanting." Our schools teach our children there are no absolute values, while our courts impose absolute sentences upon those who violate the laws that hold murder and theft as punishable along with many other crimes. Is it any wonder there are confusion and cynicism about systems that alienate large portions of our society?

The newspapers now shout headlines nearly once a week that another CEO has been accused of falling prey to greed and other criminal offenses. Graduates of Ivy League universities are astonished to find their companies as the targets of investigations of corruption within their inner sanctums. Like the Roman mob, the people have become fed up with the excesses and greed, forcing the courts to step in and remedy the wrongs.

> "Virtue is like a road—it takes a long time to build, requires consistent attention to maintain, and one little fault, one pothole, and both great and small go into the ditch."

So how do we rebuild the crumbling foundations that can no longer support a stable or thriving society? It's only possible when each person begins to see himself as part of a future solution instead of a victim of a past beyond his control.

From the haziness of examples long forgotten, perhaps we might blow away the dust and glean the wisdom that still lies there. The great leaders possessed a sense of not only their own destiny but the destiny of their people. It was not just an insatiable drive to write their names in the stars that drove them. They had a heart that beat in time with those whose dreams they would soon make a reality.

The Roman Centurion

Here is the job description of the Centurion if you're up for it. You may not be there yet, but then few others are there either. We all still have places where we can strive and struggle and continue to develop as professionals and as human beings. That is one of the great secrets of becoming a great leader—never stop becoming.

A Centurion was battle hardened—a veteran of at least sixteen years and numerous campaigns where he distinguished himself with valor.

There were no political appointments, *quid pro quos,* or smoke-filled rooms with under-the-table payoffs. You either are or aren't a veteran—whether in business or battle. It can't be a gift, and it can't be passed down from one generation to the next; it has to be earned by each person in his own right. Of course, there are examples where great scions of industry passed on their fortunes to their heirs—but they couldn't pass on the years of battle they faced to earn those fortunes and the scars that accompanied them. That is why so many inherited fortunes are lost within a single generation; their benefactors failed to force their children or protégés to struggle—to fight—to earn the right to sit at the head of the table—or lead the battle from the front of the legion.

A Centurion could carry ninety pounds of equipment at least twenty miles per day and train under the harshest of conditions. The Centurion provided his own equipment, armor, and paid for even the tools he needed to fight the battle. He was a skilled engineer and builder in addition to being the finest combat soldier.

A Centurion was the ultimate in professional competence. But it was much more than that. He carried the same weight that other legionnaires were expected to carry. There were no allowances made for persons of his position or stature. Moreover, he was expected to provide his own equipment—even the swords and shields he used in battle were wholly purchased and owned by the Centurion himself. It was a matter of honor and pride that he carry his own implements into battle. Centurions expected little or nothing from the state.

Finally, he was not just a brute beast—a Genghis Khan or a three-hundred-pound bully striking fear into all in his company. He was a skilled engineer who could build a bridge, construct siege engines to crush city gates, and build parapets and scaling ladders able to support a dozen men at a time.

The enlistment period was for twenty-five years, after which a cash payment and small plot of land were provided (unless the treasury was short of cash, in which case, commitment to service was involuntarily extended).

A Centurion understood he gave the best years of his life to Rome. He was a leader who had a destiny to fulfill, a calling upon his life that might very well cost him his life. At the end of his days, he understood that his reward was not in the pittance of land or few coins the treasury would dole out, but the knowledge and legacy he left to those who followed behind him. It was enough to know he served with courage, honor, and faithful service in the fires of battle. He had fulfilled his oath and was honored by his men as he prepared to retire.

When his twenty-five years ended, he understood his retirement circumstances were at the whims of others, and there was little he could do to change that. Nevertheless, he understood one principle that many today have forgotten: No one could take his honor from him. Only he, if he were so inclined, could give it away. No matter what else happened, he carried his honor with him on the long road home—even if he had no land or little money to show for his life's work.

To rise to Centurion was considered the highest honor a legionnaire could attain. His life expectancy was uncertain, and the Centurion always led his troops from the front.

We do not see this kind of attitude of service in leadership often enough today—from public service to private sectors, from nonprofit even to servants in the clergy. For the Centurion, it was enough that he had risen to his position through years of severe hardship and near death battles. His reward? He was elevated to stand at the head of a *century* so that his sword would be the first to touch the steel of Rome's enemies. That was the highest honor he sought—to lead from the front and to encourage his legionnaires by his courageous action. The survival statistics for Centurions were not promising, and each paid into a burial fund to cover the costs of his interment.

Yet in spite of all of these hardships, there were numerous examples of great valor while the soldiers were being ground up in the gristmill of war. One such Centurion, Spurius Ligustinus, was promoted to the rank of Centurio Prior (senior Centurion of the Legion) in 200 BC. By the time he was fifty years old, in 171 BC, he had served twenty-two years and had been singled out for bravery thirty-four times and received six civic crowns.[1] His service was notable because it was his civic work in Rome as well as his bravery on the field of battle that garnered him recognition by the civic government.

Finally, the Centurion held ultimate sway over the welfare of every man who served in his one-hundred-man century.

Punishment was swift when legionnaires fell short of the expectations of the Roman army, and the Centurion was called upon to inflict a punishment that we would consider barbaric today. It was a difficult duty because he knew each of these men personally, and most had served with him side by side in many battles. Still, he had to carry out the orders to maintain unit *esprit de corps* and strength in the entire army.

But there was a side of the Centurion that is also common among leaders who leave a legacy. Most are quiet about their personal feelings for their subordinates, and yet those who understand their responsibilities go beyond the moment, beyond the monthly or quarterly report, and reach out to walk an extra mile for their troops. The Centurion in the New Testament was one such leader.

THE ROMAN CENTURION AND JESUS

Look in for a moment upon this scene that took place in full view of Roman citizen and Jew, of oppressor and oppressed, of crowds surrounding two men seemingly oblivious to all except their own exchange—one in need, and One with infinite supply. And consider the cost that the Roman Centurion must have weighed carefully before coming to One in danger of arrest at any time.

Still, the Centurion put on his uniform and set out to find this teacher, this preacher, this strange man that he heard could do things no one else had ever done. He came understanding he might be arrested for what today would be called "conduct unbecoming an officer." He also was willing to risk the hostility of zealots from both sides who could always be counted on to add violence and death to any gathering. In spite of all of this, he came.

Do you have any idea of what it must have cost that Centurion once the news spread that he had demeaned himself and his position beneath that of an itinerant teacher for the sake of a slave? His previous reputation and all of his mighty deeds would have been for naught at the very least.

Are our times so very different in this century? Today, a general in the Pentagon speaks out about faith and the battle between good and evil, and he is eviscerated by all the powers and forces of the media, politicians, and many in the public. He is courageous enough to speak of a faith capable of sustaining anyone who will trust in a God greater than himself, but because of his conviction and courage, rage burns against him like a fiery inferno.

When officers make a public stand in a way that brings negative publicity, they pay dearly for their commitment. The current lieutenant general just pinned on his third star, and he can be sure that he will have enough enemies in Congress never to pin on a fourth. He can be sure that if there is any unpleasant assignment that needs a lieutenant general, he will receive it. If there is any task of consequence that he can be assigned to perform, he will be assigned to do it. The bureaucracy will do its best to bury this officer far from anywhere he could come into contact with the media.

When I decided to retire from the military, God had shown me He had a new path for me to follow. I had completed all my commitments and twenty-two years of service, and so I put in my retirement papers. My superiors were astonished and infuriated. How could I turn down what so few were ever offered? Yet my destiny lay elsewhere. To deny it would be to deny the very breath that gave me life.

Was it difficult? Extremely. Did I have any regrets? Yes, I had regrets, but more important, I had no doubts. I knew I was following the path of my destiny and was willing to pay whatever price was necessary to be true to my calling, true to myself, and true to the One who had called me.

Those called to be leaders—those who want to be Centurions—carry a heavy mantle of responsibility. In the movie *The Gladiator,* the character played by Russell Crowe tells his men before battle, "What we do here echoes in eternity." No truer words were spoken in that movie. What a powerful thought: What we do really *matters.* What we fail to do also matters. You have been placed into a position of responsibility for more than your success or your company's success. What you do echoes in eternity. You are the author of the book titled *You*—a book that will one day be read in eternity.

> "Whenever you are to do a thing, though it can never be known but to yourself, ask yourself how you would act were the whole world looking at you, and act accordingly."
>
> Thomas Jefferson,
> Letter, 1785[2]

For a small period of time you have been given a small measure of "power." Yet *all* power is vested in and comes from the Almighty—every ounce and measure of it. If He has entrusted some of this to you, it comes with the gravest responsibility for which you will one day be held accountable. Are you a father, a mother, a small group leader, or a CEO of a billion-dollar corporation? You have been given varying amounts of this power by the One who holds sway over the tides and courses of man. It is He who will ask how you used what you were given. Are you ready to do your duty to that responsibility, no matter the response from others?

I am reminded of the meeting between the dead Jacob Marley and Scrooge on Christmas Eve in the Dickens classic, *A Christmas Carol*. When Scrooge complimented Jacob on the business savvy he exercised during his lifetime, Jacob cried out in despair.

"Business!" he said, wringing his hands. "Mankind was my business. The common welfare was my *business*; charity, mercy, forbearance, and benevolence were all my *business*. The dealings of my trade were but a drop of water in the comprehensive ocean of my *business*."[3]

I think there is more truth in those few words than a thousand sermons I've heard. We may wear the mantle of leadership without understanding the enormous weight it conveys. With greater power come greater responsibility and accountability.

This Centurion had likely seen some twenty years of desperate battle and had been decorated for bravery on more than a few occasions. Yet he was not too hardened, too concerned for his own future, or too covetous of maintaining an unblemished reputation to act on something of greater value. When he heard that Jesus was nearby, he didn't hesitate to get up and go to Him. As a man of valor under the red skies of battle, he knew how to make decisions when lives were at stake. And now a life dearer than his own was at the precipice of death. So he threw on his cloak and flew to the marketplace where the man Jesus was teaching that day.

> "A people that value its privileges above its principles soon loses both."
>
> DWIGHT D. EISENHOWER, 1953[4]

He didn't wait for the teacher to wander away from the crowds. He didn't send a dozen soldiers to "escort" Jesus to his residence so that he could meet Him in private and protect his reputation. In full view of all in the marketplace, he made his request, and then he said words that no Roman, much less a Roman officer, would say. He told

Jesus, "I am not worthy." Think of that for a moment. Would a Nazi in World War II have entered a Jewish doctor's house asking for help, saying, "I am not worthy that you should come into my house?" This soldier had not only a Centurion's title; he had a Centurion's heart.

THOUGHTS FOR TODAY'S CENTURIONS

WE ARE FINITE BEINGS WITH BOTH A BEGINNING AND AN ending in the mortal bodies we occupy. Is it so unimaginable that one day you will take off the trappings that come with the power that has been temporarily loaned to you? When that day comes, what will you remember—what will be significant to you? After twenty-two years of military service and three command tours, I came to understand that power and all of the illusions that accompany it are a mist that disappears at sunrise. On my final tour of duty in the Pentagon, I gathered my twenty-five-man office around me on my first day, looked at each of them, and said:

"This office is going to develop the next generation of aircraft—ones that fly without pilots. I believe in you. I believe you were hired because you were the best and brightest, and I am confident that you will do all that is required to meet the challenges that we now face and those that will soon confront us. What I want to do is to assist you in accomplishing the great tasks before us. I have no desire to make this job a stepping-stone to something greater. I am content that I am here for a purpose that needs no further elevation. I am not here to make a name for myself or get promoted. And when the time comes for me to go, my measure of success will be this: 'Did I make this a good place to work? Did I create an environment where every person in this office got up each morning and felt like this was the best job he ever had?' If I do that, I know you will accomplish our mission. If I do that, whatever else happens, I will consider myself a success."

The Centurion who visited Jesus had something more important on his mind and risked personal punishment when he made the journey to meet this teacher. He had a heart-felt moral responsibility to do everything in his power to help his dying servant. This servant wasn't even a man within his company of soldiers. If he had been, we could understand the Centurion's concern as being within the purview of his military responsibilities. After all a commander, a leader, is called to look after the well-being of his people. But there was some deep sense of honor and concern for all he was responsible for that drove him to see Jesus and humble himself for the sake of a mere servant—a slave.

What would you do to help someone in need who works for you or depends upon you? Can you remember the last time you spoke to such a lowly person, much less reached out to him? Perhaps it's time to take a long, hard look in the mirror and try to recall the name of the lowest ranked person working for you. Do you know anything about him—his name, his family—anything? That person might very well be the one who makes the key input, performs a timely action, or walks an extra mile to snatch victory from the jaws of defeat for your organization. If you can't remember that person's name today, then bow your head and commit yourself to do at least this; that before you leave your position, you will not only know his name, but you will make his life better because you led.

> "Expedients are for the hour,
> but principles are for the ages."
>
> HENRY WARD BEECHER, 1887[5]

The ultimate answer of how you lead is solely in your hands. You are not the victim of circumstances, corrupt bosses, or corporations. As noted earlier, "Randomness rules less in those who steer." Most lead for self-serving reasons, a smaller number lead for the benefit of the corporation, and a few—so very few—follow the path of the Centurion. You may never hear a word of thanks, but the strength, honor, and wisdom of Centurions across the ages will echo in your soul. And though you will one day die along with all other mortals, a people yet born will one day rise up and say—"Yes, but look how he lived!"

EPILOGUE

OUR LIVES ARE MEASURED OUT IN DAYS, IN THE BALANCE scales that weigh our words against our deeds. After reading my book, you have a right to know what I have done to match these words with my life.

I would like to believe that I have years left to continue to "become" that Centurion leader. But David once said, "O Lord, teach us to number our days rightly, that we might attain wisdom." Perhaps, as much as anything else, I know that I cannot afford to allow days to slip through my fingers like water into the sand. I woke up today at 2:00 A.M. with this thought in my mind and had to put it to paper.

I no longer lead troops in the field, and my destiny lies along a different path from yours. Besides providing for and honoring my wife and children with a life they can respect, I have been given two other purposes to complete. The first you have already seen. I write of an

America that once was and can be again. I remind those who have forgotten that our freedom is a gift and a grave responsibility and that history has not looked kindly on those who refuse to defend that gift. I write to leaders to remind them that their power is momentary and we will account for how we use it one day. I pray these principles will help you have an honorable answer in that hour of life's review.

But I also have a second calling on my life—a part of my destiny that began some fifteen years ago. As I mentioned earlier, while visiting India I saw things I had never experienced before. I was exposed to nakedness, scarcity of clean water, and hunger as it ravaged both young and old. I saw the widespread devastation caused by the epidemics of AIDS and leprosy.

The images were too powerful for me to gaze long, and I turned away again and again. But God would not let me escape the pricking of my conscience. Like the Ghost of Christmas Present, who hid the two children "want" and "ignorance" under his robes, I turned away at the dire nature of their condition. And like Scrooge, I could hear him say, "They are covered for now, but they remain—they remain."

And so I bargained with God. I told him I was but a young captain living half a world away. I had four children of my own at the time and work that could occupy every ounce of my energy and every hour of my day. God was not impressed with my excuses. So I went on, saving my best argument for last.

"God, this is an ocean of pain, and I only have a spoon! This is a problem bigger than any one person, and that's all I am—one person!"

The Lord calmly answered me: "Jeff, you can make a difference here, if you are patient and do it one spoonful at a time."

One spoonful at a time? I didn't have an answer for that. Patience by the spoonful seemed almost hopeless. Yet it was the perfect answer because my perspective was completely wrong. Those words taught me a second lesson that has kept me going day after day and year after year. Never, ever, focus upon the size of the problem. It is always going to be too large. Focus instead upon the strength of your resources; look at what you *are* able to do, and start there. Then keep putting one foot in front of the other, believing that if your destiny is to complete that work, you will be given what you need at the time you need it.

And so I began—a meager, humble, and halting effort to do what good I could with what I had. A friend and I started together at first by contributing half of our flight pay to a pastor with a heart to open an orphanage for children. We started with thirteen orphans in 1990 in a rented facility on a shoestring budget of five hundred dollars a month.

The third lesson I learned in beginning this endeavor was that I had to believe in it before anyone else would. That meant investing my money as well as myself. So my wife and I built the first orphanage, buying the land and paying for the building. In 1991, we were able to do this for just under thirty thousand dollars. Today the building and land are worth nearly ten times that amount. That taught me a fourth lesson. There are doors that open in time when the Master of your destiny calls. You can go through those doors while they are open, but if you delay or demur, they will close, never to reopen. Other opportunities may come, but those left will be lost.

For three years we did this work without mentioning it to another soul. But the time came when the work grew so large that we outstripped every bit of our savings, and still there was need for more. So we began to pray, and after nine months, we felt God's release to "share" our work with others. Share—not persuade. Persuasion we would leave to the Destiny Maker. And share we did and soon received official status from the IRS as a tax-exempt organization: Mission of Joy.

Today, we house more than two hundred orphans full-time from the day they arrive until they are grown and start their own lives as Christian believers. We take care of their food, clothing, education, medical care, and Christian education. We also have brought the gospel to hundreds of villages and have opened more than fifty churches with Indian pastors whose heart is to reach their own people. We run a home for Christian widows, conduct medical care for the poor, provide AIDS and leprosy education, and are digging wells in villages without water at the rate of one a month. We feed a thousand meals a week to hungry children and in the past fifteen years have seen more than one hundred thousand seekers find Christ to be the answer to their emptiness.

As the founder and director of Mission of Joy, I will be a boss, a manager, or a Centurion. I studied the great leaders of history and know that the bar has been set very high. With God's help, I believe I can make it. No matter what, on the day when I breathe my last breath, I will be thinking of the child's smile when she took a cup of water from my hand; the grateful eyes of the widow when I handed her clothing; the man who was too sick to come to the gospel meeting so we went to him instead. I will also remember the kindnesses I received from Muslims and Hindus alike, just because we cared enough to come to their poor village and bring the good news that they had not been forgotten—that they were loved.

Finally, I will remember the night I left one village after ministering there for three days. They begged us not to leave at 11:00 P.M., even though that was when I was supposed to return the van. Their cries broke my heart, and so we stayed on, praying for the sick, feeding the hungry, and encouraging the weak. It was 2:00 A.M. when we climbed into the van and started the journey home, driving through the alley that stretched from one end of the village to the other. On both sides of that alley, about ten feet apart, were the villagers standing to watch us leave. The entire village had stayed awake and lined the alley for our departure. Then they began to clap first slowly and rhythmically, then louder and louder as we slowly drove past each of them. I looked into their eyes as they smiled, some toothlessly and others with grins from ear to ear. They gave us all they possessed that night, thanking us in the only way they could. They gave us their thankful hearts; they gave us themselves.

Until my numbered days run out, I will be doing what good I can among these people. This is my destiny to fulfill. Have you discovered yours yet? I invite you to examine the possibility of giving up your life as a boss or a manager and seek the Centurion's path. Doing so may never put an extra dime in your pocket or a dollar in your bank account, but you will never be richer either. I wish you Godspeed on your most unpredictable and fulfilling journey toward becoming what every leader should strive to be—a Centurion for the ages.

—Colonel Jeff O'Leary (Ret.)

The second book in the Centurion Trilogy series will release in 2005.

ABOUT THE AUTHOR

COLONEL JEFFREY O'LEARY (ret.) spoke to more than ten million television viewers two weeks after terrorists attacked the World Trade Center and the building in which he worked—the Pentagon. On Robert Schuller's *Hour of Power,* standing in uniform, he encouraged many and gave hope during one of the darkest days in our nation's history.

Colonel O'Leary holds the Legion of Merit, three Air Medals, four Meritorious Service Medals, the Southwest Asia Service Medal with two Battle Stars, and an Outstanding Unit Award with Valor. He served for more than twenty-two years in the United States Air Force, commanded a flying squadron, and served as the deputy group commander over three thousand people.

Colonel O'Leary completed the Executive Education Program at the Harvard Business School and was selected as a Harvard University National Defense Fellow in 1999 and 2000. He holds master's degrees in national security from the Naval War College and speech from California State University at Los Angeles. His bachelor's degree in speech was earned at California Lutheran University.

Colonel O'Leary appears on Fox News regularly as a military analyst on terrorism and Middle East politics, culture, and the ever-present crises in Israel and Iraq. He has appeared on more than two hundred television and radio programs, including Janet Parshall's *America, Beverly LaHaye Today,* and Moody's *Mid-Day Connection.* He shares his own experiences facing terrorism while serving as a peacekeeper in northern Israel during the Gulf War.

Colonel O'Leary is also the founder and director of Mission of Joy, a nonprofit organization dedicated to easing the plight of homeless children in India. He has overseen the building of four orphanages and complete care for hundreds of orphans over the past decade. Mission of Joy supports more than sixty native missionaries in remote villages in India, has built more than fifty churches, operates a home for Christian widows, and feeds thousands of meals to hungry children every week.

Colonel O'Leary is the author of *Taking the High Ground,* the *New York Times* bestseller *America Out of the Ashes,* and the CBA bestseller *Brave Hearts Under Red Skies.* He and his wife, Cindy, have been married for twenty-nine years. They have six children, five living: Jo Beth, Stephen, Kjerstin, Sean, and Shannon.

For more information on Mission of Joy, visit:

www.missionjoy.org

For information on scheduling Colonel O'Leary to speak at your event, you may contact him directly at

www.jeffoleary.com
jeffreyoleary@jeffoleary.com
or through Speak-Up Speaker Services at
(888) 870-7719
speakupinc@aol.com

ACKNOWLEDGMENTS

I BEGIN BY ACKNOWLEDGING YOU, THE READER, FOR HAVING the courage to pick up a book that is going to challenge the way you live and the way you lead. You are a unique individual as so few are willing to expand their zone of comfort. You have chosen to open your eyes to the possibility of another path, and you've picked up a leadership book to find it. It is my hope you find a life book as well. Perhaps in the reading, you will discover it is possible to leave more than just memories behind. You can also leave a Centurion legacy.

I want to thank the fine staff of Thomas Nelson. Thank you for sharing the vision of a new way of approaching leadership. Special thanks to my editor, Brian Hampton. Your scalpel was painfully precious. Thank you for taking the time to cut with care.

To Lee Hough, my agent, my friend, thank you for sharing the journey.

To Cindy, my wife—thank you for helping me in "sickness and in health." Thank you for being there in the valleys where we held hands and endured the pain, and the sun-splashed mountaintops where we lifted up our hands and rejoiced in the sweetness of His goodness. At ages twenty and twenty-one, we could not have known how low the valleys or high the mountains might be. But here we are, in love twenty-nine years later, a testimony to the power of God's grace.

To You, Lord, my daily strength, "thank You" seems so small. But . . . thank You.

NOTES

INTRODUCTION

1. *The Washington Times*, "Inside Politics," April 17, 2001, A6.
2. Interview with *Marine One* crewmember, February, 2001.

CHAPTER 1

1. Leonard Roy Frank, ed., *Quotationary* (New York: Random House, 1999), 159.
2. Ibid., 160.
3. Titus Livy, *History of Rome from Its Foundations, Books 21–39* (Republished by Viking Press in 1965 under the title *War with Hannibal*),Book 21:18.
4. Note to Reader: No Carthaginian primary sources remain. Only Greeks and Roman histories are available. The two most reliable are: Polybius (Greek, c. 204–122 BC) *Universal History*, books 3–16, and Livy (Roman, 59 BC–AD 17): *History of Rome from its Foundation*, books 21–39.
5. J. F. Lazenby, *Hannibal's War: A Military History of the Second Punic War* (Oklahoma: University of Oklahoma Press), 1998, 33.
6. Bevin Alexander, *How Great Generals Win* (New York: W. W. Norton and Co, 1993), 40.
7. Ibid.
8. Ibid., 41.
9. Ibid., 44.
10. Ibid., 45.
11. Ibid., 46.
12. Frank, *Quotationary*, 157.
13. Alexander, *How Great Generals Win*, 46.
14. http://www.enchantedmind.com/html/creativity/attributes.html
15. Thomas J. Neff and James M. Citrin, *Lessons from the Top: The Search for America's Best Business Leaders* (New York: Currency Doubleday 1999), 188.
16. http://www.creativityforlife.com/article1056.html.

17. http://www.creativityforlife.com/article1056.html.

18. http://www.riverdeep.net/current/2001/02/022101_leonardo.jhtml.

Chapter 2

1. Mike Stroh, http://www.scipioafricanus.com/courage.htm.

2. Ibid., Chapter 3.

3. Alexander, *How Great Generals Win*, 48–49.

4. Lazenby, *Hannibal's War*, 133.

5. Alexander, *How Great Generals Win*, 50.

6. Ibid., 51–52.

7. Ibid., 53.

8. Lazenby, *Hannibal's War*, 194.

9. Ibid.

10. Alexander, *How Great Generals Win*, 59.

11. Ibid., 60.

12. Ibid., 62.

13. Lazenby, *Hannibal's War*, 220.

14. Alexander, *How Great Generals Win*, 63.

15. Ibid., 64.

16. Ibid., 65.

17. Ibid.

18. Ibid., 66.

19. Ibid.

20. Frank, *Quotationary*, 265.

21. Jim Clemmer, "Successful Failures," http://www.clemmer.net/excerpts/successful.shtml.

22. Andrew Harvey, "The College Journal *Wall Street Journal*," http://www.collegejournal.com/successwork/onjob/20020814-harvey.html.

23. Clemmer, "Successful Failures."

24. "Worker Discontent Spans Ages, Income Brackets," *Washington Times*, August 27, 2002.

25. "Are You a Bad Boss?" *CIO Magazine*, April 1, 2000.

26. Sue Shellenbarger, *Spotting Bad Bosses Before It's Too Late,* College Journal.com 2000 http://www.collegejournal.com/jobhunting/interviewing/20000224-shellenbarger.html

27. *God's Little Devotional Journal* (Tulsa, OK: Honor Books, 2000), 208.

28. Harvey, "The College Journal."

Chapter 3

1. Pierre Briant, *Alexander the Great: Man of Action Man of Spirit* (New York: Abrams Inc, 1996), 14.

2. Ibid., 21.

3. Ibid.

4. Ibid., 22.

5. Ibid., 25.

6. Ibid., 41.

7. Ibid., 44.

8. Ibid., 45.

9. Ibid., 46.

10. Ibid., 50. (Diodorus Siculus, *Historical Library,* 1st Century BC).

11. J. F. C. Fuller, *The Generalship of Alexander the Great* (New York: Da Capo Press), 100.

12. Briant, *Alexander the Great,* 50.

13. Ibid., 54.

14. Ibid., 55.

15. Ibid., 56.

16. Ibid.

17. Ibid., 62.

18. Ibid., 64.

19. Ibid., 66.

20. Ibid., 69.

21. Ibid., 70.

22. Ibid., 71.

23. Ibid., 72.

24. Ibid., 78.

25. Ibid., 80

26. Ibid., 81.

27. "Under Cloudy Skies," *US News and World Report,* December 9, 2002.

28. Ibid.

29. Ibid.

30. Ibid.

31. Ibid.

CHAPTER 4

1. Frances Gies, *Joan of Arc: The Legend and the Reality* (New York: Harper and Row, 1959), 76.

2. Ibid, 78.

3. Ibid, 79.

4. *Journal du Siège, Quicherat IV,* Testimony of Dunois, Quicherat, III, 8, *160–161.*

5. Gies, *Joan of Arc,* 17–18.

6. http://historymedren.miningco.com/library/weekly/aa032698.htm.

7. Gies, *Joan of Arc,* 10.

8. C. T. Allmand, ed, *Society at War* (New York: Oliver and Boyd, 1973), 34–35.

9. "The trial record was first published in unabridged form by Jules Quicherat in the first of his five-volume work, *Procès de condamnation et de rehabilitation de Jeanne d'Arc, dite la Pucelle,* Paris 1841–1849. The best source for an English translation is the scarce work by W. S. Scott of the Orléans manuscript: W. S. Scott, ed. and Trans., *The Trial of Joan of Arc,* London, Folio Society, 1956. References in this chapter for the trial and Rehabilitation are to Quicherat's original publication." Gies, *Joan of Arc,* 261.

10. Ibid., 21.

11. Original from the *Trial of Condemnation,* Quicherat 47–48. Reprinted in: Règine Pernoud, *Joan of Arc: By Herself and Her Witnesses* (London: Scarborough House, 1982), 30. (First published in the French Language in 1962 as *Jeanne d'Arc par elle-même et par ses témoins* by Editions du Seuil).

12. Quicherat I, 131–32.

13. Quicherat II, 456.

14. Gies, *Joan of Arc,* 32.

15. Testimony of Jean de Metz, Quicherate, II, 436–37.

16. Gies, *Joan of Arc,* 36.

17. Règine Pernoud, *Joan of Arc: By Herself and Her Witnesses* (London: Scarborough House, 1994), 36 (from Quicherat's testimonial record at the Trial of Rehabilitation 19 years after her death, 94–96).

18. Ibid., 39.

19. Gies, *Joan of Arc,* 37.

20. Pernoud, *Joan of Arc,* 40.

21. Gies, *Joan of Arc,* 38.

22. Ibid., 44.

23. Ibid., 49.

24. Ibid.

25. Ibid., 50.

26. Ibid.

27. Pernoud, *Joan of Arc,* 52.

28. Gies, *Joan of Arc,* 50.

29. Ibid.

30. Ibid., 54.

31. Ibid.

32. Ibid., 55.

33. Ibid.

34. Ibid., 54.

35. Ibid.

36. Ibid., 71. (from Quicherate III 5–7).

37. Ibid., 71

38. Ibid., 72.

39. Ibid.

40. Ibid., 74.

41. Ibid., 75.

42. Ibid.

43. Testimony of Jean d'Aulon, Quicherat, III, 79, Gies, *Joan of Arc*, 77.

44. Testimony of Pasquerel, Quicherate, III, 108–9, Gies, 79.

45. Testimony of Dunois, Quicherat, III, 8, *Journal du Siège, Quicherat, IV,* 160–161.

46. Quicherat IV, 160, Gies, *Joan of Arc*, 79.

47. Quicherate IV, 70–71, (from Gies, 80).

48. Ibid., 82.

49. Ibid., 144.

50. Neff and Citrin, *Lessons from the Top*, 331.

51. Ibid., 332.

52. Maynard M. Dolecheck and Carolyn C. Dolecheck, "Ethics: Take It from the Top," *Business* (Jan–March 1989), 13.

53. James Patterson and Peter Kim, *The Day America Told the Truth* (New York: Prentice Hall Press, 1991), 1, 20, 21, 22.

54. Al Gini, *Moral Leadership and Business Ethics, Loyola University Chicago in Ethics and Leadership Working Papers* (Academy of Leadership Press, 1996)—also online at http://www.academy.umd.edu/Scholarship/CASL/klspdocs/agini_p1.htm#return2

55. 1 Corinthians 1:27.

56. http://www.biography.com/cgi-in/frameit.cgi?p=http%3A//www.biography.com/magazine/biomag/helmsley.html

57. Psalms 90:10 NLT.

58. Col 4:1 WEB.

CHAPTER 5

1. Frank, *Quotationary*, 15.

2. Charles Cecil Wall, *George Washington: Citizen Soldier,* (Mt Vernon Ladies Assn: Mt Vernon, 1988), 38–39.

3. Ibid., 43–44.

4. Ibid., 40.

5. Ibid., 45

6. James Thomas Flexner, *Washington: The Indispensable Man* (Boston: Little, Brown and Co., 1969), 170.

7. Wall, *George Washington*, 193.

8. Flexner, *Washington*, 172.

9. Ibid., 173.

10. J. A. Carroll and M. W. Ashworth, *George Washington*, v. 7, (New York: Charles Scribner's Sons, 1957), 649.
11. Flexner, *Washington*, 173–74.
12. Ibid., 178.
13. Ibid., 193.
14. Derric Johnson, *The Wonder of America* (Tulsa: Honor Books, 1999), 154–55.
15. Ibid., 90–91.
16. Ibid., 114–15.
17. Theodore Roosevelt, Speech at the University of Paris, Sorbonne, April 23, 1910, "Citizenship in a Republic," *History as Literature* (New York: Scribner and Sons, 1913), Section IV.
18. *Quotationary*, 345.
19. Claypoole's *AMERICAN DAILY ADVERTISER*, Philadelphia, September 19, 1796.

CHAPTER 6
1. Milton Meltzer, *Andrew Jackson and His America* (New York: Franklin Watts, 1993), 34.
2. Ibid., 33.
3. Ibid.
4. Burke Davis, *Old Hickory: A Life of Andrew Jackson* (New York: The Dial Press, 1977), 67.
5. Frank, *Quotationary*, 593.
6. Davis, *Old Hickory*, 69.
7. Ibid., 70.
8. Ibid., 72.
9. Ibid.
10. Ibid.
11. Ibid., 99.
12. Ibid., 105.
13. Ibid., 106.
14. Ibid., 108.
15. Ibid., 109.
16. Ibid., 102–03.
17. John Buchanan, *Jackson's Way: Andrew Jackson and the People of the Western Waters* (New York: John Wiley and Sons, Inc., 2001), 323.
18. Davis, *Old Hickory*, 115.
19. Ibid., 123.
20. George S. Patton Jr., John Hawkins at http://www.rightwingnews.com/quotes/patton.php.

21. Davis, *Old Hickory*, 143.
22. Meltzer, *Andrew Jackson and His America*, 63–65.
23. Davis, *Old Hickory*, 148.
24. Meltzer, *Andrew Jackson and His America*, 99.
25. Robert Quakenbush, *Who Let Muddy Boots into the White House* (New York: Simon and Schuster, Inc. 1986), 29.
26. http://freepages.genealogy.rootsweb.com/~prsjr/na/people/creek/selocta.htm Discussion of Native American Indian Profiles.
27. http://www.Dictionary.com
28. http://www.houseofquotes.com/quotes/persistence/
29. http://www.houseofquotes.com/category.cfm?s=11and cat=persistence
30. http://auschwitz.dk/Wallenberg.htm

CHAPTER 7

1. Stephen W. Sears, *George B. McClellan: The Young Napoleon* (New York: DeCapo Press, 1999), 1.
2. Ibid., 12.
3. Frank, *Quotationary*, 190.
4. Sears, *George B. McClellan*, 16.
5. Ibid., 25.
6. Ibid.
7. Bruce Catton, *Mr. Lincoln's Army* (New York: DoubleDay Publishing, 1951), 53.
8. Sears, *George B. McClellan*, 92.
9. Ibid., 98.
10. Frank, *Quotationary*, 193.
11. Sears, *George B. McClellan*, 107.
12. Donald T. Phillips, *Lincoln on Leadership: Executive Strategies for Tough Times* (New York: Warner Books, 1992), 43.
13. Harold Holzer, ed., *Lincoln as I Knew Him* (Chapel Hill: Algonquin Books, 1999), 134.
14. Major George F. Williams, *The Memorial War Book* (New York: Arno Press, 1979), 314.
15. Ibid., 314.
16. Ibid., 320.
17. Frank, *Quotationary*, 193.
18. Williams, *Memorial War Book*, 336.
19. Frank, *Quotationary*. 192.

CHAPTER 8

1. http://www.fortunecity.com/victorian/museum/63/profiles/csa/lee.html

2. H. W. Crocker III, *Robert E. Lee on Leadership: Executive Lessons in Character, Courage, and Vision* (Roseville CA: Forum Books, 1999), 24–25.

3. Frank, *Quotationary*, 66.

4. Hodding Carter, *Robert E. Lee and the Road of Honor* (New York: Random House, 1955), 110–11.

5. Frank, *Quotationary*, 67.

6. Major George F. Williams, *The Memorial War Book* (New York: Arno Press, 1979), 274–75.

7. Ibid., 275.

8. Crocker, *Robert E. Lee on Leadership*, 74.

9. Frank, *Quotationary*, 67.

10. Crocker, *Robert E. Lee on Leadership*, 70.

11. Ibid.

12. Ibid., 71.

13. http://www.civilwarhome.com/manassas2.htm

14. Ibid.

15. Captain Robert E. Lee, *Recollections and Letters of General Robert E. Lee* (New York: Konecky and Konecky, 1992), 416.

16. Editor, Time-Life Books, *The Civil War: Lee Take Command: From Seven Days to Second Bull Run* (Alexandria, VA: Time Life Books, 1984), 167.

17. Frank, *Quotationary*, 67.

18. Neff and Citrin, *Lessons from the Top*, inside flap.

19. Ibid., 262–63.

20. Ibid., 153.

21. Ibid., 154.

22. Ibid.

23. Ibid., 155.

24. Crocker, *Robert E. Lee on Leadership*, 93.

25. Ibid., 94.

26. http://news.nationalgeographic.com/news/2002/01/0118_020118_lee.html

27. Ibid.

CHAPTER 9

1. Williams, *Memorial War Book*, 445.

2. Ibid, 446.

3. Ibid.

4. Ibid.

5. Ibid.

6. Ibid., 610.

7. Ibid., 80.

8. Bud Hannings, *A Portrait of the Stars and Stripes* (Glenside, PA: Seniram Publishing Inc., 1988), 152.

9. Williams, *Memorial War Book*, 521.

10. Ibid., 505–507.

11. Philip Van Doren Stern, ed., *The Life and Writings of Abraham Lincoln* (New York: The Modern Library, 1940), 812.

12. Simpson, op cit, 463.

13. Ulysses S. Grant, *Personal Memoirs of U. S. Grant* (New York: Charles Webster and Co., 1894), 306.

14. Ibid., 503.

15. Ibid, 313.

16. Crocker, *Robert E. Lee on Leadership*, 157.

17. "Boss's Angry E-mail Sends Shares Plunging," *The Daily Telegraph*, Issue 2142, April 6, 2001.

18. Luke 22:25–26 NLT.

19. Newsletter from *Advanced Marketing Experts* www.adv-marketing.com, June 10, 2001.

20. Brooks D. Simpson, *Ulysses S. Grant: Triumph over Adversity, 1822–1865* (Boston: Houghton Mifflin Co., 2000), 463.

21. Frank, *Quotationary*, 154.

22. Williams, op cit, 480.

Chapter 10

1. *Birmingham Sunday Mercury*, UK, January 7, 2001.

2. Harod Holzer, ed, *Lincoln as I knew Him* (Chapel Hill: Algonquin Books, 1999) 178.

3. Ibid., 41.

4. Ibid.,

5. Peter R. Scholtes, *Leaders of People: Some Are Wonderful, Some Are Clueless. The Rest Are Somewhere In Between*, http://pscholtes.com/leaders96.cfm.

6. William Lee Miller, "The Lincoln Virtues: An Ethical Biography," *The Washington Post.com*, http://www.washingtonpost.com/wp-srv/style/longterm/books/chap1/lincolnsvirtues.htm.

7. http://www.alincoln-library.com.

8. Holzer, *Lincoln as I Knew Him*, 48.

9. Ibid., 76.

10. Ibid., 79.

11. Ibid., 80.

12. http://showcase.netins.net/web/creative/lincoln/speeches/failures.htm.

13. Paul Greenberg, "A Man for This Season, Too," *The Washington Times*, February 12, 2003, A–17.

14. Holzer, *Lincoln as I Knew Him*, 135.

15. Greenberg, "Man for This Season, Too," A–17.

16. "The 1860 Presidential Elections," http://elections.harpweek.com/5Campaigning/campaigning-1.htm

17. Holzer, *Lincoln as I Knew Him*, 119.

18. Daniel Goleman, Richard Boyatzis, and Annie McKee, *The New Leaders* (Little, Brown, 2002). Reviewed on http://www.tribuneindia.com/2002/20020728/spectrum/book5.htm.

19. Holzer, *Lincoln as I Knew Him*, 99–100.

20. Ibid., 115–116.

21. http://www.npr.org/programs/morning/features/2002/june/bosses/.

22. Holzer, *Lincoln as I Knew Him*, 88.

23. Ibid., 89.

24. Paraphrased from http://www.alincoln-library.com.

25. Donald T. Phillips, *Lincoln on Leadership* (New York: Warner Books, 1992), 14.

26. Ibid., 17.

27. Ibid., 24.

28. http://www.bogusnews.com/voafa/lincoln/80.htm.

29. http://www.theage.com.au/articles/2003/03/05/1046826436678.html.

30. Phillips, *Lincoln on Leadership,* 16.

31. Scholtes, *Leaders Are People.*

CHAPTER 11

1. Nicholas V. Sekunda, *The Caesar's Legions: The Roman Soldier 753 to 117 AD* (Oxford, England: Osprey, 2000), 71.

2. Frank, *Quotationary*, 524.

3. Charles Dickens, *A Christmas Carol* (New York: Bantam Books, 1986), Chapter 1.

4. Frank, *Quotationary*, 657.

5. Ibid.